Breakfast on the beach

Breakfast on the beach

The empty tomb
and the subsequent glory

Peter Trumper

 EVANGELICAL PRESS

EVANGELICAL PRESS
Grange Close, Faverdale North Industrial Estate, Darlington,
DL3 0PH, England

First published 1999

British Library Cataloguing in Publication Data available

ISBN 0 85234 422 8

Printed and bound in Great Britain by Creative Print and Design
Wales, Ebbw Vale

To Margaret,
whose unceasing and loving support over many years has
been invaluable, and greatly appreciated.

Contents

		Page
Preface — Note on the genre		9
Prologue: On the road to Damascus		13
1.	Hurried steps	33
2.	The third day	42
3.	The pace quickens	64
4.	News good, bad and indifferent	83
5.	Hands across the table	103
6.	Broiled fish and a honeycomb	125
7.	Further causes for astonishment	148
8.	Breakfast on the beach	174
9.	One without equal	207
10.	The rushing mighty wind	243
Epilogue: The Visitor		280
Notes		303

'Why should it be thought a thing incredible with you, that God should raise the dead?'

(the apostle Paul)

Preface —
Note on the genre

My method, when writing devotional material based upon Scripture narrative, is not without its critics! Although I believe they are relatively few in number, they register alarm at the use I make of my imagination. They suggest my approach is likely to encroach upon what the Holy Spirit has revealed and therefore to add to it, and thus confuse the reader. A reviewer once accused me of 'breaking the regulative principle'; another of 'fictionalizing' the Scriptures. Swift are they to remind me of the divine warning — one which no Christian could ever treat lightly (Rev. 22:18).

But the word 'imagination' in this instance conjures up a false picture — of the author seeking to embellish the biblical record, as if unaware of being observed from heaven. I am by no means that author, nor would want to be; quite the reverse. The aim is not to protrude my work into the Scriptures (God forbid), because to do so would be to undermine them, but rather to *enhance* the reader's understanding. The instrument I at times wield is not undisciplined in its use. It is inference, not conjecture.

There is a reason for this. How often Christians (including preachers!) refer to 'the resurrection' and 'the ascension' without an apparent second thought. The astonishment and wonder of the early church, brought about by these miraculous events, have sadly become blurred with the passage of time. The empty tomb and Christ's exaltation at the right hand of the Father are believed wholeheartedly, but perhaps more as credal statements than dynamic moments in history.

For instance, after more than thirty years of preaching, I discovered that God's people relate more to death than to life. We humans are by nature more 'at home' with the grave than with the glory! One will always proclaim the significance of Calvary to eager Christian listeners — and be thankful to see such a reaction — but when the equally glorious resurrection and ascension are mentioned and there is talk of life beyond the grave, an uneasy and embarrassed shifting in the pews is sometimes evident. If only we Christians thought as much about our eternal home as we do about our earthly one! (Phil. 3:20).

Is it wrong, just idle curiosity, for us to ask questions relating to the empty tomb? After all, it is not without its significance! I would suggest that a failure to enquire reveals a somewhat disinterested approach to a momentous historical occasion. Well might one ask, 'What actually happened at that moment of resurrection? What was it like being confronted by angels? How did the disciples feel upon suddenly meeting their Lord, who had died only hours before?' and similar questions.

Has the reader ever stopped to reflect upon these extraordinary events, and the enormous impact they made upon those who first experienced them? If not — even though this may have been in the name of a supposed reverence for the biblical text — is it not insulting to heaven to be so indifferent? Imaginative intelligence, then, under the control of God the Spirit, will do no harm, and may perhaps do a great deal of good.

It may therefore come as a shock to some to realize that great men of God employed this approach, without believing they were tampering with Scripture. For example, Luther used such phrases as 'Judas ... said to himself', and, 'Judas probably said to himself...' *(Meditations on the Gospels)*; Calvin likewise: 'It is possible that ... Paul', or again, '... and one may well believe ...' *(Commentary on Acts)*. Matthew Henry is particularly adept at applying sanctified inference, which I suspect is a good reason for his success as an expositor. One is never bored! For example, in his commentary on Genesis he writes, 'Probably it was revealed to Adam...', and on 'Acts', 'We have reason to think Stephen...' And as a consequence of these examples, William Hendriksen follows suit: 'We may perhaps picture Jesus...', and 'Is it not possible that Jesus...?' *(Commentary on Matthew)*. There are many more examples one could quote, but being in good company, I rest my case!

Peter Trumper

Prologue:
On the road to Damascus

The highway meandering from Jerusalem to Damascus was rough-hewn and baked in an unremitting heat. Clouds of dust flew up from the road's surface when horses pounded their hooves in haste upon it. Travellers were likely to be in a hurry in those days, because venturing forth on long journeys was a risky business not undertaken lightly. Many and varied were the hazards concealed behind the rocks and amid the hills covering the terrain between the two cities.

One morning, in the year A.D. 29 or thereabouts, the dust arose in gusts as numerous hooves, their number unknown, drummed their way from Israel's capital to that of Syria. The assumption is that the men were riding horses, because their business was official and urgent, and therefore speed was of the essence. There was little time to spare, as their prey was still some distance from them, having sought a measure of safety within the Jewish community among the network of narrow streets for which the ancient city of Damascus was famous.

Beyond measure

If the majority who headed north that morning did so because duty called them, furious determination drove their leader on

(Acts 9:1). This young Pharisee (see Phil. 3:5) was in no mood
to deviate from his express purpose, which was to round up
the followers of Jesus of Nazareth who had fled to a foreign
land on account of the fierce enmity they had experienced in
Jerusalem. The religious authorities (the Sanhedrin) had learned
where these people were who, in their view, had apostatized
from the faith.

Seething with rage, the young man took it upon himself to
gain the chief priests' permission to journey to Damascus (Acts
26:10), so that these apostate countrymen of his could be returned to face imprisonment, or worse. With a retinue of men,
therefore — perhaps temple guards — he had set off at speed
in possession of official letters of commendation from Caiaphas,
the high priest, to the appropriate rabbis in Damascus (Acts
9:2).

The members of the Sanhedrin would not have been surprised by the young Jew's vicious ardour (1 Tim. 1:13); his
pride in his religious orthodoxy had already revealed a ven-
omous hatred for 'the name of Jesus of Nazareth' and for his
followers (Acts 22:3; 26:9). Later, he publicly confessed his
persecuting zeal (Acts 22:19). It was as if he could never satisfy his lust for vengeance — executions, imprisonments, beat-
ings, torture (Acts 26:10-11). Saul of Tarsus' name was in-
famous among the lowly followers of Jesus (Acts 9:13).

His loathing for this new 'sect', which had arisen in the
land and been popularized by talk of its leader's resurrection
from the dead and subsequent phenomena (Acts 2), was by no
means unique. It was shared by the majority of the priests, but
it found a useful channel for expression in this eager young
man. Only a few refrained from entering the affray, and those
who did were the small minority among the Sanhedrin members who were so fearful of the consequences of their secret
belief in Jesus' claims that they kept to the shadows (John
12:42). When they wanted to make contact with him they did

so after nightfall (John 3:1-2), which reveals something of the intense hatred seething behind the scenes.

Above the brightness of the sun

Then it happened — without warning, in a flash. So unusual was the experience that, since that moment, unbelief has attributed it to the sun's intensity burning a fevered brain. In reply, believers have always expressed the desire for an epidemic of such a 'sickness', because what occurred that day helped transform the world.

It was midday (Acts 26:13), and Damascus was suddenly within sight (Acts 9:3), shimmering in the haze. True, the middle-eastern sun had reached its zenith and the parched earth baked in the intense heat, which meant that it was the time of day when cooling shades were normally sought. But later the young man was not embarrassed to admit this (Acts 22:6), because he knew that what had happened had nothing to do with the sun's rays; he was, after all, accustomed to them. Besides, everyone in the party was affected simultaneously, including the horses. Burning heat was not the cause, but rather light so dazzling that it shaded out the sun (Acts 26:13-14). One moment both horses and riders were intent upon reaching their destination as quickly as possible; and the next, the men were thrown to the ground, presumably as the frightened animals reared up. The scene was bathed in the whiteness of light at its most penetrating (Acts 26:13).

There was no question of the riders remounting and continuing their journey; the dazzling intensity of the light was too overpowering for that. Lying prostrate in the dust and grime was all they could manage, too shaken by the swiftness of the event to comment upon it. But in any case there was no time to do so, for almost immediately a sound penetrated the

shocked silence, which all but one of the bewildered and frightened travellers were incapable of hearing (Acts 22:9). The
young Pharisee heard someone speaking to him — not a member of his retinue, because the voice spoke to him in Hebrew
(Acts 26:14), the formal language of the synagogue, not conversational Aramaic. Nor was it an inner voice, such as those
which torment the mentally troubled, but one from above and
beyond him.

In retrospect, Saul the scholar would have been reminded
of Moses' famous experience at the burning bush, when he
too was mysteriously addressed by the divine voice. That occasion was also in a desert place, and it introduced the patriarch to his life's work among the Hebrews (Exod. 3). As he
crouched trembling in the dirt and dust, Saul little realized
that his ministry to the Gentiles was about to be opened up to
view (Acts 26:17-18), the fulfilment of God's covenant with
Abraham (Gen. 12:3) and the 'great light' brought to generations of those who 'walked in darkness' (Isa. 9:1-2).

That moment, within sight of Damascus, he and his companions probably longed for some of that 'darkness' to relieve
them from the dazzling splendour. Even curiosity forbade them
from lifting their heads from the ground. They could only remain where they had fallen, shielding their eyes, or keeping
them closed, against the pitiless and unremitting glare. The
proud, self-confident Pharisee, whose religious pedigree was
beyond question (Gal. 1:14; Phil. 3:4-7) — the golden ladder
to success in Jerusalem — had in seconds been reduced to the
proverbial poor man in the dust, or the beggar on the dunghill
(1 Sam. 2:8).

At a later date, when Saul of Tarsus had been elevated to
Paul the apostle (Acts 13:9), he actually saw the one who now
spoke to him (Acts 22:17-18), which was the mark of
apostleship (1 Cor. 9:1), but not during this first encounter
(Acts 9:8). It was just as well. Hearing the disembodied voice
was sufficient to cause him to cower still more abjectly, yet

despite the hatred which filled his heart to overflowing, the tone of the one who addressed him was strangely compassionate. Saul would have expected otherwise, but there was no element of stricture, but rather of tender concern. He was a defeated foe undeserving of any consideration, whose dignity had been lost in the dirt, yet the voice called to him as a family friend might have done: 'Saul, Saul...' (Acts 9:4). The enemy was clearly loved; the one who cursed was being blessed; and good was being shown to him who hated (Matt. 5:44). The proverbial 'coals of fire' were being poured upon Saul's head (Prov. 25:21-22; Rom. 12:20).

The rebuke was gracious (1 Tim. 1:14). There was no evidence of God's wrath behind the question; just a gentle enquiry, the eager young man entreated to reply. But Saul must have been shaken still further by the way the query was framed; he was asked why he was persecuting, not the *followers* of Jesus, but 'me' (Acts 9:4). That simple question flew swiftly to his conscience, opening up the festering bitterness which had controlled his actions for some time.

Hypocrisy had demanded that his religious orthodoxy wreak havoc upon those whom he, with his strict and stern beliefs, considered to have apostatized from the faith (Acts 8:3), but it was a masquerade. He now understood the truth. The motive behind the cruelty he inflicted had been, not only (as he had convinced himself and others) the honour of Israel's God (Acts 22:3), but rather his personal hatred for Jesus of Nazareth. There lay the battlefield — and it still does — in the refusal to acknowledge his claims, to 'have this man to reign over us' (Luke 19:14). In brutally striving against the communities of those who loved Jesus, and doing so even to the gates of a foreign land, Saul was merely reflecting his own loathing of the one they served. As Jesus once stated to his brothers, 'The world cannot hate you; but me it hateth, because I testify of it, that the works thereof are evil' (John 7:7).

Enmity aroused

Saul might have mused upon the time when his hatred for
Jesus had started. If so, it would not have taken him long to
discover the answer: from the very beginning. Three years
earlier something extraordinary had been taking place, as a
vast and steady stream of excited people made their way to
the banks of the Jordan river to hear a weather-beaten preacher
dressed in the rough clothing of a man who lived in the desert.
He preached the most startling of all messages: the Messiah
was about to appear! Repentance therefore was demanded,
followed by the public testimony of baptism in the Jordan
waters close by, to illustrate its sincerity — a call which produced a ready response from the assembled multitudes (Matt.
3:1-12; Mark 1:1-8). Nobody, least of all the Sanhedrin and
its supporters like Saul of Tarsus, could be indifferent to such
a challenge.

With the arrival on the scene of Jesus from the north (Matt.
3:13) and John the Baptist subsequently proclaiming the Messiah's presence (John 1:29), half the country was brought to
fever pitch (Mark 1:5). It was too much for the Sanhedrin to
accept. The situation was getting out of hand, the religious
establishment was rocked to its foundation, and there was no
way to halt the progress of this remarkable movement. Soon
the appeal of its leader was drawing even greater crowds, not
just within Judea, but to the northern outreaches of the land
and beyond its boundaries to Syria itself (Matt. 4:24). Saul,
like his superiors, smouldered with a deepening enmity. The
religious leaders would not have admitted it, but they, who
had lost the people's respect, were envious of this untrained
prophet and his ability to gather 'their' flock to his side (Matt.
27:18; John 7:15).

But envy was not the sole reason for their anger. From
Galilee there emanated startling news, summed up in a phrase

first heard when Jesus preached his most famous sermon, and such was the impact upon the hearers (which has remained undiminished today) that they were 'astonished' — as well they might have been (Matt. 7:28). Could they believe their ears? He had quoted from the moral law, and then added, 'But I say unto you...'! (Matt. 5:20-22). Everyone knew that Almighty God himself had written the Ten Commandments upon the tablets of stone carried in Moses' arms (Exod. 34:1; Deut. 10:2; Exod. 32:15), yet Jesus, with breathtaking audacity, was openly overshadowing the divine handwriting with his own presence. In the light of that, how could the prevailing rabbinical teaching match such authority, or stand up under scrutiny, in the estimation of the common people? (Matt. 7:29). It was a comparison surely noted by Saul and his superiors, and one guaranteed not to warm their hearts.

That was not all. Much worse, they considered this man not only a charlatan, but a blasphemer — something for which the law demanded the extreme penalty (Lev. 24:16). He actually claimed the sacred name of Israel's God, 'I AM' (Exod. 3:14), as his own (John 8:58-59) and even openly forgave sins! (Mark 2:7). At his trial before Caiaphas, those present had been shocked to hear his identification of himself with Daniel's apocalyptic 'Son of man', to whom ultimate dominion is given (Matt. 26:64; cf. Dan. 7:13-14). His followers later claimed he had told them that 'all power' had been entrusted to him by God, over 'all flesh' (Matt. 28:18; cf. John 17:2). Only his popularity with the people had hindered an arrest being made (Matt. 21:46). Saul seethed with indignation, as did the religious establishment as a whole.

Jesus of Nazareth was evidently unlike anyone else, which in itself was enough to cause offence. He was so awesomely pure of character, he even challenged his severest critics to detect any sin in him (John 8:46). But there were other issues too, which Saul must have heard about. There was talk of his unique powers over sickness (Matt. 4:23-24), the unclean spirits (Mark 1:27), the elements (Mark 4:39), the animal kingdom (Matt. 8:32), even death itself (Luke 7:15; 8:53-54). It was too much; an arrest was ordered, but even at that point he eluded them. The men returned to the chief priests and Pharisees without him, giving as their excuse that 'Never man spake like this man' (John 7:46). The mere presence in the land of this giant amongst men riled the authorities, particularly the Pharisees like Saul, beyond all reason. They had him killed (Acts 2:23).

But, they quickly discovered, even that was not sufficient. Three days after his execution at Calvary, accounts began to circulate of his resurrection from the dead, and of his band of disciples having met and spoken to him! Worse followed. Just weeks later, a phenomenal occurrence took place in Jerusalem. At a time when the city was crammed with vast crowds assembled for the annual Jewish feast of Pentecost, what appeared as a mighty wind gusted upon it without warning. With equal suddenness, the name of Jesus of Nazareth was on everyone's lips once more, as thousands responded to the powerful preaching of his apostles, who had emerged from hiding (Acts 2).

In no time, thousands more were added to this growing movement, which was influencing the entire city with its presence. Judaism seemed under siege, as the Sanhedrin sought to contain the 'outbreak' (Acts 2-4). But then its leaders no doubt remembered what John the Baptist had declared several years earlier: 'The axe is laid unto the root of the trees' (Luke 3:9). Jews passionate for their religion, like Saul of Tarsus, must have shuddered, especially as even priests were being influenced (Acts 6:7). Somehow it had to be stopped, and perhaps persecuting these people, 'even unto strange cities', was the answer (Acts 26:11).

Then one day Saul attended an execution, an occasion which made an indelible mark upon him, because he referred to it some time later (Acts 22:20). It was a historic moment, as the victim was this movement's first martyr. He was also a prominent member of it, one of several recently appointed to high office as a 'deacon' — a new role created by the apostles to assist them (Acts 6:1-6). Saul therefore, and indeed Jerusalem as a whole, understood the significance of what was happening. The tension between the religious authorities and Jesus' followers, which had existed for over three years, had reached breaking-point. The fact that the Sanhedrin was prepared to execute a leading member of the movement was also an indication that the chief priests recognized its importance and hold upon the people. In short, far from having destroyed Jesus' influence, they were watching it blossom (John 14:12).

But the uniqueness of the moment was not what had attracted the young Pharisee; it was the victim himself who impressed those who witnessed the scene. His name was Stephen and his extraordinary ministry in the city, described in terms of 'great wonders and miracles' (Acts 6:8), had been the cause of the disturbance which had led to his arrest. In a trial reminiscent of his Lord's (Matt. 26:60), he stood before Caiaphas and the ruling dignitaries of Israel, and in a classic incident provided all in the court with a history of the Jewish nation (Acts 7). Nobody objected, for it was the accepted way of doing things (Ps. 78) — that is, until the speaker began to apply his message. Then, with a prophet's intensity, Stephen launched into a denunciation of the Sanhedrin (Acts 7:51-53). So stern were the charges that everyone present must have had Jesus in mind (Matt. 23). Clearly, this movement had grown in stature and was not to be trifled with. But that in itself only served to deepen the antagonism.

However, there was another factor which, more than any other, left its indelible imprint upon all who saw Stephen. Perhaps it was a feature of all who shared his 'gift of the Holy Ghost' (Acts 2:38), who like Moses radiated the intimate presence of God (Exod. 34:29-35), but even his most furious opponents in the courtroom later admitted that Stephen had an angelic face (Acts 6:15). It had not been an expression adopted for the occasion but liable to melt in the heat of debate, because even when the priests, having heard his accusations (Acts 7:54), behaved as 'ravening wolves' (Matt. 7:15), Stephen's expression continued to reflect the glories of heaven.

Within the courtroom seething with fury, amidst the company of raging priests, Stephen appeared immune from the fierce expressions and gesticulating arms. Like his Lord, he committed the proceedings 'to him that judgeth righteously' (1 Peter 2:23). Instead, his contemplation was elsewhere. He gazed upwards, not outwards, because he alone in the room was privileged to have a panoramic view of heaven displayed before him. His was undoubtedly the experience of all Christian martyrs, of whom he was the first — an experience in which God's grace more than compensates for their suffering (2 Cor. 12:9-10).

The noise abated as they watched Stephen apparently looking intently up at the ceiling, though his face provided an insight into the mystery that was being unfolded (Acts 7:55). There was no point in railing against him any more; he was not listening. The room fell silent. In the stillness they heard him express his wonderment, 'I see the heavens opened...' (Acts 7:56), and they no doubt observed its theological content.

All they could see was the man, but for him heaven had for a brief moment unlocked its secrets. The veil was brushed aside and there, revealed in majesty, was the one the entire country was talking about and who himself had stood only a short time ago before these same ungodly men (Matt. 26:57). Jesus of Nazareth was not mentioned by name, but the 'Son of man' was (Acts 7:55-56) — that conspicuous title Jesus had applied to himself at his trial, causing such a stir (Matt. 26:64-66). The members of the Sanhedrin knew only too well to whom Stephen was referring. That prophet was back amongst them!

This time, however, it was not as their prisoner, but as their Judge (John 5:22).

The one who at his ascension returned to heaven in triumph (Rev. 5) and, having completed his atoning work (John 17:4) — a work which could never be repeated (John 19:30) and was sufficient to redeem 'to the uttermost' (Heb. 7:25) — *sat* in majesty at the Father's right hand (Heb. 12:2), now *stood*, compassionately interceding on behalf of his courageous and loyal servant. Stephen was not alone! The gracious High Priest was being 'touched with the feeling' of his plight (Heb. 4:15). A Christian who is conscious of that wonderful truth can pass through the deepest of waters, or the most fiercely blazing fire (Isa. 43:2).

Conviction fell heavily upon the assembly. They had been watching their prisoner staring towards the ceiling but, much as they would have wished to do so, they could not reject the incident out of hand. Stephen had witnessed the glory of God (Acts 7:55) in the face of his Redeemer and Lord (John 17:24), and his expression radiated the reality of what he had seen. There could be no denying it. The painful truth had once again been hammered home that the Sanhedrin had made the biggest blunder known to history when they had hounded Jesus of Nazareth to his death — the Prince of life, no less (Acts 3:15). Wicked men had hung him on a gibbet (Acts 2:23); God had set him on a throne (Ps. 110:1). It was a vital opportunity for Caiaphas and his colleagues to officially acknowledge the Sanhedrin's guilt in the affair and to heed the words of David: 'Against thee, thee only, have I sinned, and done this evil in thy sight' (Ps. 51:4).

But in place of cries of anguish and repentance, the court erupted with shouts of anger, as without ceremony Stephen was roughly dragged to his execution (Acts 7:57-58). It was reminiscent of the treatment meted out to Naboth, during another period noted for its rejection of God and his people

(1 Kings 21:13). The method employed for killing the two men was similar too: it was the Jewish way, by stoning (cf. Josh. 7:25). As Stephen stood in the pit, the men assembled the rocks to be thrown at their victim, and prepared themselves for the gruesome task by removing the clothing likely to hamper their movements. These were laid at the feet of the young Pharisee, Saul of Tarsus (Acts 7:58; 22:20).

Lessons from the pit

Whether Saul had been in the courtroom is unknown. Perhaps he was and later gave his account of what happened there to Luke, the historian behind the Acts of the Apostles (Luke 1:1-4; Acts 1:1). Somebody did. What is certain, though, was the impact Stephen's courageous testimony in the pit made upon Saul. He himself had inflicted much suffering upon these followers of Jesus, as if he could never be satisfied (1 Tim. 1:13; Acts 22:19; 26:11), but as he closely observed Stephen he little realized that one day he too would suffer martyrdom in the name of Stephen's Lord. During those moments at the pit Saul learned many lessons, not least in how a Christian should confront his passing, however violent the end (2 Tim. 4:6-8).

It was a pitiful sight. Stones of various shapes and sizes descended upon Stephen and found their target, for he was powerless to avoid them and there was nowhere to hide. They rained down upon him, from all directions at once, heaved by men who surrounded him with strong arms and a steady throw. No mercy was shown — none was expected — and there was no let-up. He was there to be killed. No part of his body was spared, or could be adequately protected; bruises soon appeared, wounds opened, blood trickled and limbs cracked.

Many in his position might have begged for mercy, sought ways and means of avoiding the inevitable, like the thieves who hung upon their crosses alongside Jesus (Luke 23:39), but Stephen emulated his Lord. He evidently considered every detail of his circumstances, terrible though they were, to be under the direct control of his sovereign God. That did not make the ordeal any easier to endure, the 'cup' any less full; but, like Jesus, Stephen desired only to be within the will of his heavenly Father (Matt. 26:42). Saul would have observed that he prayed, not to be rescued or for the healing of his numerous wounds, but rather as a preparation for his impending death.

But then Saul must have noticed something remarkable — in fact so disturbing, it would have deepened his loathing for Stephen and the movement he represented. As a Pharisee, expert in the Jewish Scriptures, Saul was familiar with the prayers of his people through the ages, who when in trouble called upon Jehovah. He could, for example, have recalled David's anguish when Israel's king, another Saul, aggressively pursued him (Ps. 35:1; 1 Sam. 24:1-2). Now, as the rocks repeatedly thudded into Stephen, Saul must have been shocked to hear his cry not, apparently, to the God of Israel, but to Jesus, whom he addressed as 'Lord' (Acts 7:59). This growing 'evangelical' movement, an increasing influence in the country, actually dared to equate its leader with Almighty God! To one who later described himself as a 'Hebrew of the Hebrews' (Phil. 3:5), this was an intolerable blasphemy (Acts 6:11), and yet it was well known that the prophet from Galilee had encouraged his disciples to believe in his deity. Had Saul's colleagues not been so incensed upon hearing him say as much, that they had attempted to carry out the law's demands on the spot, by stoning him for the sin of blasphemy? (John 8:58-59; cf. Lev. 24:16).

Stephen's battered body was at a low ebb. The viciousness of the attack upon him had extracted its toll, and there was not much time left for him. It is at such moments that reality is faced. To what, or to whom, will the soul cling as it hovers between life and death? How pleasant is belief in Christ when encouragements flow through the church in torrents, when it has 'favour with all the people', the Lord adding to it 'daily such as should be saved'! (Acts 2:47). But what of periods of discouragement, or when eternity looms large, as it did for Stephen crouching under a fusillade of hefty missiles? The value of one's hope is weighed at that point.

Stephen knew where to turn. He called upon God — as, indeed, the majority would in such terrible circumstances, but true faith is not something snatched from thin air in a crisis as an afterthought. Like a flower reaching for the light, it instinctively overlooks all other considerations and lays hold upon Christ, the 'anchor of the soul' (Heb. 6:19). He alone 'sits' at God's right hand (Heb. 12:2), having secured eternal redemption for his covenant people; he alone 'pleads' the merit of his blood on their behalf; he alone 'stands' compassionately interceding for them (Acts 7:56; 1 Tim. 2:5). As he is 'in' the Father, they are 'in' him and he by his Spirit is 'in' them (John 14:20). There can be no greater intimacy. Now he graciously awaits their 'home-coming' with the most cheering of all good news: 'Come, ye blessed of my Father, inherit the kingdom prepared for you from the foundation of the world' (Matt. 25:34).

Despite his crumpled and crippled body, Stephen's spirit soared beyond the immediate and clasped hold of his 'Lord Jesus', in readiness for its reception (Acts 7:59). As his observer was to write years later (and perhaps he was remembering a certain day just outside Jerusalem's city walls when he watched a stoning — Acts 7:58), 'While we look not at the things which are seen, but at the things which are not seen: for the things which are seen are temporal, but the things which are not seen are eternal' (2 Cor. 4:18).

Stephen's body had suffered enough. It could hold out no longer, and with one last effort he cried loudly for all present to hear, 'Lord, lay not this sin to their charge' (Acts 7:60). These were his final words, and the dying have every right to be heard. The message must have struck home to the listening Saul of Tarsus. Had not a similar prayer been uttered before, also outside the walls of Jerusalem and during the darkness of terrible suffering? Who could forget it? From amidst the wicked derision and cruel affliction, a gracious entreaty was heard: 'Father, forgive them, for they know not what they do' (Luke 23:34). Nobody could deny, least of all Saul, how contrary to human expectation is a loving gesture to one's enemies (Matt. 5:44). Now Stephen, 'full of faith and of the Holy Ghost' (Acts 6:5), was emulating his Master's example in a similar situation.

Jesus hanging limply upon a cross, or Stephen kneeling exhausted in the pit — these are not scenes likely to have impressed the world, until the prayerful requests were heard. Then would have dawned the realization of the enormous spiritual strength needed when undergoing such personal agonies, not only to refrain from thinking ill of the tormentors, but actually to desire their good (Prov. 25:21; Rom.12:20).

But, although the two prayers were alike, there was a subtle and noticeable difference between them. The Romans featured in the first (Luke 23:34); the Jews in the second (Acts 7:60).

At Calvary, the centurion (Luke 23:47) and the four legionaries (John 19:23) were merely on duty carrying out an unpleasant job, one which no doubt had been done many times before. Apart from the centurion, who was converted on the spot (Luke 23:47), the others had no understanding of the significance of the occasion. In response to a request from Christ himself they were therefore forgiven for their actions (Luke 23:34).

The Jews, however, were in a vastly different category. As Jesus informed the Roman governor, 'He that delivered me unto thee hath the greater sin' (John 19:11). Unbelief with regard to his claims and fear of reprisals from Rome had driven

Caiaphas and his colleagues on in the vengeful pursuit of their prey (John 11:48). The Jews were without excuse. Stephen therefore knew he could not excuse his killers; they understood exactly what they were doing, and why. Their viciousness mirrored a hatred, not so much for Stephen, but for the one he served (John 7:7). Saul of Tarsus, quite literally a stone's throw from Stephen's prayer, was deeply involved with 'this sin' (Acts 7:60) and being reminded of it would not have pacified him.

The martyr sleeps

Soon it was all over. A silence overshadowed the figure lying prone upon the blood-stained rocks. The executioners had completed their task. Their victim was dead. Or was he? Nobody present had any doubts that he was; in fact, someone would have been employed to officially pronounce the verdict. Very quickly the area cleared, except for a few of Stephen's friends, who gently carried him to his place of burial (Acts 8:2).

They were, of course, saddened by what had occurred, and deeply disturbed by what they had probably seen for themselves, but they possessed a secret known only to the followers of Christ Jesus (Matt. 13:11). Had they explained to those who had left the scene that Stephen was not dead but only 'slept', ridicule would have been the outcome. Unbelief laughed at Jesus for the same reason (Matt. 9:24). But an extremely vital truth separates 'death' from 'sleep'.

No experience known to man is more respected than death, the mourners moving slowly towards the cemetery, because there can be nothing worse than to die. In times past, men removed their hats and stood to attention when a hearse and its cortège were seen. It was not the cessation of a life which caused that reaction, but the recognition of the divine judgement upon mankind. Death is the scar upon the entire creation, from the 'wound' inflicted in Eden by the disobedience of our first parents. They were warned, 'Thou shalt surely die' (Gen. 2:17), but no notice was taken. The realm of death took over, sin abounded, and decay set in; the soil prepared itself for weeds (Gen. 3:17-18), the body for decline (Gen. 3:19), the soul for hell (Rev. 20:14). The tragic process cannot be reversed. Nothing, and no one, is excluded from the curse pronounced in Eden: '*All* die' (1 Cor. 15:22). To be born and reared in death then, as every human is, is to be enslaved to sin and inextricably drawn towards eternal damnation (John 8:24,34). To talk of a 'peaceful death', as the ignorant do, is a ridiculous phrase without relevance or meaning.

But 'sleep' — the very name conjures up a restful scene, bathed in peace, the experience of God's 'beloved' (Ps. 127:2). Death can create the appearance of sleep, but all are agreed as to which of the two is preferred! Rather the quiet stillness than the 'bondage' of fearfulness (Heb. 2:15). Death is gloom, nostalgia terminated, but sleep anticipates a bright tomorrow. How appropriate therefore that the redeemed are said, not to die, but to 'sleep' (1 Cor. 15:6).

When Jesus introduced this encouraging concept it was met with laughter (Matt. 9:24), and when he promised that his people 'shall never see death' (John 8:51) he was not believed. Death has for so long dominated the universal mind — the idyllic situation in Eden prior to the Fall having been forgotten or rejected — man finds it impossible to grasp that his great enemy can ever be defeated (1 Cor. 15:26). As death separates its victims from all they have known and loved, and does so everlastingly, the resurrection power of 'sleep' unites the beloved both in time and eternity (Rev. 6:8,11).

Stephen's ordeal over — although when viewed from the perspective of eternity it was a 'light affliction ... but for a

moment' (2 Cor. 4:17) — he 'fell asleep' (Acts 7:60) and entered into the glory of his ascended Lord (John 17:24), something of which he had glimpsed in the courtroom not long
before (Acts 7:55-56).

However, the reference to 'sleep' is by contrast immediately followed by one to 'death' (Acts 8:1), as the impact of
the martyr's testimony inflamed latent fury still further. Traditional Judaism was under threat. Persecution of the people
who belonged to this movement, the church, was therefore
considered a major priority (Gal. 1:13). Many fled from Jerusalem to escape its trauma, some travelling as far away as
Syria (Acts 9:1-3).

The cultural shock

Saul's travelling companions continued to cling to the road as
if for their very lives, overpowered by the very intensity of the
light. Suddenly, they were startled to hear Saul speaking to
someone (Acts 9:7). He did so trembling (Acts 9:6), shaken
out of his fury by this bewildering event, his chief concern
now being submission to the one he addressed. They heard
him enquire, first, who was speaking to him, and then, what
he had to do (Acts 22:10). Was it madness? Had the unremitting glare penetrated his brain? (Acts 26:24). Certainly they
could hear no other voice (Acts 22:9), but then, how could
they account for their undignified position on the ground and
the brightness of the light which kept them there? (Acts 26:13).
None of the witnesses at the site could dispute the reality of
the phenomenon.

As for Saul, he was unaware of the others, too shocked to
notice how they fared. Rather, he was riveted to the information the voice had just imparted — that it was 'Jesus' who
was speaking to him (Acts 9:5). Jesus ... Jesus of Nazareth ...

Jesus the crucified carpenter ... Jesus his arch enemy — alive? Not long before he had heard Stephen's prayer, intimating as much (Acts 7:59), and it had driven him to wreak havoc with the church (Acts 8:3; Gal. 1:13) whose leader Jesus is (Col. 1:18). And now he had been caught in the act of hunting Jesus' followers still further, with much wickedness in his heart! Although at the time he was 'alive without the law', never personally having experienced its probing exposures (Rom. 7:9), surely the enormity of his crimes leapt into view that morning near Damascus.

At a command Saul staggered to his feet (Acts 26:16). That may well have been the moment when an awful realization dawned: he was blind. The men, the horses, the landscape, the hope of rescue — they had all vanished, the voice of the triumphant Jesus the only reality left to him. What price could be placed upon his religious pedigree now? (Phil. 3:5-6). The proud Pharisee had nothing left to say; his persecuting zeal was in ruins; but there was much to hear. A turning-point had been reached for Saul, the church, and even for the world.

As he stood silently, and sightless, bathed in the splendour of Christ's presence, the 'heavenly vision' to which he was about to swear obedience was outlined to him (Acts 26:19). It was filled with paradoxes unlikely to be forgotten. He who was a 'Hebrew of the Hebrews' (Phil. 3:5), and as such hated all Gentiles (Eph. 2:11), would spend the rest of his life ministering to them; he who was at that moment blind would 'open their eyes' (Acts 26:18); he who had known great spiritual darkness (Acts 9:1) would be instrumental in leading them into the light he now shared (2 Cor. 4:6).

Saul the Pharisee had been reared in the belief that a legal involvement with God's covenant with Abraham was in itself sufficient to save his soul (Luke 3:8), and that the Gentiles were beyond redemption, 'without God in the world' (Eph. 2:12). He was later to learn the stunning truth (which would

have come as a tremendous cultural shock), that both the Jews
and the Gentiles 'are *all* under sin' and have 'come short of
the glory of God' (Rom. 3:9,23). In which case, *all* are by
nature under Satan's dominion (John 8:44). Saul's task, through
the proclamation of Christ's gospel and fervent missionary
endeavour (Acts 13:2-3), would be to bring the good news to
the Gentile races (Acts 26:18). In short, his commission was
the exact opposite of what Saul would have formerly believed
was possible, or what he would have desired (Eph. 2:11-17).

Led by the hand

What pride had been swallowed! However, the message was
over, the light had faded from the scene, and Saul and his
companions were alone once more. How long the extraordinary experience had lasted is unknown, and those present would
have been unable to say. They were all too shocked to estimate it; too bewildered to care.

But Saul knew what he had to do (Acts 9:6). He, who had
sped to Syria with an evil intention, was now obliged to enter
the city more slowly. He, who had intended arresting the followers of Jesus there, now headed towards them in need of
their help (Acts 9:8-19). It was a scene filled with pathos.
Pride and fury had given way to humility and tranquillity, as
the blind Pharisee was led by the hand like a child towards
Damascus (Acts 22:11). A new life had begun for him — a
new heart had been given him too (2 Cor. 5:17) — and a new
era for both the church and the world. But what had led to
that phenomenon?

1.
Hurried steps

Built upon Jerusalem's Temple Hill stood the magnificent palace of Antonia, once the home of Herod the Great, but now the residence of the Roman governor when visiting the city from his villa in Caesarea, seventy miles away to the northwest. He did so three times annually for the major Jewish feasts (Deut. 16:16). This was necessary as these occasions were opportunities for uprisings against the Roman occupation (Mark 15:7). Antonia was therefore also a fortress in which the legionaries were garrisoned, and was situated close to the mighty temple itself, the pivot around which the feasts revolved.

Jerusalem is 2,500 feet above sea level, a fact which encouraged the original inhabitants to believe it was impregnable (2 Sam. 5:6). However, Antonia's bulwarks reaching to the sky from the heights of the Temple Hill made it a very imposing edifice indeed, adequately reflecting the grandeur of imperial Rome. From this lofty position the city's scenic splendour was displayed panoramically on the widest of canvases, a view which must have impressed even a cynical Roman governor like Pontius Pilate.

Laid out in front of the grand palace, with its marble colonnades and wide, steep steps, was a huge open flat space adorned with porticoes, fountains and colourful mosaics. It measured 3,000 square yards, and was known by the Jews as *'Gabbatha'*, or 'the Pavement' (John 19:13). On the first 'Good Friday' it had been the scene of much drama, as one of the most notorious moments of all history was played out there when the vacillating Pilate and the vociferous crowds combined to condemn heaven's favoured Son. The precincts reverberated with the cries of the mob, baying for Barabbas' freedom and Jesus' blood (Matt. 27:19-25).

The following day, crossing its wide expanse, a large group of priests could be seen heading towards the main doors of the great building. From the statement in Scripture that 'the chief priests and Pharisees' (Matt. 27:62) were on their way to see the Roman governor, it would appear that the entire Sanhedrin was involved. Their mission was evidently one of great importance, which had necessitated an emergency sitting; otherwise this august body, consisting of seventy men 'plus two' (cf. Num. 11:16-30), would not have concerned itself with it.

Swallowed pride

The priests wore a frown. Communications between legalistic Judaism and pagan Rome were never straightforward, but this occasion was going to prove particularly difficult, for more than one reason. Pilate had done a great deal to offend the Jews right from the start of his rule: first, setting up overnight the Roman insignia in the heart of Jerusalem; then dipping into the sacred treasury *('Corban')* to pay for the building of an aqueduct; instigating a massacre; and even stooping to sacrilege in the achievement of his purposes (Luke 13:1). Now, the visitors knew, the tormentor of the Jews had them at a distinct disadvantage, and not only because they were obliged to step on to Roman territory.

To begin with, it was the sabbath (Matt. 27:62), a day on which the priests would normally have been engrossed in religious duties and would have kept themselves as far removed from Roman influences as possible. However, on this occasion they found themselves having to break the sabbath in order to seek assistance from their enemy. They, who were the first to point to the letter of the Fourth Commandment (Exod. 20:8-11) when instructing the people (although conveniently invoking the spirit of it instead when it suited them to do so — Matt. 12:11), must have resented the shattering of their image as strict observers of every detail of the law.

For his part, Pilate was no stranger to the priests' hypocrisy, aware that envy of the prophet from Nazareth had motivated their behaviour the previous day (Matt. 27:18), not loyalty to the laws of their God. Now once again their religious scruples were being swept aside in order to gain access to the Roman ear. 'Uncircumcised' Gentiles may have been 'defiled', but they had their uses! (Eph. 2:11-12).

How swiftly the collective conscience could be manipulated! Only hours before, when these proud leaders of Jewish society had taken their famous prisoner to Pilate (Rome alone could sanction an execution), they had refused to enter the building because of their fear of religious contamination (John 18:28). But on this special day, the sabbath, the priority was conveniently overlooked, such was the urgency of the matter the priests had arrived to discuss.

Confronting Pilate

The governor must have groaned when told about the priestly delegation at his door once more. No doubt the trauma of the previous day was still taking its toll upon him — not least the intrusion of his wife into the affair, with her ominous warning about Jesus of Nazareth (Matt. 27:19). What did they want *this* time?

Pilate was not a fool, nor could he afford to be, with the mighty Caesar as his employer, which meant he was constantly having to glance over his shoulder to assure himself that he had not incurred displeasure in Rome. Dealing with guile on the part of the Sanhedrin was one of the less agreeable tasks in his unenviable role as the custodian of the peace among a people deeply resentful of the occupying power. He therefore had to be on the alert when confronted by this troublesome body.

He quickly learned the nature of their request (Matt. 27:63-64). Not content with having witnessed the condemnation and crucifixion of their sworn enemy, the priests now wanted the tomb sealed and guarded to prevent rumours of a resurrection. Their victim had promised such a miracle 'after three days'; this was day two and time was short. The tomb would surely soon be raided by his disciples.

Although a pagan, Pilate, as ruler over the Jews, would have been cognizant of their basic beliefs, and aware that the Sanhedrin's concern did not ring true. It might even have caused him a certain cynical amusement. Standing before him were both the chief priests and the Pharisees, the one party diametrically opposed to the other on the subject of the spirit world. For example, the chief priests Annas and his son-in-law Caiaphas were Sadducees, appointed by Rome and more akin to the Tiber than the Jordan. Although they were the official custodians of the temple worship, they were, ironically, without a belief in an afterlife, belonging to the party which 'say that there is no resurrection, neither angel, nor spirit' (Acts 23:8). On the other hand, the Pharisees believed in both, so why on this occasion had the two groups united to make common cause in approaching their Roman enemy? After all, they did not require the governor's permission to have the tomb sealed and protected, as he made plain when he irritably reminded them they had temple guards to do the job (Matt. 27:65).

Priestly alarm

Pilate knew the answer. The priests had a special interest in stifling any rumour about Jesus of Nazareth's empty tomb. At all costs the carpenter-teacher's body had to remain 'imprisoned', his reputation destroyed and his popular appeal in the land made null and void.

They had watched him cut a swathe through the land, in the spirit of ancient prophecy, in his role as the appointed Shepherd of God's flock (John 10:11-14). There was no doubting his claims to be the Messianic shepherd-prince (Ezek. 34:23-24), and he evidently likened his 'sheep' to their neglected, spiritually 'wounded' and scattered forefathers, comparing the priests themselves with the ungodly 'pastors' of Jeremiah's day (Jer. 23:1-2). He even ploughed up the parched earth of traditional rabbinical teaching, condemning these men for having rejected God's Word (Matt. 16:11; Mark 7:1-13), and teaching his followers it was imperative that their righteousness should exceed that of the scribes and Pharisees if they were to enter heaven (Matt. 5:20).

Among the people his authority had rivalled theirs (Matt. 7:28-29) — something which had never been known before. In fact, at one stage he had even, in their eyes, established his own 'Sanhedrin', when seventy men (the number was significant — see Num. 11:25) were sent through the land in his name (Luke 10:1). It was vital therefore to justify themselves before the nation, and prevent any possibility of Jesus' influence taking root through the spread of rumours. They were later to be very disappointed, and extremely irate, when they realized that they had not been successful (Acts 4:1-2).

The opportunity to seek a vindication of their cause had arrived at Calvary. With their prey trapped and pinioned to a tree, the chief priests, scribes and elders gathered to take a cruel pleasure in watching Jesus suffer and die. It was a moment

of apparent triumphant victory for them, and they used it to
proclaim the most vitriolic of 'sermons' (Matt. 27:41-42), ironically failing to appreciate that their exultation had been foretold a thousand years earlier (Ps. 22:8).

The 'fiery darts' of stern, black-robed wickedness were
aimed at Jesus (Eph. 6:16), but found a lodging-place only in
the tree upon which he hung (Deut. 21:22). Like the blind
guides he had revealed them to be, 'weeds' that would one
day be rooted up by his Father (Matt. 15:13-14), these custodians of divine truth which they were incapable of fathoming
could not penetrate beyond the wood of the cross. In their
view, *he* did not embrace *it* for the salvation of sinners; *it*
clasped *him* a prisoner. Escapology, not theology, was their
major interest; the magic arts, not biblical truth, their main
concern; entertainment, not salvation, their chief delight (Matt.
27:41-42).

They played the riskiest game of all, as so many do, barter-
ing the glorious claims of Christ for the 'pottage' of their resolute refusal to believe them. One can gamble for no higher
stakes than to risk one's soul; no greater calamity can befall
the losers (Matt. 7:24-27). The possibility of an empty tomb
was too awful to contemplate, or even gossip surrounding it,
especially since this young man from Nazareth had referred to
himself as 'the resurrection' (John 11:25). If he rose from the
dead, they too would rise, with all their sins, to face a dreadful
judgement (2 Cor. 5:10).

Had they not aggressively opposed him when he identified
himself with the glorious 'I AM' of ancient history — in fact
stooped so low as to throw stones at him for doing so? (John
8:58-59). With what authoritative confidence he had used the
sacred title, 'I AM':

    ... the living bread (John 6:51);
    Before Abraham was... (John 8:58);

... the door [of salvation] (John 10:9);
... the good shepherd (John 10:14);
... the resurrection (John 11:25);
... the light (John 12:46);
... the way, the truth, and the life (John 14:6);
... the true vine (John 15:1);
... [the] king (John 18:37);
... Alpha and Omega [in fact, God] (Rev. 1:8).

Yet, through a travesty of justice and 'by wicked hands' (Acts 2:23), they had killed him! They had every reason to be sensitive about any talk of a resurrection.

Anxieties within

As for Pilate, even he would not have been immune from secret anxieties, hard Roman though he was. Could he have forgotten his wife's warning the previous day — one no doubt repeated at home behind the scenes? Claudia Procula (as history records that she was called) had dared to intervene at a most inappropriate moment. Acting upon a dream, if not a nightmare, she informed her husband he should have nothing to do with the condemnation of 'that just man' (Matt. 27:19). Caught as he was between the belligerent accusers, the innate nobility of the accused, his emperor in Rome and his conscience, the warning served to expose Pilate's weakness. He dithered, sought comfort in ambivalence, in the washing of his hands and the pathetic cry: 'I am innocent of the blood of this just person...' (Matt. 27:24). Nobody believed him, or had cause to do so.

The events of Skull Hill over, the drama continued inside the castle of Antonia, if only within Pilate's spirit. The public rinsing of his hands could not have washed away the ominous foreboding overshadowing him. In his official capacity as governor he would often have ordered the scourging and execution of men, but this situation was strangely different, and not one he could easily shake from his mind. There can be no doubt that the time spent in the company of the one whose crucifixion he had ordered had made an enormous impact upon him, despite what he might have said to the contrary. How could it have been otherwise?

Pontius Pilate and Jesus of Nazareth — the contrast between the two could not have been starker, the chasm deeper or wider. Their paths had both ploughed furrows across the nation — the one for good and the other for ill — but had never crossed. That Friday morning was the first time, when within the judgement hall the governor summoned his prisoner to approach (John 18:33). The arrogant Roman eagle, massive wings outstretched and talons at the ready, hovered over the lowly Lamb poised for the kill. At least, that is how the scenario must have appeared to an observer. In fact, it was far from the case. The 'eagle' appeared distinctly ill at ease (John 19:9). It was uncanny, and no doubt annoying to him. After all, *he* was not the captive! But there was a certain something about the Jew standing before him — a serene nobility, an authoritative confidence, which his awful circumstances had failed to take away from him. The guards who arrested him the previous evening had experienced a similar reaction. Before his arrest, so awesome had been his presence that they had been overcome and had actually fallen to the ground (John 18:6). Jesus could not, then, be dismissed out of hand, but had to be taken very seriously indeed, however reluctant the governor may have been to do so.

Pilate must also have been aware of the unusual change in his relationship with the manacled young man. To begin with, it was that of interrogator and dishevelled prisoner. Soon, however, the governor found his influence over the proceedings diminishing, as Jesus elevated the conversation to heights above and beyond the mundane (John 18:33 - 19:12). What was the proud magnificence of the empire, compared with the kingdom 'not of this world' about which he spoke? How could Roman power be matched against the decrees of heaven, from where all things are determined? (Acts 4:27-28). What was the worth of Roman (or Greek) philosophy, when heaven's King was truth personified (John 14:6), and his followers (unlike pagans everywhere) were guaranteed to know and understand it? (John 16:13).

Pilate was shaken, as his questioning revealed. He was ignorant of what was being said to him (as he showed when he asked, 'What is truth?'), but he nevertheless sought answers. There was an urgency about it, perhaps even a certain desperation, as if his dilemma (seeking to please everyone, even the prisoner) could only be solved by this carpenter from Galilee. Agitated, he enquired, 'Art thou the King of the Jews? ... What hast thou done? ... Art thou a king then? ... What is truth? ... Whence art thou? ... Speakest thou not unto me? ...' (John 18:33 - 19:10). He was an unhappy man, and remained that way, until his eventual suicide years later in Gaul.

For once, then, the troubled Roman agreed with the priests, had something in common with them. The young man being dead — he had made sure of that (Mark 15:44) — and the body entombed, it had to remain that way at all costs. It was important to Pilate that out of sight should also mean out of mind. Of course, he was troubling himself unnecessarily, as nobody had heard of the dead escaping from a tomb, and although the prisoner had spoken of his resurrection (Matt. 27:63-65), there was no possibility of it happening, was there? Surely not.

2.
The third day

Jerusalem slumbered in the final few hours or so before the dawn. The bright yellow tips of the sun's rays hovered coyly over the horizon, giving notice of the light which would shortly bask the landscape in the morning glare. Some would have already been up and about, but the narrow, dusty streets were still quiet, except perhaps for the sounds of a heavily laden mule or two, escorted by weary travellers, or for the scuffling of mangy dogs hidden away in dark alleyways. Soon the city gates, always securely shut at nightfall (Josh. 2:5), would be flung wide open, heralding the bustle of a new day.

Nearby was a beautiful garden — one of a number in the more prosperous sections of Jerusalem — where the tranquillity was in sharp contrast to the sounds of daytime activity within the highly populated city. These gardens invariably contained an olive grove and were profuse with colourful arrays of flowers, the air sweet with the heavy scent of blossom. There is no reason to believe that Joseph of Arimathea's was an exception. However, its beauty belied the use others might have intended for it, because in a peaceful and shady corner, hewn into the craggy rock-face, was a tomb.

A respected and wealthy member of the Sanhedrin, Joseph, like others in his position, probably desired that in death his remains should lie as close to the temple as possible (Luke

23:50-53). However, that was not to be — at least not in the tomb built for that purpose — because although this tomb contained a corpse, it was not that of Joseph.

Within the tomb

Shadows may still have been dancing in the half-light, and overhanging branches silhouetting grotesque shapes of various sizes. Certainly, at that time of day a cool breeze would have wafted through the trees, the silence broken only by the rustling of the leaves in the garden. Even the birds had not yet burst into song.

There were also shadows of a more recognizable kind to be seen, and probably whispers to be heard as well. Two or more men, temple guards, might have been seen pacing to and fro in front of a huge boulder which effectively sealed the tomb (Matt. 28:4). Attempting to keep warm after a night's vigil would not have been unusual, as they dutifully carried out their unenviable task of guarding a corpse in such eerie surroundings. They surely longed for the shift to end, after hours of boredom, and without anything to report. Little did they realize that, at that precise moment, something astonishing was about to happen. Had they, or even the entire world, been told of it, they could not have believed it. Within feet of them, death was on the point of giving way to resurrection, human impotence to divine omnipotence.

The tomb would have been no different from others of the period, similar to the one in 'Gordon's garden' in Jerusalem today: a small cave, with a narrow entrance, stone flooring and a ceiling just high enough to prevent a man of average height from stooping. Cut into the furthest rock-wall was a niche, and there, wrapped in a white linen cloth, with a separate 'napkin' covering his head, lay the body of Jesus of

Nazareth. Time was suspended in the bitter cold; the stillness possessing the razor-sharpness of ice.

The moment of resurrection

Profound mystery pervaded every recess of that sacred spot, beyond the sight of man, but those who are privileged to possess 'the mind of Christ' through his indwelling Spirit (1 Cor. 2:16; 3:16) are able to understand something of what transpired during that remarkable experience known as 'the resurrection'.

To begin with, a display of the divine splendour is never sheltered by shadow; the cry will always be heard: 'Let there be light' (Gen. 1:3). In which case, a candescence, a white radiance, must have filled the tomb's interior, sweeping aside in an instant all vestiges of shadow and chill. The one who was both human and divine, God 'manifest in flesh' (1 Tim. 3:16), and had lain for two full days in 'the dust of death' (Ps. 22:15) now, in a brief moment, was adorned with a 'glorious body' (Phil. 3:21), one not limited by time, but capable of elevation above and beyond it. The impotent passivity of the once crumpled form, bearing the hallmarks of death — sallow flesh, languid expression, hollow eyes, sagging mouth, twisted arms and legs — gave way to a rapid surge of divine strength. Death's sickly pallor surrendered to the radiance of death defied; the power of darkness (Col. 1:13) to 'the power of an endless life' (Heb. 7:16).

Yet — the mystery deepens! — Christ, although different, was as recognizable lying on the rock-shelf, aglow with glory, as he had been hanging upon the cross. The viciousness of crucifixion could still be seen in the lacerated hands and feet (Ps. 22:16) and the gash made by the spear-thrust (John 19:34), because these are the stimuli behind heaven's eternal acclamation: 'Thou art worthy ... for thou wast slain, and hast redeemed us to God by thy blood out of every kindred, and tongue, and people, and nation' (Rev. 5:9). This is the national anthem of the 'new Israel' (Eph. 2:13-18). For that reason the mutilation of his flesh will remain everlastingly, even though the flesh is now glorified (John 20:27).

The hope of centuries rested in what happened next. Within the silent realm of the tomb, where sound is a stranger, the whispered intake of breath could be heard. What then? The stirring of a finger, a foot, an arm? Curiosity is idle speculation. One thing is certain: as if ascending from the depths of the blackest and deepest of pools, his head thrusting through the surface into the brightness of daylight, Christ opened his eyes! It was a simple act, yet the most profound known to man, signalling that the finality of death could be overcome; the living no longer needed to be sought among the dead (Luke 24:5). Heaven had burst into that confined space. Christ is risen!

As dead men

Outside, the scene was set for the dawning of yet another day. The sun's rays inched their way towards the skyline, the chill of the night slowly submitting to the glow of dawn, while the foliage dripped with dew. The guards surely waited impatiently for their duty to end. It had been an uneventful night, as boring as it had promised to be! Now they thought only of returning home. But they little realized that at that precise moment the Son of God was walking towards the entrance to the cave, the giant rock which blocked it no longer a hindrance to him. He was not a ghost (Luke 24:39), but his was an experience which soared beyond the finite, and one in which physical considerations no longer held sway. He could have entered the garden leaving the boulder in place, but the world had to be made aware of the awesome power of God and the triumph of his risen Son.

They did not have long to wait. The one who had twelve legions of angels at his immediate disposal (Matt. 26:53) required only one to fulfil his purpose. This one angel swooped from heaven, the vanguard of a 'great earthquake' that concentrated its intense power upon the small tomb (Matt. 28:2).

A warning of what was to happen next would have been irrelevant, for resurrection never requires one and 'the watch' were present at the scene as a result of the machinations of men, and not by divine appointment (Matt. 27:62-66). They had no business being there, yet they found themselves within feet of the most remarkable moment since the creation of the universe. They were tragically ill-equipped for what transpired.

Throughout the night they had kept an eye on the silent darkness 'out there' for possible intruders, not, of course, anticipating the wonder of the resurrection taking place behind them. Unbelief, as always, was looking in the wrong direction, though in any case it can never hope to obstruct God's intentions. How could these guards, mere dupes in the hands of experienced knaves, hope to combat the power of one for whom no object is immovable or force irresistible? When Almighty God miraculously breaks through into time, there can be no escape from the swiftness of his approach, as men from the days of the patriarchs to the time of the apostles discovered. The men on duty at the tomb learned this too, the hard way. In the briefest possible space of time they found themselves cast into the vortex of divine intensity, one moment casually contemplating a return home after their night's work, the next petrified when confronted with the unleashing of heaven's majesty.

The garden would have been bathed very suddenly with brilliance, which swept aside all shadows. As if they were seeking to stare into the face of the sun, the speechless men must have found they had to shield their eyes, as their numbed minds groped for an understanding of what was happening. Within a short space of them stood one whose radiance was the beauty of eternal glory (Exod. 34:35), clothed in the brilliance of white light (Matt. 28:2-4). The ignorant guards wallowed in the deepest of quagmires beyond reach of reality. They just stared, their minds having been wiped clean of all thought.

No time elapsed for any adjustment to the remarkable moment, if such a thing was possible. With the appearance of the angel the tranquillity of the garden was shattered. Rapid was the onslaught, as from every direction within that confined space could be heard the sounds of nature's response. The men must have thought the world had ended, as with the heavy rumbling of the earth beneath their feet, the violent shaking of the trees scattering their olives and the cries of terrified birds, heaven heralded the glorious resurrection with an impressive display.

Nature though, however fierce, cannot match the realm of God for producing terror in the unprepared (Luke 12:5; Heb. 10:31). The 'watch' looked on in fear and trepidation as their angelic visitor performed the task, which no human could undertake single-handedly, of removing the boulder from the tomb's entrance (Matt. 28:2). Unbelief had sealed it (Matt. 27:64), but God derided the paltry attempt at keeping intruders at bay, by providing one of his own. Against him, even an entire army of 'keepers' would have proved useless, as Jewish history tragically records (2 Kings 19:35; Isa. 37:36).

There was no struggle, and no word was spoken. Unbelief's employees were reduced to being 'dead men' as they trembled abjectly before the visitor. He in turn, without uttering a word, triumphed in heaven's great victory by sitting upon the boulder in full view of his opponents (Matt. 28:2,4). They fled, while he waited for the first to arrive upon the scene. He did not have long to wait.

The first arrivals

The citizens of Jerusalem had been unaware of the fact that
the new dawn heralded one of the most significant days in
history. Startled, the city opened its eyes much quicker than
anticipated. What was that? The question hung upon many
lips. From close at hand, the unmistakable rumbling preceded
the briefest of explosions, as compressed energy was unleashed
upon its target. 'Great' earthquakes are not known for their
stealth (see Matt. 28:2).

It was not the first disturbance that weekend, or the first
quake. In fact, the many thousands packed into the city from
all over the known world for the Passover feast had almost
grown accustomed to the unusual phenomena which had been
a feature of the occasion. The focal point had been Skull Hill,
the scene of Jesus of Nazareth's crucifixion, where the Creator and his creation gave vent to their wrath. A violent storm
lashed the mound (Ps. 18:4-18), the terrain shook and trembled, and for three long hours the sun disappeared behind black
skies which stretched over the entire land (Luke 23:44). That
was not all. Graves were opened, their occupants raised from
the dead, and the temple's embroidered veil, separating the
most holy place from prying eyes (Exod. 26:31-33), was mysteriously torn apart (Matt. 27:51-52). In all its long and event-
ful history, the city of David had not experienced anything like
it. Now there was this earthquake.

The quiet approach

A group of women could be seen making their way through
the narrow streets which criss-crossed the city, intent upon
arriving at their destination as quickly as possible. The previous evening they had bought spices with which to anoint a

body (Mark 16:1), as was the custom, and the sabbath being over, they hurried towards the spot where the body lay (Luke 23:55-56). Some of them had witnessed the trauma of their Lord's crucifixion at close hand just two days before (John 19:25), and emotional stress must have driven them on in haste.

How many were in the group is unknown, since Luke refers to 'certain ... other women' (24:1,10), but there would have been safety in numbers, as danger lurked around every corner. The reason for this was that they were all associated with Jesus' intimate disciples, who had fled when the authorities arrived to secure his arrest (Matt. 26:56) — a fact anticipated by Scripture (Zech. 13:7). Now they were in hiding. Their womenfolk were therefore extremely vulnerable, with arrest on the instructions of the chief priests or abuse from the people always a real possibility.

This was especially so in the case of Joanna (Luke 8:3), who was married to Chuza. Her husband's employer was the notorious Herod Antipas, a son of an equally evil father, Herod the Great. It was a remarkable providence, replete with historic irony, in view of the fact that the father had sought to kill the infant Jesus (Matt. 2:1-13) and the son had cruelly victimized him as an adult (Luke 23:11), that the Herodian family should have in its midst one of his followers. A similar situation occurred years later in Rome, although this time it was Caesar himself who unwittingly found himself harbouring a church under his roof (Phil. 4:22). Almighty God has no enemy he cannot overthrow.

It was therefore a brave as well as a loyal party which headed towards the garden, led by Mary of Magdala, or Mary Magdalene, who had featured so prominently among the loving band of women who provided service and comfort to Jesus and his disciples and whose tender-heartedness and generous spirit was surely a constant source of encouragement. A few of them accompanied her now (Luke 8:2-3). Their lowly support was invaluable, mirroring Sarah's example (1 Peter 3:6), and one to emulate by sisters in Christ everywhere.

At least two of the group had particularly strong ties with Jesus, since they were mothers of prominent apostles. Mary of Magdala appears to have been a close friend of one of them, referred to as 'the other Mary' (Matt. 27:61), 'the mother of James the less and of Joses' (Mark 15:40). Was this unusual description, 'the less', a reference to his size, as has been suggested in the intervening years? If it was, one could not imagine a mother appreciating it! Equally, drawing attention to someone's disadvantageous physique would not have received encouragement from his Lord. This James carried with him the epithet 'the less' to distinguish him from his older namesake, one of the sons of Zebedee (Matt. 4:21). It was neither of these two who wrote the famous New Testament epistle. That was yet another James, Jesus' brother on the human level (Acts 15:13; Gal. 1:19). The father of James 'the less' was the unknown Alphaeus (Matt. 10:3), which suggests that Matthew (who simply refers to his mother as 'the other Mary' — Matt. 27:61; 28:1) was in fact James' brother. Some commentators disagree, on the grounds that, unlike the pairings in the Gospels of Peter and Andrew, James and John (Matt. 10:2), Matthew and James 'the less' are never paired. True, but then why are both these apostles referred to as 'the son of Alphaeus' (Matt. 10:3; Mark 2:14), if it is to be believed they did not share the same father?

The two Marys, Mary Magdalene and the mother of James 'the less' (and probably also of Matthew) — whose husband's name history has blurred so that it is variously recorded as Alphaeus, Cleophas (John 19:25) and Clopas — both shared a fervent devotion for their Lord. In fact, they accompanied each other on several occasions during that momentous weekend, the first being at Calvary, when they stood with Jesus' mother and the apostle John at the foot of the cross (John 19:25). With what courage they faced the unimaginable horror of it all. Then again, after John had removed Jesus' mother from the gruesome scene to his own house, as his dying Master had requested (John 19:26-27), the two women accompanied the party carrying his body to the tomb (Matt. 27:61). Now they found themselves together again on their way to it.

As for Zebedee's sons, James and John just mentioned, their mother was also in the group. Her name was Salome (Mark 15:40; cf. Matt. 25:56), and she was probably Jesus' aunt, as she may have been his mother's sister (see John 19:25). In which case, the brothers would have been Jesus' cousins. If that were the case, it was not unnatural or unusual that Salome should believe she had some influence over her nephew, as her sister had also thought (John 2:1-3). Whether that was so or not, one day her maternal instincts got the better of her. She audaciously requested Jesus that her sons should feature prominently in the kingdom of heaven, seated on either side of him, no less (Matt. 20:20-21). The incident revealed Salome's immaturity in theological matters — although this was equally true of the apostles themselves at that time — but her love for Jesus was undoubted. It was much more than that of a blood relationship, rather an unshakeable faith in his claim to be the Messiah.

The garden reached

By this time the sun had appeared above the skyline and was slowly reaching for its zenith; another day had begun with pristine freshness (Mark 16:2). The city gateways would already have been bristling with activity: bustling women, playing children, aloof priests, merchants with their overloaded mules, vendors plying their wares, beggars competing with each other for attention. Jerusalem had arrived at 'the third day' (Matt. 16:21).

Despite all the chatter there must undoubtedly have been relating to the 'great earthquake' the city had experienced a short time before (Matt. 28:2), there was still much ignorance about what had actually happened, and where it had taken place. This was probably due to the fact that the incident was over so quickly. Certainly, when Mary Magdalene and her friends arrived in Joseph's garden they appeared not to have known about it. They assumed the opening to the cave would still be blocked (Mark 16:3).

Perhaps it was the emotional strain the women were under which accounted for it — the horrors witnessed, the fears and alarms — but practical people though they were, they had overlooked a basic requirement, the removal of the 'great stone' (Matt. 27:60). It would have been far too heavy for women to move — Mark refers to it as 'very great' (Mark 16:4) — but it was only when they entered the garden that they began asking the question which should have occupied their thoughts before leaving their homes: 'Who shall roll us away the stone from the door of the sepulchre?' (Mark 16:3). They had completed the task, normally performed by women, of preparing the necessary spices and ointments (Luke 23:56), but had forgotten the role men would also need to play in the situation.

Within the garden

Approaching the grave where the remains of a loved one lie is never a simple matter, especially when the aura of death hovers overhead and tears are still fresh. How much more poignant were the feelings of this group of women that Sunday morning, one of whom had lost a relative and all of them a Lord. Bewildered, they must have wondered what the future held, incapable as they were of imagining what life would be like without Jesus. It was not to last, but for these women as they approached the tomb, instead of death being swallowed up in resurrection victory (Isa. 25:8), to all intents and purposes, death might have triumphed over the promise of resurrection.

Memories of the grotesque scenes at Golgotha, so aptly described as 'a place of a skull' (Matt. 27:33), were deeply etched upon their hearts. There was no way these remembrances would ever be erased. The cacophonous event, chilling in its viciousness, had been no place for sensitive ladies, especially for those emotionally involved. A few of them, including Jesus' anguished mother, who no doubt bore in mind Simeon's thirty-year-old prophecy, 'A sword shall pierce through thine own soul also' (Luke 2:34-35), had even managed to remain rooted to the spot at the foot of the cross throughout the appalling ordeal (John 19:25). Only abounding love and grace could have produced such courage. The entire proceedings had been harrowing in the extreme, but now they were back in the garden accompanied by a plethora of haunting thoughts, the sublime as well as the unpleasant. The symmetry of the trees against the skyline, the generous splash of colourful flowers, the gentle birdsong — how incongruous was the sight of a solitary and silent sepulchre against such a backcloth

The silent spectator

The good women suddenly stopped in their tracks. They had stumbled across the unexpected. Having arrived within sight of the tomb, they were surprised to discover that their initial query had been answered. Somebody had already shifted the boulder. But who? As they puzzled over the matter, they would have been even more amazed, had they realized they were being quietly observed by an angel (Matt. 28:2-4). And was it not also probable that, amidst the cluster of trees which inhabited such gardens, might have been seen the silhouette of a man?

Bewildered, they glanced around in all directions, but could not find answers that would solve the mystery — and solve it they intended to do! But in their haste, they overlooked the importance of the moment in more ways than one. To begin with, how quickly they had forgotten that this was the noted 'third day'. '… and be raised again the third day', their Lord had said (Matt. 16:21). They had visited the garden in a sombre mood when in fact rejoicing was called for, and now they expected the worst instead of anticipating the best. Sadly, the believer's gaze towards heaven is at times easily distracted by events upon earth (Phil. 3:20-21). Faith is not always as fervent as it is fickle.

Then again, the unexpected removal of the great rock (Mark 16:4) had focused their attention upon the immediate, preventing them from hearing the prophetic voices calling to them over the generations. Had not David, a thousand years earlier, anticipated that Christ's body would 'rest in hope', it being impossible for the power of death to have the final say over him? (Ps. 16:9-10; Acts 2:24-28). Was not death expected to be swallowed up in victory (Isa. 25:8), its fearful grip unloosed? (Ps. 49:15; Hosea 13:14). Resurrection hope was no newcomer to the world, but despite Jesus' repeated references to it (e.g. Matt. 22:23-33), the glorious certainties were lost on the women who loved and cared about him most. In that, they were not untypical of believers since, their faith more at ease with an occupied cross than an empty tomb.

There was something else. Shock had quickly given way to suspicion. If the sepulchre had been opened, then Jesus' body had surely been removed. Alarm gripped them. At that point, they must surely have felt more vulnerable than at any other time since they had known him. Throughout the previous three years they had played a supportive role, secure, living in the large shadow cast by the Lord and his apostles (Luke 8:1-3). Although they were only on the periphery of the circle, their menfolk would have shared with them much of what they had seen and heard: how that 'The blind receive their sight, and the lame walk, the lepers are cleansed, and the deaf hear, the dead are raised up, and the poor have the gospel preached to them' (Matt. 11:5).

They had shared vicariously in this amazing ministry, free, to a large degree, from the cut and thrust of daily controversy in which the men were engaged. Now, however, the situation had altered drastically. The eleven disciples (Judas having committed suicide — Matt. 27:5) were in hiding, and not only had Jesus died, but it appeared from where they were standing that they were not even in possession of his body. They were alone. For the first time, they were having to exercise their new faith in the true manner, without props of any kind. What were they to do? It did not take long for them to make up their minds; the situation was plain. They must immediately get word to the men of what had happened. They would know what to do!

At this point one has to be careful.[1] The tendency is to assume that all the women entered the tomb, and a superficial reading of Mark's account might create that impression: 'They said among themselves ... they looked, they saw ... and entering ... they saw...' (16:3-5). Yet, John informs the reader that Mary Magdalene, having noticed the removal of the boulder, 'then she runneth' to tell him and Peter (John 20:1-2). In other words, she ran immediately. And Mary's words to the men bear this out. There is no reference to having seen angels or receiving a message from them (a somewhat unusual occurrence), but rather her concern was with the Lord's missing body, which for her was implied by the removal of the boulder.

Mary, it appears then, probably younger and swifter of foot than the others, set off without a moment's hesitation to see Peter and John (John 20:2), whom she seems to have known were together. In the meantime, her friends were to inform the rest of the apostles. But first, hesitant though they were to draw near to the bleak darkness of the tomb, being practical women they had to make sure their assumptions were correct — that Jesus' body was indeed no longer there.

The living among the dead

With Mary Magdalene now on the way to find Peter and John, that left her women friends to walk hesitantly towards the entrance to the tomb. The aperture was black and uninviting; beyond it lay mystery, and much more of it than they could possibly have anticipated.

The interior of a tomb would have been familiar territory to them, it being traditionally a woman's task to anoint the deceased with specially prepared spices (Luke 23:55-56), and therefore the friends were no doubt used to such places. The cool, claustrophobic stillness of death, and the morbid fears associated with it, would not normally have held any special terror for them. However, that early morning the circumstances were very different.

One of them must surely have peered through the opening towards the slab of rock at the farther end of the cave, only to confirm what they had suspected: it was bare. The body of Jesus had gone (Luke 24:3). Without further hesitation, curious to find out as much as they could, they entered. It was at that moment, before they had time to express their bewilderment, that they suddenly realized they were not alone. There was someone else in the cave with them — in fact, two others! (Mark 16:5; Luke 24:4).

In that environment, in such a situation, surprise quickly turns to shock. It is easy to picture the probable scene. Their hearts pumping furiously, the women turned sideways, and gasped. One of the strangers was a 'young man' dressed 'in a long white garment' (Mark 16:5), which could only mean one thing: angels! How often they must have listened to Jesus' mother, their friend Mary of Nazareth, relating the account of Gabriel's visit to her over thirty years before and also recalling the angelic appearances to Zacharias and the shepherds (Luke 1-2). But now it was their turn, and hearing about something is less alarming than experiencing it at first hand.

Beings swift of flight

But what are angels? Rising and descending upon the magnificent court of heaven are hosts of them (Gen. 28:12), countless myriads swarming through the reflected candescence of the divine presence, where worship is ceaseless and at its most profound (Ps. 89:7). To fly with these flames of holy fire ((Ps. 104:4; Heb. 1:7) is to exult in the being of God, to marvel eternally at the realization of unrivalled unity within unquestioned trinity; to be ceaselessly fascinated and ecstatic by the surprises that Deity reveals to those outpoured in energetic devotion. It is to bathe in the fervent love which flows through every recess of the heavenly circle, in an affectionate glow of joyful response. It is to give vent to innate ardour with outcries of acclamation: 'Praise ye the Lord from the heavens: praise him in the heights. Praise ye him, all his angels: praise ye him, all his hosts' (Ps.148:1-2).

They do indeed praise him, but, vast though these worshipping armies are (Heb. 1:6), their limitations are known to all within the royal court (Job 4:18). They are ever aware of the radiance of the divine face, reflecting an aspect of it in their own (Acts 6:15), but are not permitted to see it. They over-shadow the throne of grace but cannot sit upon it; they possess feet but humbly cover them lest they be tempted to stand and linger before the one to whom they minister (Heb. 1:14). They know of his love (1 John 4:8), but instead cry, 'Holy, holy, holy' (Isa. 6:2-3). Obeisance is their duty, reverential awe their delight.

In submission to the divine will and purpose, the angelic myriads step aside to usher into heaven's glory vast and innumerable multitudes (Rev. 7:9-12) with more right to the favour of the thrice-holy Potentate than they (1 Tim. 6:15). These are privileged members of the family, not mere servants (Heb. 1:14). Their eyes do not need to be covered, for they bear the family likeness (1 John 3:2). Nor do they require to cover their feet (cf. Isa. 6:2), for to be seated on the throne of grace (Rev. 3:21), or to stand before it (Rev. 7:9), are things that would be expected of them. Those who belong to the family of the King-Priest (Mark 3:33-35; Zech. 6:12-13), who in fact have been made a kingdom of priests (Rev. 1:6), are not only joyful observers of ultimate glory (John 17:24) but also sharers in it (Rom. 8:30).

But in the meantime

Too awestruck to speak, too terrified to run away, the women just stared at the strangers, their minds numb. Besides, language is not the most adequate expression of communication when confronted by those from beyond the horizons of time. They waited for the next move, and it was swift in coming. An unusual question was put to them, in a matter-of-fact way, which seemed to imply that the trembling group should have known the answer. The angel asked why they were seeking for the living among the dead (Luke 24:5).

Unlike those outside the covenant of grace, heaven looks compassionately upon its favoured children. The guards were dealt with sternly and driven from the scene (Matt. 28:4,11), but the ladies were smiled upon, as Mary and the shepherds had been all those years ago, and their trembling stilled by the gracious words: 'Fear not'. It must in later years have been a constant source of contemplation and thanksgiving to the friends that their spiritual relationship to Jesus had made all the difference and was, in fact, the sole reason for it (John 14:27).

The angel of light, aloof from the frailties to which humanity is prone, could have spoken sternly, as from one who is sinless to the sinful. Instead, heavenly wisdom 'that is ... pure ... peaceable, gentle, and easy to be entreated' (James 3:17), paved the way in the unequal relationship between those within the tomb. Instruction and the calming of the situation were substituted for a terror which would have robbed them of an understanding of what had happened.

Having assured them of his friendliness (Mark 16:6), one of the angels established the fact that he knew why the women were there (Matt. 28:5). Idle curiosity was not their motive, or merely the desire to satisfy an intellectual quest, but a genuine love for the Son of God. It was as well that this was so. They would have received short thrift had it been otherwise, for toying with revealed truth (Matt. 22:29), or playfully tinkering with the spirit of discipleship (Luke 14:25-27), does not meet with heaven's approval. The empty tomb, like the church itself (1 Tim. 3:15), is not a debating chamber where the 'pros and cons' of Christianity are critically scrutinized, but rather a place of pilgrimage for those already convinced by the Spirit of truth (John 16:13).

Then again, the angel referred to 'Jesus', even 'Jesus of Nazareth' (Matt. 28:5; Mark 16:6). The mysterious stranger, whose adoration of the triune God is intimate and eternal (Isa.

6:1-3), could have referred to his Master (Heb. 1:4), the Lord of glory (John 17:24), in high theological terms. He could have reached deeply into heaven's treasure box of truth, leaving his hearers bewildered and bereft of understanding and even more terrified. However, not wishing to alarm his friends still further, he set the boundaries of the conversation to include them and to put them at their ease. They knew their Lord as 'Jesus', and therefore he too called him by that name (Matt. 28:5). Preachers, whose theological grasp is far inferior to his, can learn from this angelic example! Baffling the unsophisticated with élitist theological expressions may enhance a reputation, but it could also damage a soul.

He also referred to Nazareth (Mark 16:6), associating himself, not with matters beyond their grasp, but with that lowly 'dry ground' (Isa. 53:2) they had trodden with Jesus so often. In fact, the reference to the town where he had been reared (Matt. 2:22-23) would also have reminded them of other angelic visitations associated with Nazareth (Matt. 1:20; Luke 1:26-27). There was indeed nothing to fear.

The irony of the occasion was unknown to the women, and their angelic friend had no intention of revealing it, but at that moment he could probably have pointed through the opening of the tomb to the garden beyond to where their risen Lord might have been seen. There is no reason to believe he was not watching what was happening to his beloved followers, as subsequent events seem to reveal (John 20:15).

But the angel had no intention of making matters easy for the women, for faith is always weaker when it is permitted to stroll along smooth paths. Instead he pointed to where Jesus' body had lain and no doubt observed their reaction closely. What lessons an empty, cold slab can teach! Heaven's messenger was brief and to the point, his message simple and convicting. It consisted of three succinct phrases, 'He is not here ... he is risen, as he said' (Matt. 28:6), like small arrows shot from the bow, and each one hitting the target accurately. The wives of Alphaeus, Zebedee, Chuza and the others could not have misunderstood the message ('as he said'), which, although they would not have known it, was a preparation for their meeting Jesus shortly afterwards, to prevent them from being too overcome when he suddenly appeared in front of them (Matt. 28:9).

The slab was empty: 'He is not here.' Their Master's body was no longer lying prone upon it; but why did they expect it to be there? Mary and Salome had sons who had been present on the occasion when Jesus had raised Lazarus from the dead; they must therefore have heard about the astonishing account. If Jesus *is* 'the resurrection, and the life' (John 11:25), as he had on that day authoritatively declared, why should they be surprised that his body was not still helplessly lying in the tomb? As Peter was later to proclaim triumphantly, 'Whom God hath raised up, having loosed the pains of death: because it was not possible that he should be holden of it' (Acts 2:24). Death can no more tie down the resurrection than man can manacle God.

It was a much-needed lesson. How unhappy the women had been as they hurried towards the tomb that morning, harbouring in their hearts the assumption that nothing could possibly alleviate their sorrow. They believed in the resurrection of the body, as the Pharisees had taught them (Acts 23:8), but, like Martha of Bethany, no doubt sought comfort from the belief that 'He shall rise again in the resurrection at the last day' (John 11:24) — and that was probably a long way off! Then sadness had turned to anxiety, when they thought it likely that the boulder would prevent access to the sepulchre (Mark 16:3).

In other words, 'He is risen' (Matt. 28:6) was not one of the ideas uppermost in their minds, but the angel had stated the fact as if he considered it should have been. Like the men,

they too were 'slow of heart to believe all that the prophets
have spoken' (Luke 24:25). It did not take an educated rabbi,
or even a fine tooth-comb, to discover the wonderful
resurrection promises contained in their Scriptures. How often
they must have witnessed in the synagogue the unfolding of
the appropriate scroll by the rabbi, and heard the mighty prophetic words. Had not Job in his suffering been prophetically
confident that his Redeemer lived: 'For I know that my redeemer liveth, and that he shall stand at the latter day upon the
earth'? (Job 19:25). And had not David stated that the 'Holy
One' would never experience 'corruption'? (Ps. 16:10).

The women's response might have been to think that if their
menfolk were equally remiss in their understanding of scriptural
truth (Matt.16:21-22), what chance did they have, who were
only on the periphery of the circle? However, they might have
remembered the sister of Martha and Lazarus, yet another
Mary, whose eagerness to learn had found her quite literally
sitting at Jesus' feet (Luke 10:39). If she could do that, why
could not they? The excuses for ignorance about that which
God has revealed, and has written down in one's own mother
tongue, are very few indeed (Luke 11:28). As a great man
once said, to ignore the Scriptures is to ignore Christ.

However, it was the third and final 'bolt' shot from the
angel's bow which must have buried itself deeply into their
consciences: the three accusing little words, '… as he said'
(Matt. 28:6). This was such a simple phrase, assuming a child-
like trust. Had Jesus not told his friends, and through them the
women as well, that following his arrest and execution he would
'be raised again the third day'? (Matt. 16:21). That day had
arrived. Why then were the men in hiding, and the women in a
quandary, if they all claimed to love their Master and believe
his teaching? For them, as for many others since, the discovery was made that 'fair-weather' belief is a puff of wind, and

that faith should never be confused with mere fervour (Matt. 16:16,22-23).

Mary, Salome, Joanna and the other ladies received the gentle rebukes in silence. They should have paid 'more earnest heed' to what they had heard from Jesus, instead of allowing their memories to 'let slip' the good news (Heb. 2:1), which the angelic newcomer at their side continued to remind them about. Seeking the living among the dead was no way in which to prove loyal to the one they held dear (Luke 24:5-8).

Still, the triumphant and long-awaited resurrection day had arrived and heaven was ablaze with acclamation (Rev. 1:18). It was therefore not a time for solemnity but rather for haste to impart the joyful news to those first favoured to hear it (Mark 16:7), just as Anna had done about his birth (Luke 2:37-38). Christ had risen!

The women left the tomb hastily and breathed the early morning air with relief. Startled into silence, their pulses racing, they made their way through the garden to the outside world. It was wonderful news they had to impart to the men and they hurried on their way as fast as they could. Nothing and no one was going to cause them to deflect from their purpose (Mark 16:8).

3.
The pace quickens

In the meantime, Mary Magdalene was unable to share in the tremulous rejoicing of her friends. Her sadness and alarm still lingered. We can imagine her hurrying through the narrow alleyways and streets which traversed the city like ruts in a field, her thoughts still in the garden. What could have happened? At that stage, angelic visitations heralding the resurrection of her Lord were unknown to her. All she knew was that the large boulder which had sealed the tomb where Jesus' body had lain had mysteriously been shifted. But how, and by whom? Although she had not actually looked inside the tomb, one fact occupied her mind: the body had been removed. That being so, more than one person must have been involved.

At last she arrived, breathless and seemingly distressed. Before Peter and John could enquire what was wrong, she had blurted out her thoughts: 'they' had removed the Lord's body and she and the other women had no idea where they had taken it (John 20:2). Of a spiritual frame of mind though she was, the contents of her concern were practical and strangely untempered by faith. It had not registered that the one who had 'raised' her from the clutches of seven devils (Luke 8:2) could raise himself from death's embrace (Acts 2:24).

A mother's reaction

It is not known whether Jesus' mother was present and heard the news. Since John had been entrusted with her care, as soon as her son had died she was taken to the bosom of her nephew's home (John 19:26-27). Was that where Mary Magdalene headed, knowing she would discover Peter there? (John 20:2). Certainly, if the deceased's remains have been removed from their resting-place, there is never a question that the next of kin are told about it first. It would have been extremely unkind, even cruel, to have kept such alarming news about a dead son from his mother. She would need to know straight away of anything untoward having taken place, and the angel had not overlooked this fact when he instructed Mary's friends to 'tell his disciples and Peter' (Mark 16:7), without mentioning Jesus' mother. He was concerned with geography, not etiquette, as the mention of Galilee implied.

Whether Mary was there or not, one can easily imagine how she would feel on being told there had been a violation of her son's tomb. Her anguish must have deepened. How much more suffering could she take? She had anticipated it for over thirty years, since her remarkable meeting with the godly Simeon in the temple at Jerusalem. As she held the infant Jesus in his arms, the old man had looked at her and spoken of the sword-thrust that would penetrate her soul (Luke 2:34-35). She had experienced it during her vigil at the cross (John 19:25). But now this — having killed her son, the authorities apparently could not even leave his body to rest in peace.

Presumably, if the others had failed to remember Jesus' teaching about his resurrection on 'the third day' (Matt. 16:21), Mary had overlooked it also. It would not be surprising if she had. Her household had hardly been conducive to spiritual contemplation, her eldest son being regarded as 'an alien' (Ps. 69:8) by his unbelieving brothers (John 7:5), a domestic

situation which no doubt entailed all the stresses within the
family unit which normally accompany such a state of affairs.
Even his friends and relatives considered Jesus to be 'beside
himself' (Mark 3:21). It had evidently been such an ordeal for
Mary that, knowing all about it, even during his agonies on
the cross her caring son had taken the trouble to commit his
mother into John's hands (and therefore away from his brothers and sisters — Mark 6:3), so that she might end her days in
fellowship with his disciples (John 19:26-27).

The race to the garden

Onlookers would have wondered what had caused such a flurry
of activities, since in Israel's climate it was unusual for its citizens to run. Besides, the length of the robes hampered speed.
Mary Magdalene would not have run with the men even had
she been capable of keeping up with them, for it was not in
accord with traditional modesty for a woman to do so. She
intended returning to the garden (John 20:11), but at a respectful distance from Peter and John (John 20:3-4).

As he ran, Peter's thoughts must have been many, and not
solely of Mary's startling news, about which he and John were
decidedly sceptical (Luke 24:11). His subsequent reaction to
the emptiness of the tomb (John 20:10) revealed that resurrection was far removed from his mind, as it had been at
Caesarea Philippi when Jesus had introduced the subject. Then
Peter's reaction had been so carnal that the rebuke from his
Lord, 'Get thee behind me, Satan', must have shrivelled his
confident impetuosity (Matt. 16:21-23).

But there was something else even more pressing. The
mystery surrounding the apparently empty sepulchre had stirred
an already troubled conscience and the latent misery deep
within him. How proud had been his assumption — indeed,

obscene on such an occasion — that he, of all men, would never be offended in his Lord! (Matt. 26:33,35). Why, he was prepared to die with him! Pride had come before the fall (Prov. 29:23), as much boasting led to many tears when reality finally measured up to dreams (Matt. 26:75).

There must have been an air of desperation about Peter as he ran. The apparent finality of Jesus' horrific death, which unlike John he was unable to watch at close quarters (John 19:26), had thrown a blanket over his spirit. It was crushed under the weight of guilt. He yearned to see Jesus once more, to make amends, to say 'sorry', to step back in time. If only he could reach the happy moments and relive them! It was too late, and the realization only made matters worse. The future therefore seemed bleak. He would never be able to forget that, when his Lord needed his support most, he was seen in the wrong company vehemently denying that he knew him (Matt. 26:69-74). Still a young man, he would have to live out the remainder of his life under the dark clouds of treachery and wretched weakness in a brief moment when great strength had been required.

He was unaware of the words he would write many years later to his troubled brethren and sisters in Christ. Like Peter on his way to the garden, they too would suffer, but because of faithfulness to Jesus, not through disloyalty to him. How painful it must therefore have been for him in later life to be reminded of that period when, despite having actually walked with the Son of God, he still denied him (Mark 14:66-72). His readers, on the other hand, had never seen Jesus, but because of their love for him, were having to bear patiently 'the trial of faith' (1 Peter 1:6-8). Peter was indeed in a most unhappy frame of mind as he ran, each step seeming to emphasize his guilt.

On the other hand, John had cause to be troubled too. He had not openly disclaimed knowledge of Jesus, as Peter had done, but was not his hasty escape from Gethsemane with his brethren that dreadful night also a denial? (Matt. 26:56). Of course, John would have been familiar with Zechariah's prophecy related to the event, 'Smite the shepherd, and the sheep shall be scattered...' (Zech. 13:7), but knowing he was one of those 'sheep' would have been of little comfort to him at the time! Besides, Jesus was his cousin, Mary of Nazareth his aunt. Family ties surely dictated his duty to have supported his loved one, especially as theirs was a very close relationship (John 13:25).

Still, he and Peter had sought to make amends for their timidity as soon as Jesus' arrest had been effected. They had followed the procession, at a respectful distance, as it made its solemn way from the garden with its captive (John 18:12-15). This was a daring thing to do, to be within such a short distance of the temple guards who sought their arrest.

Perhaps it was Peter's suggestion, seeking to give credence to his boasting earlier that evening (Matt. 26:33), but he and John tried to get as close to Jesus as possible in the courtroom ruled over by Caiaphas the high priest. The fact that John was known to him, presumably through business connections (John 18:15; Mark 1:19-20), assisted them in their attempt. In retrospect, John must surely have realized their folly, because the evening ended in Peter's bitter tears and John's strange disappearance, for which there is no known explanation (Matt. 26:69-75).

Whereas the experience had understandably driven Peter into hiding, John showed tremendous courage by being within feet of that central cross on Skull Hill, although not as much as Jesus' mother and the other women with her did. Theirs was an astonishing display of devotion in the face of extreme adversity (John 19:25). With John, the 'apostle of love', they shared a unique and gruelling experience, the most dreadful in a weekend of great emotional stress. At close quarters, they

witnessed the twisted features of a loved one suffering excruciating agony, heard his groans (and those of the thieves), saw
the rivulets of blood dripping to the red-soaked earth from
nail-pierced hands and feet (Ps. 22:16), and yet remained rooted
to the spot despite the outpouring of divine fury manifested in
nature — an earthquake, lightning, thunder, violent wind, tor-
rential rain and hailstones (Ps. 18:6-15).

They did not, could not, leave; a profound love prevented
it. They stood riveted to the spot. If only they could have eased
the appalling situation in some way! But they were unable to
do anything but 'watch and pray' (Matt. 26:41). The helplessness deepened their distress. For John, though, there was an
added dimension. Each minute he spent at Calvary, with the
Roman and priestly authorities within touching distance (Luke
23:35-36), he risked being recognized and arrested. One glance,
a suspicious mind and enquiring curiosity — that is all it would
have taken.

Providence, though, overshadowed the humble group at
the foot of that central cross, protecting it from the wrath of
God and man, because it was their privilege to hear the whispered compassion of their dying Lord, instructing John to take
good care of his mother, Mary of Nazareth. Shortly afterwards,
the end came with the triumphant words for which Calvary is
famous: 'It is finished!' Christ's atoning sacrifice had reached
its fulfilment; its highest peak (John 19:25-30).

But if John had run *from* the garden of Gethsemane, he ran
even faster *to* the garden tomb. What would he find? He had
only Mary's hurried and scant report to assist his imagination
(John 20:2), which by this time had been stirred, although like
everyone else's, not in the right direction.

Years later, in retrospect, John had marvelled at the momentous privilege which had been his and that of the other
apostles. They had glanced at, gazed upon and even touched
the eternal Word of life, and so amazed was he by the wonder

of it that when he wrote about the remarkable experience he repeated the claim, as if to make sure his readers had taken in what he had said (1 John 1:1-2).

But as a young man heading towards the tomb with great speed, John did not appear like one who had 'beheld' the glory of the Messiah. His haste had more to do with the practical than the spiritual, the apparent disappearance of Jesus' body than with any expectation that 'the only begotten of the Father' (John 1:14) had actually risen from the dead, or was capable of doing so.

However, had he not been present on the astonishing occasion when Lazarus, their friend from Bethany, left his tomb where his corpse had been lying for four days? Four days! Was it not possible, therefore, for Jesus to leave his own tomb after two? 'Lazarus, come forth', had been the divinely authoritative command, and without hesitation the dead man heard his voice and responded (John 11:43-44). It has been suggested that if Jesus had omitted his friend's name, there would have been a general resurrection! (John 5:28). Had not Martha, Lazarus' sister, told John about Jesus' unusual yet comforting words to her that day: 'I am the resurrection, and the life: he that believeth in me, though he were dead, yet shall he live'? (John 11:25).

No one, least of all John and his fellow apostles, could have mistaken the wonderful teaching: their Lord exercised ultimate authority over the realm of the dead (John 5:25) — in fact possessed 'power over all flesh' (John 17:2). In which case, why had they been such poor students? One lesson had been learned, however: how simple it is to rest one's head on Jesus' chest when he is present, but how quickly faith wanes when he appears to have left the room! As John headed for the tomb his face would have worn a frown, not the triumphant joy it should have registered.

Mary, on the other hand, would have lagged behind the muscular fishermen as all three, at irregular intervals, hastened through the crowds to the quiet spot beyond the city walls. She had already run to her friends as quickly as decorum permitted her to impart her news (John 20:2), and now she was having to run all the way back again. She must have been exhausted. The emotional strain, the anxiety, the fearfulness, the haste, and maybe the men's scepticism — all surely were taking their toll.

If as they ran the men looked grim, Mary was suffering from increasing despair, her mind occupied with just two thoughts: 'They have taken away the Lord ... and I know not where they have laid him' (John 20:2,13). Within those two clauses lay not only the crux of her immediate dilemma, but the summing up of her entire life. Mary pre-empted the apostle Paul's testimony by many years: 'To live is Christ' (Phil. 1:21).

The reason why this was so is well known: she had been delivered by Jesus from demonic powers of such intensity that the very special number seven was attributed to them. How this terrible affliction was manifested is unknown — nor is curiosity profitable — but clearly Mary was dominated and controlled by evil spirits. Then Jesus entered her life and, in saying that, one has said everything there is to say. Like 'Legion', she too sat at her Lord's feet in her right mind. How could either of them ever cease from loving him — in fact, do anything other than desire to 'be with him' always? However, whereas 'Legion' was instructed to return to his own people, to proclaim what 'great things Jesus had done unto him', Mary was committed to the same task by joining many other women in ministering to his practical needs and, presumably, those of his apostles (Luke 8:2-3,35-39).

But now he had gone and, with what appeared to be the removal of his body, Mary must have felt an even greater sense of emptiness in her life. Like the brethren, the sisters had also imbibed the gloom which hovered over them all, the feeling of anti-climax resulting from their Lord's death (Luke 24:21). They had expected so much — in fact everything — but the entire experience of seeing him treated so mercilessly by the authorities had devastated their confidence and left them wondering what remained of the hope he had given them. It was too much for Mary, who probably sobbed as she ran — as she certainly did shortly afterwards (John 20:11).

Second-hand cloth

Probably because he was younger than Peter and could run faster, John arrived first within sight of the tomb, and one can imagine his feelings. Mary was right after all! At least, he could see the boulder had been removed, but whether Jesus' body was still inside had yet to be ascertained. His walk towards the opening was surely hesitant, as if fearful of the truth, because at first he evidently had no intention of entering the cave (John 20:5). Instead, he merely peered inside, considering a cursory glance sufficient, but it was shortly to prove otherwise. Not far away were the grave-clothes, and that was all of any significance — or so he thought, except for the uneasiness lingering can cause in such circumstances. For this reason, John was probably pleased when Peter joined him, although he was not to know his every move was observed by spectators! (John 20:11-14).

Peter's impetuosity was renowned: he was invariably the first to eagerly step forward, whether to express the desire to walk on water (Matt. 14:29), confess his Master's lordship (Matt. 16:16), boast about his own loyalty (Matt. 26:33), or refuse the washing of his feet (John 13:8). Now he probably regretted not having been first at the tomb, but once he had arrived at John's side, unlike his friend, he entered without a moment's hesitation (John 20:6).

It was a good thing he did, because he noticed something of importance which John had missed. Not only was the rocky niche vacant which had once been occupied by Jesus' body, but there was something unusual about the grave-clothes. John's momentary glance had failed to spot it (John 20:5). First was the fact that they were there at all. Officials removing a corpse would surely have kept the body covered in its special shroud. On the other hand, had vandals broken into the tomb, would they have stopped to unwind the clothing, and then carefully have folded the head wrapping and placed it neatly to one side? (John 20:7). There was something odd about it.

Peter suspected it, and probably beckoned John to join him. The two then considered the matter together within the cave (John 20:8). The tomb was empty, but if not because of the authorities or grave-robbers, what then? Whatever their conclusions — if any — they were certainly not rooted in Scripture. Not therefore considering the possibility of Jesus having risen from the dead (John 20:9), they returned to the fresh air even more puzzled than before.[1] By that time Mary had breathlessly arrived and the two men obviously would have told her of their discovery: that she had been correct, the body was missing (John 20:2). It was too much for Mary. She wept. Her worst fears had been realized. Uncertainty can often prove even harder to bear than bad news.

Angels unawares

Peter and John then acted strangely. The tomb was empty. Jesus' body was missing. Mary was weeping. Yet they went home! (John 20:10-11). It was unusual behaviour in the circumstances, and one can only assume that 'home' meant John's house, where Jesus' mother was staying (John 19:27). It was imperative that the news reach her as soon as possible. For that reason, Mary Magdalene was left by herself outside the tomb.

Alone, Mary continued to give vent to her feelings, questions mingling with her tears (John 20:11). Who had desecrated the tomb and removed the body? Why had it been taken? Where was it now? And what would become of it? She had no answers to any of these queries, nor to the most practical question of all: what would become of the brethren and sisters who made up Jesus' band of followers? The more questions she asked, the further away answers appeared to be. Despair had taken up residence.

There seemed no point, but before leaving the area and despite what Peter and John must have told her, Mary decided to glance into the tomb to see for herself — just in case! (John 20:11). How could she leave the garden, drawn as she was to the spot by an irresistible fascination? As she stooped before the narrow opening, without her being aware of it, the three silent spectators closed in upon her. Since the dawn, they had witnessed the bewilderment, the anxiety, the 'comings and goings' and, above all, the gossamer-like faith of those who had gathered at the sepulchre that morning. Mary's tearful concern (1 Cor. 15:19) was the moment to spring the most joyous, and sweetest, moment known to mankind.

She peered into the tomb, not expecting to see very much except the cloths Peter and John had mentioned, but instead... She gasped. It was already occupied! As with her friends earlier that morning, she was incapable of running from the scene; shock had riveted her to the spot. She just stared disbelievingly, for the darkness had given way to radiant light, solitude to companionship. Seated at each end of the slab, like cherubim in the most holy place overshadowing the mercy seat, were two angels (John 20:12; cf. Exod. 25:22).

At first, no doubt, her mind refused to accommodate to the reality of what her eyes were telling it to believe. Was she really seeing angels? Presumably, she had not experienced anything like it before, but there was no question as to what these two beings were. She stared at them. What does one say to an angel, or, even more so, to two of them? What can one say? The realm they inhabit is beyond the great divide separating heaven from earth. Like those of the sovereign God, their thoughts and ways were not to be compared with Mary's, but were above her reach (Isa. 55:8).

Human speech, therefore, is superfluous when, without warning, they suddenly appear. In that situation the shepherds to whom the wonderful proclamation about the incarnation was revealed had remained silent until they recovered their composure after the angels had gone (Luke 2:8-15). On the other hand, Jesus' mother spoke only when reason persuaded her to do so, and that was merely to ask a question (Luke 1:34).

Mary, more tearful than fearful, was still peering into the tomb when one of the angels spoke. It reveals a great deal about this remarkable woman that her devotion for her Lord far outweighed whatever alarm she might have been feeling for herself. The angel noticed this. Jesus' mother (Luke 1:30), the shepherds (Luke 2:10) and Mary's friends (Matt. 28:5), were all told not to fear, but not Mary Magdalene. She was asked why she wept (John 20:13).

How uncontrollable were the tears; how compassionate was heaven's messenger (Heb. 1:14); how gentle was the question; how doleful was the answer. For most of that morning, Mary's entire concentration had been centred upon two matters: the removal of Jesus' body and the fact that she did not know where it was (John 20:2,13). Nothing else had mattered — not being seen running through the streets, being left alone by Peter and John with her distress, or even meeting with angels unawares (Heb. 13:2). Having delivered her from the deepest

of pits, represented by those 'seven devils' (Luke 8:2), her
Saviour was the light and love of her life. He had laid down
the principle when referring to someone else: the lower the
descent, the greater the ascent; the more arduous the rescue,
the more extensive the relief and ardent the thankfulness (Luke
7:47).

In life and death, Jesus meant everything to Mary — a depth
of devotion to which few since then have attained. Perhaps it
was the ethos of heaven's graceful tranquillity which her visitors had generated, but Mary revealed much more to them
than she had done before. To Peter and John, Jesus had been
referred to simply as 'the Lord' (John 20:2), a respectful title
used by all his followers through the ages. Now, though, within
the privacy of this precious moment, she did not attempt to
hide her true feelings. Her heart was in any case an often-read
book to God. She claimed the Saviour, 'my Lord' (John 20:13),
as her own.

The private purse

She had every right to do so. In that declaration, Mary had
grasped, as few Christians today appear to do, something of
the privileged and precious relationship between them and
their God. She clutched her Redeemer and Lord to her heart:
he was 'all mine'! But this was only true because she herself had been grasped to his heart in a similar manner. Her
pure passion for Christ could only be measured by his for
her. As one of her companions at the sepulchre that day
was to write many years later, 'Not that we loved God, but
that he loved us' (1 John 4:10). That is always the correct
order of priorities.

Her other companion was also to reflect upon the subject
at a much later date (1 Peter 2:9). Surely, thanksgiving to God

is inevitable from those drawn into 'marvellous light' from the embrace of spiritual darkness. It had been accomplished against the backcloth of his mighty acts on their behalf, all of which have their roots in Old Testament history and theology. They are chosen citizens of a holy nation (Deut. 7:7-8). Almighty God has 'a delight ... to love them' (Deut. 10:15). They are members of the royal household of God, priests of the royal court of heaven (Rev. 1:6).

In fact, just as the Roman invariably carried a purse with him containing his personal possessions, a *'peculium'*, God also has a 'purse' — a very large one. His elect fit comfortably into it — a 'peculiar' and precious people, about whom he says they are 'all mine!' When Mary, therefore, suggested that Jesus belonged to her, calling him 'my Lord' (John 20:13), she was theologically correct, although whether she appreciated the fact to that depth is doubtful. Nevertheless, she certainly was his too, tucked away securely in his purse, 'elect, precious', just like her Lord (1 Peter 2:6).

From the loftiest to the lowliest

As Mary spoke, she seems to have become aware of movement somewhere behind her, distracting her so much that she failed to give the angel an opportunity to respond to her appeal (John 20:13). It was a most unusual thing to do. Angels are expected to have the last word about the termination of a conversation! Yet Mary turned her back upon them (John 20:14). Would she have done this, exchanging a meeting with heavenly beings for one with someone who she assumed was a fellow human being, unless, of course, she had seen something in the angels' manner which indicated that a 'better one' had drawn near? (Heb. 1:4). Had they pointed towards the opening of the cave, indicating that this was so? Whatever the reason for her behaviour, when she turned from the angels, all she saw was a 'gardener'. How disappointed she must have been! At first sight, it seemed as if her search and enquiry had descended from the highest to the most lowly.

Her mind was a whirligig of confused thoughts, lurching in every direction as she sought someone, anyone, who could satisfy her craving for the return of her Lord, even his corpse. Mary clearly had lessons to learn about the mysteries of the kingdom (Matt. 13:11), superstition not being an aspect of them.

What a morning it had been for her! She had left home before dawn, had been surprised by the discovery that the sepulchre had been opened, had run to Peter and John and blurted out her story before hastening back to the tomb, where she met the angels — all in quick succession. Now the 'gardener' entered the equation. Mary's anxiety had reached fever pitch, to the point of tearfully reaching out to this supposed stranger for help and a vestige of hope. It revealed how desperate she was. She wore the appearance of a lost child — panic-stricken, forlorn, helpless and alone. Not even angels could assist her, so she thought, but Mary was about to receive one of the biggest shocks, and most wonderful surprises, that history has recorded (Mark 16:9).

In a foreign land and not expecting to see anyone he knew, the author of this book once stared closely at a friend for some time without recognizing him. So surprised was he, his mind refused to accept what his eyes were seeing. Something similar happened to Mary in the garden. She actually 'saw Jesus' (John 20:14), her friend whom she knew so well and the central figure of the morning's activities, but her tears had washed away reality. As for the two disciples later that day (Luke 24:16), the one she most wanted to see was the person she least expected to meet. Anxieties had driven hope away; weeping had dissipated faith.

The scriptural record reveals how unusual the event was, because strange things occurred. To begin with, pointing to the tomb, Mary might have said excitedly to a stranger, 'You'll never guess who I've just been speaking to in there!', which in the circumstances would have been the obvious thing to do. It was surely how the shepherds must have reacted once they had recovered from the shock (if they ever did) of being surrounded by angelic hosts. In spreading the news of Christ's birth, they could not have resisted telling everyone they met who had imparted it to them (Luke 2:17). But Mary did not respond in that way, being more taken up with death than life. The thoughts of Jesus at that moment, although unfathomable, can nevertheless be imagined in some measure, as he quietly observed this woman for whom he had done so much (Luke 8:2).

What a remarkable parable Joseph's garden had told that Sunday morning, contrasting the resurrection power of God with the flurry of fallen humanity. During that weekend, while heaven had majestically placed its foot upon the serpent's neck at Calvary (Col. 1:13) and in bursting open the tomb had taken death its prisoner (Acts 2:24), those most profoundly affected by the glorious victory were in sad disarray. While the majority of them hid away fearfully and tearfully, the 'gardener' had watched the few from a short distance rushing to and fro like startled rabbits, as if they had never heard his comforting words '… and be raised again the third day' (Matt. 16:21). Hours later, he very sternly made his feelings known on the subject (Luke 24:25).

The sweetest moment

From within the shadows cast by the rising sun, for the radiance of his appearance remained concealed from Mary, a gentle

voice was heard. It could have been the trumpet blast of the
one whose name is I AM, heralding triumph, like that heard by
John on the isle of Patmos (Rev. 1:10), but ascension had yet
to supersede resurrection (John 20:17) where victorious acclamation would mark the fulfilment of the divine purposes
(Rev. 5). Instead, the manner was one which under normal
circumstances Mary would have recognized, quiet and graceful, stilling the storm within her. But not that morning. What a
contrast between the vertical and the horizontal! Heaven was
rejoicing; Mary was weeping.

But Jesus was expert at building conversational bridges, as
a certain Samaritan woman discovered (John 4:1-30), slowly
prising open the oyster of concealment with an apt phrase or
compassionate gesture. The starting-point was the mundane,
not the sublime; the practical, not the abstract. In the case of
the woman of Samaria he began with talk of water (John 4:7);
in Mary's with the subject of her tears (John 20:15). These
thinnest of threads grew stronger as the rapport between each
of the women and the stranger deepened, spiralling upwards
beyond their fears and failings to heights where souls are satisfied (Phil. 3:20).

Dawn had broken, the sun had risen, and with it the solemn
stillness of the night broken by birdsong cheerfully welcoming
the new day. Nature could not remain unheard when resurrection had burst open death's tomb, and the Son of God stood
amidst his creation wearing the smile of victory. It was one of
the ironic moments of history that the Creator of every leaf,
petal and blade of grass in Joseph's garden, before whom they
all bowed (Col. 1:16-17), should be mistaken for the gardener
who tended them.

The voice was gentle, the questions subtle, but Mary was
in too deep a pit to recognize the moment when help was near
(John 20:15). Why was she weeping? She thought she knew
the answer: the removal of the body, and not its resurrection,

was her concern, but she was miserably unaware of how wrong she was. Her gracious Friend was not asking politely after the welfare of an obviously distressed woman but, with a gossamer touch, seeking to wipe her tears away by urging her thoughts heavenward. Why was she weeping? Her sobs blurred the wonderful fact that there was no more need to do so. It was resurrection morn, and where fountains of 'living water' (John 4:10) spray their refreshing balm, tears have no place (Rev. 7:17).

He tried again, gently opening the shutters of her mind, preparing her for the shock she was about to receive. Whom was she looking for? (John 20:15). In her agitated state, Mary might have wondered at the 'gardener's' ignorance, as he presumably spent so much time tending the flora and fauna close to the tomb. Was not everyone aware whose body had been placed in it? Now it was empty, and he asked whom she was looking for!

However, had their positions been reversed, Mary would surely have asked him *what* was he looking for. Property is more often lost than people. Why should this 'stranger' assume she was looking for a person? On the other hand, since he had apparently expressed ignorance as to why the sepulchre was empty, why did Mary assume he knew she was talking about its recent occupant? He had merely asked who it was she was looking for, but she did not answer his question. Instead, without mentioning a name, she replied, 'Sir, if thou have borne him hence, tell me where thou hast laid him, and I will take him away' (John 20:15). If he had no idea to whom she was referring, how could he tell her where the body was?

It was an unusual conversation, but such was her distress, the strangeness of it eluded her. There was not even the thinnest glimmer of understanding filtering through her mind, no revelation, however obscure. In fact she turned away from him, in what seemed to be her last line of enquiry, the 'gardener' apparently of no more interest to her (John 20:16). But she could not have taken more than a step or two when she heard her name softly spoken in the early morning breeze: 'Mary!' (John 20:16).

Her mind froze. Time and logic were suspended, the garden erased of all its contents save that of the voice. How often she had heard its gentle tone! It could only be...! But he was dead. She had been nearby when they had taken his body to the garden, and watched it being carried to its place of rest (Matt. 27:61). He could not possibly be alive, of course not, and yet...! Her thoughts trailed away in a haze of confusion and insipid hope, as if in a dream. Then, as if she was rising from the depths towards the sunlight shimmering on the surface, there suddenly burst upon her the dawning of an over-whelming realization: it was Jesus — alive!

She swung around, and saw the smiling 'gardener'. Questions must have flown at her, like darts from numerous directions: 'How...? Why...? When...?' But although there were no answers, the morning's misery was swept aside instantly in an overriding thankfulness. Words were in short supply, futile, and all she could whisper breathlessly was, 'Master!'— and ran eagerly towards him (John 20:16-17).

4.
News, good, bad and indifferent

Not far away, Mary's friends continued on their way to the apostles as fast as they could, eager to impart the angel's message (Luke 24:4-9). They probably hurried along in silence, too excited to speak, too breathless to make the attempt (Mark 16:8). As older women, two of them at least with adult sons, they must have found the startling events of those few hours exhausting. So much had happened, including miraculous events; it was surely as much as they could cope with. Still, they walked as swiftly as possible, but such was the wonderful news they harboured in their hearts, they probably considered the journey endless and their progress a mere snail's pace. After all, had they not been instructed to 'go quickly'? (Matt. 28:7). They were anxious to obey, but probably wished their legs were younger!

How astonishing — Jesus was alive! The thought was so remarkable — that death could be overcome, the helplessness and finality of it suddenly transformed into vigorous hope. There was no doubting the fact that Jesus had died. After all, 'the other Mary' and her friend Mary of Magdala had been present when his body was placed in the tomb (Matt. 27:61). The body had been cold, the death-dew upon the brow; yet now he lived! Who could possibly understand it?

The turn of events was so dramatic and traumatic it was difficult for their minds to adjust. They had left their homes

that morning (had it really been only a few hours earlier?) griev-
ing at the 'loss' of a loved one (Salome especially, as Jesus'
aunt) their hearts aching and their spirits despondent. Now
their excitement could scarcely be contained. Jerusalem was
filled with unhappy people, yet these women possessed the
most joyful secret in the world, one which cried out for publicity on a grand scale. How difficult it must have been to keep
the news to themselves! Anna had been unable to do so when
Christ was born (Luke 2:38).

True, they had not actually seen the Lord for themselves,
and were unaware that Mary Magdalene had done so, but what
had happened to them within the tomb had been the next best
thing. Not everyone has spoken to an angel, especially in such
circumstances. Even their menfolk had not known anything
like it. They may have remembered the experience of Jesus'
mother (Luke 1:31). If the incarnation had exploded upon the
world's stage, just think what *their* news would do! They must
have longed to tell everyone they passed in the street.

They might also have considered Sarah. She too had received astonishing news — that at the age of ninety she would
give birth to a son. Her husband Abraham was ten years her
senior and they had both laughed (Gen. 17:17; 18:12). In human terms, it was impossible. But it happened, according to
the purposes of God. The old couple were 'strong in faith,
giving glory to God' (Rom. 4:20). Isaac's miraculous birth
was also in its own way a 'resurrection', equally remarkable.
He was delivered from a womb that was 'dead' (Rom. 4:19);
Jesus from the 'womb' of death.

'Hello!'

The route the women took is unknown, but at some point a
quiet spot was reached, perhaps an open plain, or more

probably one of Jerusalem's shadowy side-streets. At any rate, suddenly they heard the voice of a man speaking to them from near at hand, courteously and cheerfully. He merely said, 'All hail!' or 'Peace, goodwill, be unto you!' (Matt. 28:9), a greeting reminiscent of the angelic declaration of his birth: 'Glory to God in the highest, and on earth, peace, good will toward men' (Luke 2:14). How eager Christ is to extend warmth and loving friendship to his people, whose understandable fear of him is counterbalanced by his love for them (Rom. 8:28).

The softly spoken voice, in sharp contrast to the fearful sounds of the thunderous waterfall that it could have been (Rev. 1:15), nevertheless startled them. Since leaving the garden they had made every effort to avoid speaking to anyone, not wishing to be delayed, or tempted to divulge their thrilling news before informing the apostles (Mark 16:8). In any case, it would not have been their habit to stand talking to strange men. But this was different. He appears to have stood directly in front of them, blocking their way, so that they were unable to pass him.

It happened so suddenly and, not for the first time that day, they were speechless. They had not seen him approaching: he just 'met them' (Matt. 28:9). They halted in their tracks, no doubt breathing heavily from their efforts to cover as much ground as possible. Time hovered. Slowly their minds registered, that it was — no, impossible! — Jesus? 'Surely not! ... It can't be! ... Could it be? ... Is it *really* him?' They had last seen him slumped in death, but here he was standing a few paces from them alive. 'Jesus...? Is it...? How...? It is!' They had not doubted the angels' word, but seeing certainly is believing, sweeping away the last vestige of 'reservation' from the recesses of the mind.

With the suddenness of the appearance itself, the women, without a glance at each other or a spoken word, all reacted in unison. They rushed towards him with the same intention as

Mary had shortly before (John 20:17): to worship him, overwhelmed with relief at seeing him again (Matt. 28:9). Submissively, they fell at his feet, as if, like Moses, they had been privy
to the sight of 'the body of heaven in his clearness' beneath
the feet of Israel's God (Exod. 34:8; 24:10), and as Salome's
son, John, would do many years later at the sight of Christ in
majesty standing before him (Rev. 1:17). What else would
covenant children want to do? What greater delight can there
be than to fall before the one to whom they owe so much?
(Luke 7:37-38).

There was, however, a more mundane reason for clasping
his feet in a gesture reminiscent of the Shunammite woman's
reaction to Elisha (2 Kings 4:27). They wanted to hold him
down and keep him imprisoned in their grasp. If he could
mysteriously appear without warning, he could also vanish
just as quickly, as he was to do later that day (Luke 24:31).
They gripped his feet tightly. Having 'lost' him once, they did
not want to 'lose' him again. So much still needed to be learned
— not least, that if the power of death had failed to manacle
the Son of God (Acts 2:24), what hope had mortality's frail
female hands of doing so?

They were afraid, trembling no doubt, as they had been in
front of the angels (Matt. 28:10; Luke 24:5), overcome by the
extraordinary events of that morning. How much more could
they have borne, after all the shocks, the excitement, the anguish and the ecstasy? Some have testified of such glory experienced during intense moments in prayerful fellowship with God
that they have not been able to bear it. How much more so for
Salome, Joanna, 'the other Mary' and their friends, whose day
had begun with intentions of visiting a corpse! (Matt. 28:1).
Now they were at the centre of the most profound mystery
known to man, if not actually caught up to the 'third heaven'
(2 Cor. 12:2), at least peering through the keyhole of its door
(Rev. 4:1).

But Christ is practical. The resurrection is a historic fact, rooted deeply in an understanding of the plan and purposes of God. It has nothing to do with the mystic spirit, and the three devoted followers were not permitted to pander to it. They gazed adoringly up at him as they clasped his feet, and clearly had no intention of moving, but there were things to do. Encouraging them to get to their feet, he simply reiterated the message they had received from the angel (Matt. 28:7,10), as if jolting them back into action. They had not to forget they were on a specific mission. Much as they wanted to stay with him, it was not possible. They continued on their journey to where the apostles were gathered, with the message they had been given.

A joyful reunion

The New Testament makes no reference to a reunion of the women at this point, but it is difficult to see how there would not have been one.[1] In which case, the following scenario might capture something of what it was like.

As they entered the crowds in the morning bustle of the great city, hurrying on towards the apostles, the group was at last joined by Mary Magdalene, whose relative youthfulness had enabled her to catch them up. They had not seen each other since earlier that morning, when they had approached the tomb (Mark 16:1-4). Then the scene had silenced them, but now they had a great deal to talk about.

The situation would have had its amusing side: neither party was aware of the other's wonderful news, that Mary had spoken to their risen Lord in the garden, and her friends had just been kneeling before him. It must have proved difficult to get a word in edgeways! Surely, no detail was excluded. It would have been impossible to refrain from squeezing the stories dry,

because the resurrection of Christ, although beyond comprehension, for that very reason demanded examination from every
possible angle because, of course, it was one of history's greatest moments, and certainly the most significant.

Once their thrilling accounts had been shared, their excited
joy no doubt noted by the passers-by, it was time to move on.
Soon the brethren would hear the tremendous news and rejoice with them, especially Peter and John, who up till then
had no further knowledge than the fact that the tomb was empty
(John 20:3-10), and then *everyone* in the country would hear!
The Lord Jesus, who had been crucified by the Sanhedrin (Acts
2:23), his Messianic claims having been officially rejected, was
on that third day openly vindicated by God (Acts 10:40). The
proclamation was about to be heard: 'Christ is risen from the
dead' (1 Cor. 15:20). The friends were obviously looking forward to telling the apostles, to see the expressions on their
faces, but they little realized what would greet them when
they did.

From good to bad news

Not far away, in another part of Jerusalem, others were shocked
by what had happened, extremely so; in fact consternation had
broken out. Just when the members of the Sanhedrin believed
a new era of calm had begun, following the traumatic events
of the previous three years of trying to deal with Jesus and his
claims, they received news which caused them both anger and
dismay. After all their attention to detail in the attempt to rid
themselves of this man and his influence in the nation, from
the crucifixion to obtaining Pilate's agreement to seal the tomb
(Matt. 27:41,62-64), they now heard it was empty. There must
have been much pacing up and down the corridors of power,
with heads thrust into hands, in sheer exasperation. Now, this!

The 'short straw' dilemma

The resurrection story is not told from the standpoint of the temple guards, but theirs was a dismal experience, made worse by the fact that eternal mysteries forbade them from understanding it (Matt. 13:13-17). This would account for the time-lapse between their running from the garden in fear and trembling and the appearance of 'some' of them at the Sanhedrin's door, at the very moment the women started on their way again to tell the apostles the wonderful news (Matt. 28:11). Their joy was the guards' misery.

Within that period much had obviously happened: the group of women seeing the shifted boulder (Mark 16:1-4); Mary Magdalene running off to tell Peter and John (John 20:1-2); and her friends meeting the angels before hurrying to inform the brethren (Luke 24:3-8). Then Peter and John arrived at the sepulchre (John 20:3-10), followed by Mary, who remained behind weeping; after which she held a conversation with the angel and then the 'gardener' (John 20:11-17). Shortly afterwards Mary's friends met the Lord (Matt. 28:7-9), and then were joined once more by Mary (Luke 24:10). None of these events could have passed hurriedly, yet it appears it was only after Mary had joined her friends that the guards went to see the chief priests (Matt. 28:11). As fit men, they would not have taken long to head straight from the garden to report the news, so why the delay?

The following seems a likely scenario: after rushing from the quake zone in a panic, they would not have scattered in all directions. Frightened people cling together seeking solace in each other's company. Undoubtedly traumatized (Matt. 28:4), they were in no state to report the news immediately. Instead, together they sought a solitary place where they could calm down and discuss a strategy for what lay ahead for them (Matt. 28:11).

Through no fault of their own, they found themselves in a
dreadful situation. As soldiers attached to the temple in Jerusalem, Israel's most holy site (Matt. 24:1), they had been given
the responsibility of carrying out their employers' demands.
The members of the Sanhedrin were anxious to prevent the
followers of their greatest enemy from removing his body overnight from its resting-place (Matt. 27:64), lest by doing so
they should be able to vindicate his promise that he would rise
from the dead (Matt. 16:21). Now, not only was the tomb
empty and the corpse nowhere to be seen, but the blame for
this disaster was about to be laid entirely upon them. What
were they to do?

One could not have been surprised in the circumstances
had their imaginations run wild. The whole of Jerusalem would
soon be demanding answers. First, there was the officer to
whom they were accountable, who surely would not have been
part of 'the watch'. What would he think? The interrogation
would be lengthy, the questions flung at them numerous: Where
were they when the body was removed? The sealed rock at
the tomb's entrance was large and could not be shifted easily,
so why had they failed to notice what was happening? Had
they moved it? At what time had they left the scene, and why
had they done so? Were they absent without leave? Why...?
How...? Where...? When...?

But if the truth was told, they would have to say, 'Well,
you see sir, there was this angel sitting on the rock...!' (Matt.
28:2). For that remark, despite its being the truth they could
be charged with insubordination ('An angel indeed! A likely
story! And sitting...!'). Perhaps not Jewish temple guards, but
Roman legionaries certainly were thrashed to death by the
centurion's vine-cane for such breaches of discipline.

Then what of their comrades back at the barracks, the general public and even Roman soldiers with whom they came

into daily contact? The list seemed endless. The laughter would ricochet around the city, if not the country. It might have crossed their minds to overlook the angel, and refer only to the earthquake. Why not? It would provide some credence to their claims, and might even rescue their reputations, if not their lives. How strange that men associated so intimately with the temple of God, the priestly custodians and military guardians, were more likely to be impressed by a 'natural disaster' than by the one who caused it! (Matt. 28:2).

But what would undoubtedly have caused the greatest trepidation was facing the high priests. These fearsome men were behind the death of Jesus, the prophet from Galilee (Deut. 18:15), whose corpse the troubled soldiers had been seeking to protect. What would happen to them now, having failed in their duty? Would Annas and Caiaphas in their fury seek ways and means of having them executed? It was possible. Not long after, when the apostle Peter had been miraculously rescued from prison by an angel, Herod 'examined the keepers, and commanded that they should be put to death' (Acts 12:19). The hapless temple soldiers had much to think about. If night-duty guarding a corpse had been an unenviable task, the fact that it was now missing was proving a nightmare.

But that was not all. What had happened had also set off a chain reaction, reaching to Rome itself, which they were powerless to stop. Their military superiors were responsible to the Sanhedrin, which in turn answered to Pontius Pilate the governor, and his reports were sent to Caesar in Rome. In the meantime, the emperor's hard eyes were known to penetrate the furthest reaches of his domains for signs of unrest among his conquered territories, and news of the prophet's missing body might cause Israel to remember his promise to rise from the dead (Matt. 16:21). The unpopular Sanhedrin's (Matt. 7:29) insistence upon having him put to death (John 11:47-53) could stir the massive following he had once known (Matt. 4:23-25; John 6:15). Beyond the city gates, confronted by a crisis of epic proportions, the soldiers had cause to shudder.

But they could not remain where they were indefinitely, so what should they do? A decision was called for, but they knew that, whichever way they turned, only trouble awaited them. Desertion not being an option, they realized the awful fact that they could not avoid the inevitable. The military and religious authorities would have to be informed of what had occurred overnight in Joseph of Arimathea's garden, and the best approach to be made was to tell the whole story, however ridiculous it would appear. They knew, though, that the hope of leniency was slim.

However, they sought to help themselves as best they could by deciding to split up as a group. In this way their problem might be halved. Perhaps lots were drawn (the 'short straw' approach), and while the rest of the temple guards probably reported nervously to their commanding officer, 'some' returned to the city 'and showed unto the chief priests all the things that were done' (Matt. 28:11).

Giving an account

Caiaphas was the incumbent high priest (John 18:13), his father-in-law Annas having been forced to retire from the same office about twenty years earlier (A.D. 14), when one of Pilate's predecessors (Valerius Gratus) deposed him. However, the title was retained for life, and with it a prominent seat in the Sanhedrin. It was not unusual, therefore, that as high priests related to each other, even if only by marriage, the two should work together in opposing Jesus and his followers. It appears they even shared the same palatial residence (John 18:13-27). In other words, they were a formidable duo, especially to the men they were about to meet, men whom in the normal course of events they were not likely to come across socially.

When the anxious guards arrived at the gates with their guilty secret, they must have wondered what the next few hours would bring forth for them — in fact, the next few minutes. After three years of trying (John 11:49-57), they had at last succeeded in having Jesus arrested and executed, and his influence buried with him — or so Annas and Caiaphas assumed. But within one weekend, all their meticulous planning had been demolished, and these smallest of cogs in the Sanhedrin machinery were about to be held responsible.

The sight of these dishevelled and obviously panic-stricken men standing outside was sufficient to gain them entrance into the palace, for it would not normally have been possible to do so without prior arrangement, and for a very good reason. Thus they found themselves in the presence of Israel's chief priests, the most important men in the nation, and it was for the culprits without doubt a fearful occasion (Matt. 28:11).

Upon seeing them Annas and Caiaphas must have immediately suspected the worst, because there could only be one reason why these men were standing before them. The sepulchre had been broken into! Their worst fears had been realized: Jesus' disciples had, after all, managed to snatch their leader's corpse from its resting-place (Matt. 27:64). Now rumours of his rising from the dead would be rampant throughout Jerusalem, and even the entire country. All because of the inefficiency of these men and their equally inefficient colleagues!

How could it possibly have happened? True, during the arrest of this preacher from Galilee, one of his disciples had suddenly produced a weapon (Matt. 26:51), but surely a few zealous devotees could not overcome professionally trained and armed guards? The questions would have continued, from two overwrought and furious priests to the men, who were no doubt trembling in anticipation of what would happen to them.

What time was it when they were attacked? Did they not hear sounds of approach in such a quiet spot? Were they all asleep? How could it happen? It was, as anticipated, a question of 'Why...? How...? Where...? When...?'

But eventually, the answer which the guards gave was the last the chief priests expected, or would have wanted to hear. It was not the reference to the earthquake, the noisy arrival of which must have been heard far afield, probably even in the high priest's palace, but rather the persistent claims of these men to having witnessed the supernatural at work: 'Well you see, this angel...' (see Matt. 28:2-4).

Annas and Caiaphas would not have been able to believe they were hearing correctly. They must have glanced at each other in disbelief: 'An angel? How preposterous! Angels do not exist!' But the guards were adamant that was what they had seen. The garden had been bathed in candescent beauty, matched only by the radiance of the heavenly being who sat upon 'the very great stone' which had been blown aside by the earthquake which he had caused (Mark 16:4; Matt. 28:2). By this time, the atmosphere in the room would have been almost as explosive.

However, the account the guards were giving, both in unison and without any hesitation at all, was becoming alarmingly realistic for the two high priests. As Sadducees, they held no belief in the realm of the spirit (Acts 23:8). Any talk of angels would have proved an irritant. The guards had obviously concocted this story to conceal their neglect of duty. But the sophisticated always have a good idea whether those who are less so are telling the truth or not. There was something about this account which demanded investigation, if only for the fact that those who told it did so with such alacrity. Reluctant though Annas and Caiaphas would have been to probe further, they were forced into doing so.

The guards were sent from the room, perhaps even the palace, to await events. There was no turning back now: the die was cast, and they were in the thick of a controversy which could reach to Rome itself. In the meantime, Annas and Caiaphas remained behind to discuss the matter. It had evidently impressed them much more than they were prepared to reveal to their subordinate employees, because an emergency, but limited, sitting of the Sanhedrin was assembled (Matt. 28:12).

Not surprisingly, they were crafty in their choice of who should attend the meeting — not 'all the council' as at Jesus' trial (Matt. 26:59), but just a relatively few elders (Matt. 28:12). This could have been due to lack of time, the need to discuss the unexpected crisis in a hurry, but a more important reason was probably to keep the Pharisees and scribes at bay. Unlike the Sadducees, they strongly believed in the spiritual realm (Acts 23:8), and as there were about 6,000 Pharisees in Israel at the time (supplying them with an excellent representation in the Sanhedrin), they were much more likely to accept the soldiers' account of the angelic appearance. The Sadducees Annas and Caiaphas had no intention of being in the minority on such an important issue, but the chief priests' guile did not work to their advantage.

Bribery and corruption

The session with the elders completed, the guards were summoned again to appear before the high priests. This was it! They stepped into the spotlight once more, extremely apprehensive, this time to hear the verdict which would determine their future. At the very least they could expect to lose their jobs, or be arrested and imprisoned, and at worst be detained for eventual execution (Acts 12:19). But no, instead, they heard the chink of many coins! (Matt. 28:12).

Clutching their bags of shekels in shocked disbelief at the strange turn of events, the bemused men heard the furious high priests speaking to them through clenched teeth as if from afar. Within a haze of bewilderment, and utter astonishment, they listened as the instructions from the hastily convened council were given them. They were to spread the lie that Jesus' body had been stolen by his followers in the night, and this had been due to the ineptitude of the culprits, who slept while on duty (Matt. 28:13). In other words, nothing less than a public confession of guilt was called for, even if it was a false one. They had no choice.

So the leather pouches filled with coinage had very long strings attached! The 'culprits' holding them were assured of the money, but the price was high: they would become figures of fun, the butt of much laughter, from fellow Jews and Romans alike, for years to come. The story would be told that these professionally trained guards had been overcome by a band of amateurs, who had robbed the tomb under their noses while they were fast asleep. It was not a scenario guaranteed to assist the Jews in their daily confrontation with the Roman occupying force, with the temple guards held up to ridicule.

The only apparent consolation they received was the promise that should Pilate hear about the débâcle (as he surely would), the priests intended in some way to protect them from the Roman eagle's fierce talons (Matt. 28:14). It sounded encouraging, until they realized that even here the priests were shifting the blame from themselves to the guards, when in fact Pilate had placed the onus of keeping the tomb secure, not on the guards but on the Sanhedrin (Matt. 27:65).

In any case, the corruption the troubled men were now entangled in may not have provided these 'scapegoats' with much hope that the ecclesiastical authorities would really intercede for them, especially as the governor's contempt for the Sanhedrin was very evident (Matt. 27:65; John 19:19-22). In short, their souls had been done great harm by those whose official emblem was: 'Holiness to the Lord' (Exod. 28:36). Not only were they capable of bribery, but of selling their innocent employees to the accusers and mockers, in order to save their own reputations.

But there still remained a mystery. The lie to be told was that 'His disciples came by night, and stole him away...', but was that not the situation the Sanhedrin feared most, the reason why its members had visited Pilate in the first place? Had they not anticipated widespread rumours, to the effect that Jesus had risen from the dead, and as a consequence 'the last error' would be 'worse than the first' (Matt. 27:64). Now, they were back to square one, but why? What had made Annas and Caiaphas, the leaders of the council, suddenly capitulate to the pragmatic view? Evidently, they had learned something dramatic to make them radically change their minds.

It must have occurred when they had met with the elders (Matt. 28:12), because there was no other opportunity. By this time the guards' commanding officer had no doubt reported on his interrogation with the other 'culprits'. They too had recorded exactly the same incident, and with equal intensity. Of course, it could have been an invented story, but they would all have had to have been outstanding actors to portray the same traumatized condition and at the same time. Clearly, something remarkable had happened in Joseph of Arimathea's tranquil garden, and that would have been the majority opinion among the priests. They could not have helped themselves.

In other words, secretly behind the scenes, the appalling recognition was made by those most opposed to the notion that, if the robbers did not exist, the resurrection probably did. Was not this the 'sign' the scribes and Pharisees had sought

from Jesus, and had he not supplied it by giving them a name
— that of 'Jonah'? Everyone knew the story about the prophet
to the Ninevites, and his providential 'entombment' within a
whale's belly, an appropriate symbol for what happened in
Joseph's garden. The guards' testimonies must have caused
the incident to rear up and confront the priests. In that case,
they could not have forgotten the chilling application to the
prophecy, from one who openly claimed to be greater than
Jonah: 'The men of Nineveh shall rise in the judgement with
this generation, and shall condemn it: because they repented
at the preaching of Jonas' (Matt. 12:38-41). There were some
anxious expressions on solemn faces within the Sanhedrin.
Truly, God had arisen (Ps. 68:1), and 'scattered' his enemies
(Num. 10:35).

Yet even as the awful truth hovered in the air, the Sadducees,
although outnumbered, were having none of it. Angelic visitations were far beyond the framework of their thinking, as
was any talk of divine interventions (Acts 23:8), and pride
hammered unbelief still deeper into their hearts like sturdy nails.
They had no intention of behaving as Nehemiah's enemies had
done on discovering Jerusalem's wall had been rebuilt in rapid
time and against all the odds, when they had been 'much cast
down in their own eyes, for they perceived that this work was
wrought of our God' (Neh. 6:16). On the contrary, Annas and
Caiaphas and their ilk hardened their hearts still further, as
Peter and John were later to discover, when 'The Sadducees
came upon them, being grieved that they taught the people,
and preached through Jesus the resurrection from the dead'
(Acts 4:1-2).

Excited hammering on the door

The nearer to their destination they had got, the more the
women must have wanted to shout aloud their thrilling news

to everyone passing by that 'Jesus is risen!', but they restrained themselves. The apostles had to learn the truth first. Yet how slow had been their progress, hampered as they would have been by the increasing numbers of busy people who filled the network of narrow cobbled streets on a typical hot Jerusalem morning. But this day was the most untypical of any in history, one which demanded joyous acclamation. Eternity thrilled to the news (Rev. 5), then why not time? There is, after all, 'fulness of joy' in the presence of the Holy One whose body did not 'see corruption' (Ps. 16:10-11). It would have been in that mood that the women hammered on the door, their faces radiant from the glorious news they had to tell, and almost bursting with anticipation.

Descent into gloom

Whoever answered to the eager knocking was likely to have been brushed to one side in the rush, as the women, probably led by Mary Magdalene, pushed passed him shouting, 'Jesus is alive!' But once the euphoria had reached its climax and the angelic message had been delivered safely (Matt. 28:6-7), the contrasting atmosphere in the house must have struck the new arrivals with the force of a wet blanket thrown into their faces. They were suddenly aware that if they were joyful, the eleven apostles were weeping (Luke 24:9; Mark 16:10). One half of the room exulted in resurrection; the other wallowed in the ruin of their hopes!

The brethren wiped the tears from their eyes (and the dismayed women, no doubt, the smiles from their faces), as they listened half-heartedly to what the sisters had to tell them. Male chauvinism not being a new concept, they were unimpressed, and could easily explain the euphoria which had just burst into the room. 'Idle tales' indeed! (Luke 24:11). There was a need to be level-headed, and to resist emotional responses to the situation. What had evidently happened was that all of them were suffering from shock following a weekend of gruesome events. In one way or another, they were bound to have received emotional bruises, the men responding to them in one way, and the women in another. It was therefore understandable that the longing to have Jesus back again had led to thoughts among the sisters that they had seen him, and that he had actually spoken to them. It was all straightforward!

Far from remembering his words about the impending resurrection (Matt. 16:21), or even biblical teaching in general (Isa. 25:8; Hosea 13:14), the apostles had nailed their thinking to the floor. Like those often found within the church whose 'conversation' cannot quite reach heaven (Phil. 3:20) and who therefore shelter in practical substitutes, they answered faith with 'sweet reasonableness'. Strangely, such people invariably have the greater say, nudging the more spiritually meek to the sidelines. So it was on that memorable day, the brethren flowing with words but with a meagre faith; the sisters full of faith but with few words. When they did speak they found it impossible to convince the men their experiences were genuine. Even the mothers failed to impress their sons; the two Jameses, Matthew and John were just as sceptical as the others — and this at the very moment when the members of the Sanhedrin were trembling that it all just might be true (Luke 24:11). The day was filled with irony. It was not an encouraging start to the apostles' role as the foundation upon which, with the mighty prophets, Christianity is built (Eph. 2:20).

Ripples everywhere

There was no point in remaining within this house of doom and gloom, and as the apostles had not insisted they remain silent about what they claimed to have seen and heard, the discouraged but not undaunted women set off in all directions to spread the wonderful news. Would they, could they, have done otherwise? It was too astounding to be silenced. There were at least 120 followers of Jesus hidden away in secret who had yet to be told what heaven had done for them (Acts 1:15). Fearful as they were of reprisals from the authorities, the shaft of 'marvellous light' was about to shine all around them, inspiring them with new courage (1 Peter 2:9).

Like the aged Anna who, having seen the baby Jesus for herself, hurried off as quickly as she could and 'spake of him to all them that looked for redemption in Jerusalem' (Luke 2:38), the women undoubtedly shared a similar enthusiasm. Who can deny that they must have gone through the city in search of the true people of God, who were now more numerous than in the days of Simeon, Anna, Zacharias, Elizabeth, Mary and Joseph? Even if the apostles were saying gloomily, 'Jesus is dead!', the women's message could not have differed more sharply: 'Jesus is alive!' Wherever there were disciples the news would have spread rapidly. The humble hearth, the dusty streets, the shaded alleyways, the open fields, the hills where shepherds watched their flocks — soon the excitement was infectious: 'Jesus is alive! Christ is risen!' Many believed; some would not; but all were astonished by what they heard (Luke 24:22). Could it be true?

In search of Jesus

While the news circulated widely, the apostles sat hugging their grief, resolute in their refusal to be caught up with the euphoria displayed by their womenfolk. Undoubtedly, pride had much to do with it. If what they had been told was true, they may well have wondered resentfully why their Lord had not appeared first to them. After all, they were supposed to be the apostles, not the women! A sulky sadness hung over them like a silken shroud.

But they could not sit around moping for ever. It appears that Peter was unable to tolerate the situation any longer. Suddenly, and with typical impetuosity, he jumped to his feet. Whatever his fellow apostles intended doing, he was determined to find out for himself whether the women were correct. In which case, there was only one thing to do: he must go once more to the tomb. Before, it had been with John and Mary Magdalene (John 20:2-10), but this time he went alone (Luke 24:12). Luke and John each record one of Peter's two visits.[2]

Running, Peter weaved his way through the crowds, until he arrived breathlessly at the tomb once more. Within it, where the women had said angels heralded the resurrection of Christ (Matt. 28:5-6), he believed lay the secret after which he hankered. Earlier that morning, whereas John had 'stooped' at the tomb's entrance but did not venture inside, without hesitating Peter 'went into the sepulchre' (John 20:5-6). But on this second visit, there was an element of apprehension as if he was wondering what he might see, 'stooping down' before gingerly peering inside (Luke 24:12). Would those angels still be there? If so, would they tell him where Jesus could be found? He, who had publicly disowned his Lord (John 18:25-27), now wanted desperately to meet him again to make amends, to be forgiven.

But as he glanced inside the tomb, he knew he had no need to enter. It was as cold and empty as it had been on his first visit. No heavenly radiance cast its warmth, no risen Lord stood waiting to greet him, not even an angel to console him. Nothing! He was alone. Jesus was nowhere to be seen, the voice silent, the garden and its quiet tomb empty. There was not even a 'gardener' to excite his curiosity.

5.
Hands across the table

What a breathtaking morning it had been! Jerusalem, though, was no place in which faint hearts could linger — at least any among the followers of Jesus of Nazareth, condemned by the Sanhedrin and crucified under Roman law. Those capable of plotting his death would not have hesitated in having them arrested. Indeed, aggression was still being experienced weeks later, when Peter and John were arrested for preaching 'through Jesus the resurrection from the dead', threatened (Acts 4:1-22) and shortly afterwards re-arrested and beaten (Acts 5:18-40). It was therefore felt expedient by some of his company to leave the city, under cover of approaching darkness (Luke 24:13,29).

Solemn thoughts in springtime

Along a road then, which led from Jerusalem into the surrounding countryside, two men could be seen walking (Mark 16:12). To a passer-by, they would have appeared unusually engrossed in murmured conversation, perhaps sufficiently so as to create suspicion. It was springtime, yet nature's blossoming environment and the sweet singing of birds went unnoticed. Clearly, they were not out for a relaxing stroll. In fact, they appeared intent on reaching their destination as soon as possible.

These companions had solemn matters on their minds which quickened their pace, as they headed towards a typically small and obscure village called Emmaus (Luke 24:13-33), which lay seven miles away, and was far enough from the aggressive hub of the city to grant them a modicum of comfort. This alone was sufficient to hasten their step; the further from the city gate they strode, the more at ease they felt. In any case, what business had they in Jerusalem now that their Master was dead?

What a weekend! An unbearable tension, stretched to its limits, hung over the city like a pall, as satanic influences flowed through it. The Jewish authorities and Roman officialdom loathed each other; when therefore on this unique occasion they joined forces to destroy Jesus, the mixture was lethal (Matt. 27:1-2). With his arrest and travesty of a trial, the entire city appeared to erupt, as latent animosity generated by the guile of the Sanhedrin gave vent to dark emotions. Vast, jostling crowds filled the streets: the excited, the voyeuristic, the curious and those who bayed for the blood of a victim (Matt. 27:20,25).

You should have heard the noise! Through the throng the pitiable procession had slowly threaded its way: a centurion, four legionaries, two villains and the one whose presence indelibly etched the occasion upon the annals of history. The shrill shrieks of the mob, the harsh shouts of the soldiers, the raucous curses of the felons, the swish of the centurion's vine-cane, the crack of whips, the groans of the victims — the ugly scene was witnessed by the strained and tearful followers of Jesus, urged on by trembling devotion to within sight of Golgotha (Luke 23:49). Who among those who loved him could stay away, or turn their backs? Of the men though, the apostle John alone stood loyally beside the cross, providing what comfort he could to the pitifully few brave women (John 19:25-27).

But now two days had passed since Calvary had reverted to its emptiness and solemn silence and the crucified prophet (Acts 3:22) had been carried to his waiting sepulchre. Strange things had occurred that very morning — at least, according to the women in their company. They claimed that Jesus was alive. Angels had told them! (Luke 24:23).

There was much for the two travellers to discuss between themselves as they strode on, their minds in turmoil, a plethora of notions vying with each other for recognition. A conflict of priorities existed between the rational and the supernatural and, judging from the fact that they continued on their journey *out* of Jerusalem, it was plain that despite their initial 'astonishment' at the news (Luke 24:22), reason was gaining a victory over faith.

Reason always feels more comfortable when unaccompanied by faith, preferring to paint life's canvas with its own colours, and pride leaps high when the mind of man is exposed as being merely finite. The discovery of an empty tomb would not have been a problem in itself — the removal of the corpse by officials or vandals could have supplied an answer — but why bring angels and a message of resurrection into the equation? Surely, a rational explanation was all that was required. How cynical men are when mention is made of the unseen, how embarrassed by talk of faith, as if the latter is not the 'evidence' of the former! (2 Cor. 4:18; Heb. 11:1).

But reason had excuses at the ready. The hallucinatory 'vision of angels' (Luke 24:23) and the message they were supposed to have given the women acted as a balm to their fears, there being a need for them to raise their spirits above the depths of despair. After all, Peter and John had also visited the spot but had seen nothing more than grave-clothes (John 20:3-10). That surely was the answer, and at that point, reason turns its back and walks away satisfied, discovering only what it wants to find, its mind locked and barred to any other possibility. As the mysterious stranger was shortly to illustrate, groping in the darkness for rational answers to metaphysical problems, and no doubt believing it possible to be successful, is a game played by fools (Luke 24:25).

Incarnation through to resurrection

The travellers should not be judged too harshly, though. If their initial astonishment had turned to bewilderment and a hasty departure from the city when mention had been made of a resurrection, it was because they viewed the incarnation through a haze. Like the unravelling of wool, if the mystery behind Christ's birth is misunderstood, then gradually the entire fabric of revealed truth is unwound in one's thinking: Christ's righteous perfection, lived under the demands of the law, his substitutionary atonement, bodily resurrection, triumphant ascension, as well as the anticipation of his glorious second advent. All these mighty truths receive their value, and are seen at their finest in Bethlehem's manger. 'God was manifest in the flesh'; the mystery of godliness is truly great (1 Tim. 3:16).

As with all the disciples, these men were products of the eschatological thinking of the age. They had been within the Jewish fold all their lives, and found it well-nigh impossible to rid themselves of the prevailing teaching regarding the Messianic hope. When they first encountered Jesus, Judaism was a melting-pot filled with ideas concerning the Messiah. The Pharisees, for example, represented one of two schools of thought. The first was optimistic in its outlook, and certainly more akin to biblical teaching than the other (Rom. 11). Jehovah would eventually arrive from beyond many horizons

(Luke 23:42), because he loved his people. The nation would repent and be restored triumphantly. Here was true hope, reflected in the 'Psalms of Solomon' (63 – 45 B.C.).

However, the majority were students of the other school, in which Israel's hope depended upon the nation being ideally obedient to Jehovah. When that day arrived, he would look with favour upon his chosen people and send the Anointed One to establish his kingdom. The Messiah was pictured, not as a Saviour of sinners, but rather as the nation's Great Avenger, bringing vengeance upon Israel's enemies. That reasoning continued when Jesus claimed to be the Messiah (John 8:24), the assumption being that his prime function was the setting up of a political kingdom in order to terminate the Roman occupation of the land. Having misunderstood the prophet (Isa. 61:1-3), they sought after a political, not a spiritual, 'redemption' (Luke 24:21).

At times, the disciples reflected this teaching in their behaviour, seeing themselves occupying important posts within the governance of a restored and triumphant Israel. In fact, as we saw earlier, Salome, the mother of John and James, went so far as to ask Jesus whether her sons could sit on either side of him in his kingdom (Matt. 20:20-21). They all 'thought that the kingdom of God should immediately appear' (Luke 19:11), yet after three years in which they had been in his company, Jesus still had not attempted to overthrow the establishment.

Despite assurances to the contrary, as explained to Pilate (John 18:36), the disciples persisted in their belief that the new heavenly regime was about to be set up, and that national prestige would be elevated to a position not witnessed before. Jesus' entry into Jerusalem, with the waving palms and excited crowds (Matt. 21:1-9), had proved a major disappointment. Had not the prophet told of a day when, amid great rejoicing, 'Thy king cometh ... riding upon an ass...'? (Zech. 9:9). Yet, although the multitudes had shouted their expectancy, this had been followed by nothing more than a skirmish in the temple (Matt. 21:9,12). Jesus had still refrained from ascending to the throne. He had even allowed himself to be arrested without a struggle. The apostle Peter had been ready for such an event, and carried a sword, which he used to minor effect, but Jesus commanded him to refrain from violent behaviour (John 18:10-11), and even refused to call upon the angelic guardians which he claimed to have to fly to his support (Matt. 26:51-53). The disciples were confused by their Lord's unexpected reaction. The glory of Israel was at stake!

The death of their Master, then, was a crushing blow to all they had waited and longed for. Even weeks after the resurrection, their shock and joy at seeing him again were tempered by the old question asked with the same impatience: 'Lord, wilt thou at this time restore again the kingdom to Israel?' (Acts 1:6). These were the topics which engrossed the travellers as they continued on their journey to Emmaus: 'We trusted that it had been he which should have redeemed Israel...' (Luke 24:21).

From the sisters to the brethren

There was nothing haphazard about the heavenly procedure; there never is. The fact of the resurrection had already been revealed through the sisters among the disciples; now it was the turn of the brethren to receive the news. There were several reasons why first Mary of Magdala (Mark 16:9) and then her friends were honoured in this way. To deal with them in reverse order, one reason was the graciousness of their Lord. He considered their emotional needs, especially those of his mother, whose horrendous experience at Calvary had fully lived up to the 'sword-thrust' Simeon had prophesied over thirty years earlier (Luke 2:35). Would it have been possible for the women, whose love for their Saviour could not have been greater, to have borne much more? They had watched Jesus' cruel death (Luke 23:49), a few, including his mother, at close quarters (John 19:25), and two of them had observed as his body was carried to the tomb (Matt. 27:60-61). Then, as if that were not enough, there was the discovery of its disappearance, removed for all they knew by the uncaring (John 20:13). It was therefore typical of heaven's love for them, from 'the Father of mercies, and the God of all comfort' (2 Cor. 1:3-4), that they were the first to be comforted in the joyful realization that their suffering was at last over.

But, of course, there was another, and even more important, reason: the need for the apostles to receive a sturdy rebuke and for their faith to be strengthened. Paul was later to command the Christian brethren of Corinth to 'Stand fast in the faith, quit you like men, be strong' (1 Cor. 16:13). It was an instruction greatly needed at Gethsemane, when those who had boasted of their loyalty to Jesus were seen scampering from the garden, leaving him to the mercy of his captors (Matt. 26:35,56). The fact that Zechariah the prophet had foretold the incident was no excuse for their weakness, either of faith or of character (Zech. 13:7; Matt. 26:31).

True, it had been a fearful occasion, but had they not been in the company of 'the Christ, the Son of the living God', and did they not hear his assurance that angelic hosts were close at hand? (Matt. 16:16; 26:53). Yet despite these comforting reminders, they preferred to trust in carnal instincts rather than rely upon faith and seek the shadows. What followed was a dismal display, but in the circumstances, to have been expected: Peter's denials of his Lord (Mark 14:66-71), the general air of distress and uncertainty among the brethren, even tears (Mark 16:10). They were in no position to make light of the sisters' wonderful news of the resurrection, or to discourage them with scorn (Luke 24:11). It is, therefore, not surprising that the apostles were kept waiting, before their Lord favoured any of them with his risen presence. The point made, it was now their turn to be encouraged.

The listener to every conversation

'When I soar through tracts unknown' wrote Toplady in his famous hymn, 'Rock of Ages' — graphic poetry, but poor theology! The apostle Paul provides the definitive explanation, 'absent from the body ... present with the Lord' — instantly (2 Cor. 5:8). How wafer-thin is the barrier which separates eternity from time, leaving no time to 'soar'! Likewise, note how swiftly prior to his ascension did the risen Christ appear at his followers' side. One moment Cleopas and his friend were unaccompanied, and the next they had been joined by a 'stranger' (Luke 24:15).

Normally, the instinct would have been to look behind them as they heard someone quickly approaching, but mystery is the master of silence. He 'drew near', and walked beside them — an encounter not without its humorous side. Without their knowing it, the one they were discussing assisted them in their discussion! It was reminiscent of the occasion when God the Son, manifested in a theophany as 'the angel of the Lord', informed Gideon, 'The Lord is with thee...' (Judg. 6:12), and he literally was.

Cleopas (not to be confused with Cleophas, or Clopas — John 19:25) and his friend suddenly realized they had company. They turned and looked straight at the newcomer, and he at them, and although probably standing closer to him than Mary Magdalene had been when she saw him in the garden (John 20:14), they nevertheless failed to recognize that their queries were answered. Of all the people of their acquaintance, the one they were least expecting to see was the one most likely to want to see them. On the other hand, if it is possible to grant hospitality to 'angels unawares' (Heb. 13:2), as Abraham did (Gen.18:1-8), to entertain the risen Lord so soon after the mighty event would have been even more mysterious.

The fact that the 'stranger' broke into the conversation, which on any other occasion might have been considered an impertinence, did not cause annoyance. With Jerusalem humming with news of the weekend's drama, and this man apparently unaware that anything untoward had occurred, the normal rules of courtesy played no part in their thinking. Everyone was talking about the events, gossiping about the rumours: the execution of the mighty prophet, the sun blanketed out for three hours, earthquakes, alarming weather conditions (Ps. 18:6-15), the miraculous exposure to view of the most holy place in the temple, the disappearance of the prophet's body. Where had the man been all this time? (Luke 24:18).

However, it was not only the earnestness of their conversation the 'stranger' had noted, but their sadness (Luke 24:17). He would, of course, have known what they were talking about and understood the complexities of their distress, but others would not have done so, merely observing two despondent men. 'Happy is that people ... whose God is the Lord', David the inspired psalmist declared (Ps. 144:15), but that sentiment was not shared that day on the road leading to Emmaus. How often, and easily, the messenger can be a hindrance to the message!

Their sadness, shared by many 'believers' today, should not have surprised them. Several factors caused it. The main one was their misunderstanding of the gospel. God had been progressively revealing his great scheme of redemption throughout history, from Eden (Gen. 3:15) through to Christ. These men, however, were victims of the prevailing malaise. Their knowledge of the Jewish Scriptures was sparse, and what little they knew was not fully understood. As a consequence the wonder of what God had accomplished was tragically over-looked. Like the majority of their contemporaries, and most people today, they trusted their teachers rather than the Word of God. 'Reasoning' had been substituted for faith (Luke 24:15,21,25).

They recognized Jesus as the prophet foretold by Moses (Deut. 18:15); his ministry revealed it — the miracles (Matt. 11:5), his astonishing teaching and authoritative preaching (Matt. 7:28-29). Here was one whom both heaven and earth recognized as supreme (Luke 24:19). But then Cleopas and his friend stumbled, as everyone does who has not been tutored by the Spirit (John 16:13). He alone reveals these marvellous mysteries, this 'hidden wisdom' (Matt. 13:11; 1 Cor. 2:7).

They valued their Master's person, testified of his greatness, had no difficulty in appreciating his peripatetic and powerful ministry, but the events at Calvary were observed with a total lack of understanding. The cross, as always, had proved a hurdle (1 Cor. 1:23); it had not even featured in their reckoning. The friends were more concerned with morality than theology. They were aghast at the treatment meted out to Jesus by those who in their view should have known better, but as to the redemption secured through atoning blood, nothing could have been further from their minds.

To them, Calvary was about the machinations of men cruelly delivering the prophet to death (Luke 24:20), rather than the 'deliverance' being the result of 'the determinate counsel and foreknowledge of God' (Acts 2:23). They were unable to look higher than the horizontal, beyond the human level, with the result that Christ's work remained hidden in the haze. New birth was urgently required — an experience so essential heavenly matters cannot be perceived, or heaven itself entered, without it (John 3:1-7). On the Emmaus road, the two men were unregenerate and therefore sad, there being no greater tragedy than to trust Jesus in time but to be unable to do so for eternity. As Paul would later write, 'If in this life only we have hope in Christ, we are of all men most miserable' (1 Cor. 15:19). Cleopas and his friend were very miserable indeed.

However, such 'trust' as they did have was suspect, more akin to the fervent political ethos wafting through the land than to God's remarkable plan of salvation; the desire for the glory of Israel rather than the glory of God; the one mistaken for the other (Acts 1:6). When it appeared that Jesus might ascend to the Messianic throne as Zechariah's 'king priest' (Zech. 6:13), and overcome the Gentile occupation of his kingdom, the men's loyalty to him could be counted upon. But, to their utter dismay, he had been ignominiously 'defeated', shamefully crucified — killed! (Luke 24:20).

An extremely thin line exists between adulation and disillusionment, and it never takes long for that line to be crossed. The brittle dreams of a 'redeemed' Israel, restored to her former glory as in the days of David, were dashed. A light had been switched off, the door shut and bolted. From a few of the women there had been talk of angelic appearances and a resurrection, but an examination of the evidence had proved inconclusive (Luke 24:22-24). Besides, how could emotional rumours about angels, an empty tomb and a disappearing corpse possibly be substituted for the expectation of Messianic grandeur? To Cleopas and his companion, trust had toppled to the ground with a thud; hope had splintered. And they were by no means alone in their grief and despondency. The apostles felt the same (Mark 16:10).

Ignorance is folly

'O fools!' (Luke 24:25). The two men were surely startled; it was enough to stop them in their tracks. What was that? Had the 'stranger' really called them fools (Gk, *'anoetus'*, 'unthinking')? The word 'fool' is a special one and many-faceted, best left to God and the Scriptures (Luke 12:20; Ps. 14:1). In fact, those who 'play God' in the use of this sensitive word (Gk: *'moros'*, 'rebel'), are warned by his Son about the danger of facing 'hell-fire' (Matt. 5:22).

The sudden challenge silenced the two men for some considerable time — in fact for what appears to have been the remainder of the journey (Luke 24:28) — as they felt obliged to permit the 'stranger' to have his say. There was obviously something about him which forbade argument. Instead they listened carefully as he accused them of being both unthinking and unbelieving — 'fools', no less. They still had not recognized who he was (Luke 24:16), although readers since have had the advantage of knowing, but they were about to enter one of the most epic situations in history and to be the envy of every Christian since that day, receiving a comprehensive study of the Old Testament from the Son of God, whose person and ministry is central to the understanding of it (Luke 24:26-27). The travellers listened spellbound.

Keeping within bounds

First, they would probably have noticed that he confined himself to the limits of the recognized Old Testament canon (from the Greek *'kanon'*, meaning 'standard'), and its threefold development: 'Moses' (the Torah), 'the Prophets' *(Nebiim)* and 'all the Scriptures' or 'Writings' or 'Psalms' *(kethubim)* (Luke 24:44). Here lay the scriptural authority, beyond which the Teacher would not venture (Luke 24:27). He never tolerated the traditions of men, which have always sought to rival God's pure Word (Mark 7:1-13).

The 'Torah', or Law, or Pentateuch (Genesis to Deuteronomy), was acknowledged — and still is — by Judaism as divinely authoritative. Moses was known to have written 'all the words of the LORD' (Exod. 24:4), which he later handed to the priests as the custodians of God's Word (Deut. 31:9-11). His successor, Joshua, read it to the entire nation (Josh. 8:35). Certainly by B.C. 721/722, when the Assyrians captured Samaria, the existence of the Samaritan version of the Pentateuch was evidence that the 'Torah' had been accepted widely as canonical.

Then the prophets' *(Nebiim)*: these mighty men of God were the anointed mouthpieces for his message (2 Peter 1:21); therefore it was essential their words should be recorded on parchment (Jer. 36:1-4). Equally, it was considered imperative to remember God's sovereign activities in history (Deut. 7:18-19). Consequently, the inspired writings ('Thus saith the Lord...') of the 'former' prophets (Joshua, Judges, Samuel and Kings) and those of the 'latter' (Isaiah to Malachi, excluding Daniel, which the Jews have always considered apocalyptic rather than prophetical) were added to the existing canon (1 Chron. 29:29). Not surprisingly, a large number of the Psalms written by David were also included (Acts 2:25-28).

If the collation of the scrolls appeared to have been partially accomplished by the time of the Exile (B.C. 605-586) — for Daniel refers to the 'books' and specifically to 'Jeremiah' (Dan. 9:2) — it was certainly completed with the close of the prophetic voice. As one of the prophets states, it was God, and not a council of scholars, who determined when that point had arrived (Zech. 13:2-5). The unique prophetic ministry gradually dried up, creating the 400 years of the intertestamental period. These 'silent years', as they have been called, were not broken until the sudden appearance of John the Baptist (Mal. 4:5).

As for 'the Writings', or 'Psalms' *(kethubim)*, (called 'Hagiography' in the Septuagint or 'LXX' the Greek translation of the Old Testament), this section consists of material acknowledged by the Jews as being authentically 'of God': Chronicles, Ezra, Nehemiah, Esther and Job. Some of it had originally been associated with 'the prophets' (Ruth with Judges, Lamentations with Jeremiah), but was later transferred to this section to be part of the 'volumes' (*'Megilloth'*, Ps. 40:7) to accompany the Song of Solomon, Ecclesiastes and Esther. Daniel, on the other hand was included here (see above). The Apocrypha was not considered inspired, and was therefore excluded.

The official date for the completion of the Old Testament canon is uncertain, but in B.C. 200 a reference was made to the three sections in *The Wisdom of Jesus ben Sirach*. In other words the canon had been fixed, and it was to this that Jesus of Nazareth referred when he stated, 'Thy word is truth' (John 17:17). His companions on the Emmaus road were therefore left in no doubt where the roots of their belief lay.

They would also have observed that he did not question the fundamental theme of their 'Bible', or suggest that it required scholarship to discover it. On the contrary, the Scripture, which could not be 'broken' (John 10:35), was within the grasp of everyone to whom the 'mysteries' had been revealed (Matt. 13:11). They would 'know the truth' (John 8:32), having been guided into it by the Spirit (John 16:13). For such people, a straightforward question was all that was needed: 'Ought not Christ to have suffered these things, and to enter into his glory?' (Luke 24:26).

But why that question, and what would have inspired them to ask it? The answer was obvious: because the mighty prophets were primarily concerned with the subject. As the apostle Peter would later remind the church, their function, under the anointing of Christ's Spirit, was to testify 'beforehand the sufferings of Christ, and the glory that should follow' (1 Peter 1:11). To overlook, or refuse to believe, what the prophets had to say about Christ is folly indeed; the rich man and multitudes of others might not be in hell had they responded to 'Moses and the prophets' (Luke 16:31).

The master-class

At no time did the 'stranger' insist, or even casually suggest, that his two friends should return to Jerusalem. Instead, he walked with them towards Emmaus, and as he did so gradually unfolded the grand scheme of redemption, the Messianic hope of succeeding centuries. They listened in complete silence, with rapt attention, absorbed by what they were hearing and undoubtedly impressed, as the rabbinical teachers had been in his youth, by his remarkable grasp of scriptural truth. Then, about twenty-one years earlier, 'All that heard him were astonished at his understanding...' (Luke 2:47).

He would have employed the Jewish method, recounting the history of his people (cf. Deut. 1-4; Acts 7), before slowly but surely starting his epic journey through the Word of the living God — 'Moses ... all the prophets ... all the scriptures' (Luke 24:27), about which he always spoke with such reverence (Matt. 4:4; cf. Deut. 8:3). The Teacher could not have been more qualified, the subject more wonderful, the students more privileged, or more eager to learn (Luke 24:32). He reached into the deepest of pools, the revelation of truth, and from it there surfaced a panoramic splendour guaranteed to satisfy the mind and soul of every serious enquirer.

No one knows whether mention was made of *all* the 332 prophecies related to him and his ministry; the two-hour journey to Emmaus would surely not have been long enough, but any one of the following references was likely to have been used. We may read them in a different language from the one spoken on that day (Aramaic), but all who have heard the voice of truth (John 18:37) will rejoice as Cleopas and his friend did at what heaven has made known.

Moses

Gen. 3:15; 12:1-3; 14:18; 15:5; 22:2; 49:10.
Exod. 3:14; 12:13; 16:4 (cf. John 6:51); 20:1-17 (cf.
    Matt. 5:17); 28:29.
Lev. 1:4; 3:7-11; 16:10.
Num. 8:3 (cf. John 8:12); 12:7 (cf. Heb. 3:5-6); 20:11
    (cf. John 4:14); 21:8 (cf. John 3:14); 24:17.
Deut. 18:15 (cf. Acts 3:22; 7:37); 32:1-4.

The Prophets

The former prophets

Josh. 3:11; 5:13-15; 18:1 (cf. Gen. 49:10).
Judg. 6:11-16; 13:1-21 (cf. Isa. 9:6).
2 Sam. 7:16-29 (cf. Luke 1:32-33).

The latter prophets

Isa 1:18,25; 6:7; 7:14; 9:6-7; 11:1-2,10,12; 12:1-3; 25:8;
    26:12; 27:9; 32:17; 35:4-10; 40:2-3 (cf. Luke 3:4);
    40:10; 41:8; 42:1-4,7; 43:5-10; 45:4-6,22; 49:1-9;
    52:7,13-15; 53; 55:3-7; 61:1-3 (cf. Luke 4:16-21);
    62:10-12; 63:1-4.
Jer. 2:13 (cf. John 7:37-38); 7:9-11 (cf. Mark 11:17);
    8:22 (cf. Matt. 9:12); 23:5-6 (cf. 1 Cor. 1:30); 30:9
    (cf. Luke 18:38); 31:10 (cf. John 10:11-14); 31:15
    (cf. Matt. 2:16-18); 31:31-34 (cf. Heb. 8:7-13; 10:15-
    17); 33:14-16; 50:34 (cf. Heb. 4:15; 7:25).
Lam. 1:12; 2:15; 3:14-15,19,22-30.
Ezek. 21:25-27 (cf. John 1:49); 34:15,22-24,26 (cf. John

10:1-18); 36:24-27 (cf. Acts 2:1-13); 37:5 (cf. John 6:33); 37:15-28 (cf. Rom. 11:15-27); 38; 39; 40-42; 43:7-9 (cf. Rev. 21; 22); 47:1-12 (cf. Rev. 22:1-5).
Dan. 7:13-14,22,27 (cf. Matt. 24:39; 26:64); 9:22-25 (cf. Matt. 21:1-10); 9:26 (cf. John 19:30); 9:27 (cf. Matt. 24:15); 12:1-2 (cf. Matt. 24:21-22).
Hosea 1:10 (cf. 1 Peter 2:10); 3:4-5 (cf. Rom. 11:25-26); 11:1 (cf. Matt. 2:15,21); 13:14.
Joel 2:28-32 (cf. Acts 2:16-21).
Amos 5:27; 6:14 (cf. 2 Kings 17:3-6); 9:11-15 (cf. Acts 15:15-17).
Obad. 15-19 (cf. Rom. 9:13), 21.
Jonah 1:17 (cf. Matt. 12:40).
Micah 4:1-7; 5:2 (cf. Matt. 2:6).
Nahum 1:15.
Hab. 2:4 (cf. Rom. 5:1); 3:17-19 (cf. Matt. 21:19-22).
Zeph. 1:14; 3:14-20 (cf. 2 Thess. 2:2).
Hag. 2:6-9,21-23.
Zech. 3:8; 6:12-13; 9:9,16 (cf. Matt. 21:5); 11:11-13; 12:10; 13:1,6-7; 14:3-8.
Mal. 3:1,17 (cf. Matt. 11:10); 4:5 (cf. Matt. 17:10-13).

The Writings

Ps. 2:7,12 (cf. Heb. 1:5); 16:10-11 (cf. Acts 2:25-28); 22:1-19; 32:1; 40:6-7 (cf. Heb. 10:5); 45:6-7 (cf. Heb. 1:9); 69:8 (cf. Job 19:13); 89:26 (cf. Heb. 1:5); 97:7 (cf. Heb. 1:6); 104:4 (cf. Heb. 1:7); 110:1-2 (cf. Acts 2:34; Heb. 1:13); 132:17-18.
Ruth 4:13-22.
Job 19:13-21 (cf. Ps. 69:8); 19:25-27.
S. of S. 2:1-4 (cf. Isa. 35:1-2)

Emmaus reached

Time had sped swiftly by. Never had so much been said, or
such depths reached, in so short a space of time. The two who
had set out from Jerusalem solemn, if not sullen, were now
enraptured by what they had heard. Like infants tasting life for
the first time, they breathed the fresh, clean air of refreshing
truth, after years spent imbibing the stale legalism of dead religious observance (Matt. 7:28-29). They had learned much
— were almost overwhelmed by it — but what was now clear
was that it is not religion that sinners require, but grace; not
the cold formality of rites and ceremonies, but the warmth of
knowing God (John 17:3). They had been wading in Judaism's
stagnant pools, but now were bathing in the 'living water'
(John 7:37) that flows from the throne of God (Rev. 22:1).
How it sparkles! Offered freely to the darkest of sinners (John
4:10), it fills the soul with joy (John 15:11), when drawn from
the deep well of salvation (Isa. 12:3).

Equally it is not stern dogma that sinners require, nor on
the other hand sentimental 'devotion', but doctrine that stimulates the areas where love is expected and desired by God
(Deut. 6:5; Matt. 22:37). They now knew what Jeremiah meant
when he confessed, 'His word was in mine heart as a burning
fire shut up in my bones' (Jer. 20:9), because they too felt the
same way (Luke 24:32). Everyone born of the Spirit (John
1:13) appreciates exactly how Cleopas and his friend felt.

They will also guess how the two would react once the
village was sighted, and the moment had arrived to say good-
bye. Throughout the journey not once had they asked their
new friend where he was heading, assuming the village was
his destination also, but when he went to leave them they hankered like the newly born for him to remain with them. He had
imparted so much; how could they let him out of their sight?
Lydia was later to react in the same way to Paul: having had

her heart opened by the Lord when she heard the apostle's teaching, she yearned for his fellowship and that of his missionary party (Acts 16:14-15).

Heaven's infants always behave in that way, instinctively reaching for the 'breast' of God's Word, nourishment being the soul's first requirement (1 Peter 2:2). Their new friend had opened the Scriptures, switched on the light, revealed the divine hand behind all things historical and personal (Isa. 40:21-31). Now they understood the 'secret' (Matt. 13:11). Yes Christ is the key, the Creator and centre of the cosmos (Col.1:12-20), the Word made flesh (John 1:14). His incarnation, his unique life, his sacrificial death, his resurrection, his ascension and second advent — once this realization dawns, everything slots efficiently into place, along whatever avenue is walked. That is it; they had the answer!

At the table

For those touched by the 'marvellous light' of grace (1 Peter 2:9), there is a fascination about the examination of the Scriptures which cannot be equalled. To sit at the Master's feet, literally or through his Spirit (Acts 1:2), and be introduced to 'hidden wisdom' (1 Cor. 2:7) is an enviable position to be in, as Mary of Bethany discovered (Luke 10:39).

Cleopas and his friend wanted to share in that experience; they would no doubt have liked the study begun on their journey to continue, perhaps well into the night. With darkness descending quickly in those parts, they therefore begged the 'stranger' to remain with them, as Lydia would later do with Paul (Acts 16:14-15). He agreed (Luke 24:29).

Whose house it was is not known. Perhaps it was a caravanserai, a wayside 'inn', an overnight hostelry (Luke 10:34; 2:7). Whatever it was, after the weekend's traumatic events

and the strain they produced, it was a welcome relief to find
shelter miles away from the aggressive hubbub of the big
city. By comparison with Jerusalem how peaceful Emmaus
was! But the little village was about to reveal surprises of
its own.

On entering the house, the travellers would immediately
have found the signs of welcoming hospitality which every
respectable Jewish home contained (Luke 7:44): the jar filled
with water beside the door with the accompanying towel lying
close by, to bathe and ease the travellers' weary feet after hours
spent striding the dusty roads wearing open sandals (John
13:4-5). Then, when the meal was served, they reclined upon
the *triclinia* laden with large cushions, doing so in the cus-
tomary manner, turned towards the table, their feet stretched
out behind them. Clearly a pleasant evening was anticipated
with their guest (whose name the two men remarkably never
enquired after), the quest for truth flowing through the conversation. It was not to be.

In fact, the meal had scarcely begun when the hosts for the
evening received the biggest shock of their lives — of that
there can be no doubt. It arose, as is so often the case, when
least expected and from the most mundane of circumstances.
As he was their guest, they invited their new friend to divide
the bread for each of them — unleavened (Exod. 12:8) because leaven symbolized corruption (Matt. 16:6) — and to
offer thanksgiving to God for it. There was nothing unusual
about this, or indeed sacramental; it was an everyday occurrence in Jewish homes across the land.

They watched as he gently took the bread from the plate
and proceeded to snap each piece into segments ready for dis-
tribution to the others. Had either of them been present in a
certain 'upper room' in Jerusalem the previous Thursday
evening (Matt. 26:26), the truth would have dawned sooner,
but it was not this action which startled them. Nor was it

necessarily the prayer which followed, although it should and could have done; it was something else.

Surely at the very least their discernment was dimly stirred when he prayed, even without having heard him commune with his Father in that room a few days earlier (John 17); for who had such intimacy with heaven as he? (Matt. 6:6). He stood with his eyes opened (John 17:1) and arms uplifted (Exod. 17:12) as was the Jewish custom (1 Tim. 2:8) — a precious moment!

The contents of the prayer are unknown, but the reason for it is not: he gave thanks for the bread. Unlike others, he did not take this substance for granted, the staff of life through many centuries. Bread nourishes the body, providing it with the necessary strength and vigour (Lev. 26:26). The peasant spent his days toiling under a blazing sun to provide enough for his family's daily bread, as the one who prayed once reminded his listeners (Matt. 6:11). God warned Adam following the Fall: 'In the sweat of thy face shalt thou eat bread' (Gen. 3:19).

The irony of the situation was that the quiet moment was lost to Cleopas and his friend, who did not realize that the one who gave thanks for the bread was in fact its Creator (Col. 1:16). Again, did not the grain 'fall into the ground and die' (John 12:24) before producing the wheat from which the bread came? Is he not the 'true bread' who had given his life (John 6:32-33) just a couple of days before, and who sprang as the choicest of the 'wheat' from the 'dry ground' of Nazareth? (Isa. 53:2). And did he not once make a remarkable statement that 'I am the bread of life; he that cometh to me shall never hunger'? The redeemed receive their daily spiritual nourishment from the most pleasant of all 'food', this satisfying Bread which came from heaven (John 6:32) .

The prayer over, the guest for the evening would have placed some pieces of bread upon two plates, and then stretched across the table and handed them to his hosts. As he did so, the sleeves of his outer garment must have inched their way up his arm. At that precise moment the truth dawned. The two astonished men stared incredulously, dumbfounded. They had spent over two hours in his company without realizing! They had been so caught up with their doubts and dismay, like Gideon when complaining to 'the angel of the LORD' (Judg. 6:12-13), that they had failed to appreciate who was speaking to them.

Their minds were in turmoil. There was so much to say, so many questions to ask. Where could they begin? It is not recorded which of them had noticed first, perhaps both at once. Neither is it recorded what was said, or thought, but an intelligent guess can be made. 'His hands — look at his hands!' (Luke 24:35). The nail-prints were distinctly discernible (John 20:25). But he had gone — vanished (Luke 24:31).

6.
Broiled fish and a honeycomb

They stared at the spot where he had reclined a moment before, their thoughts jumbled by the phenomenon. Who could
possibly fathom what had happened, so suddenly and swiftly?
It was Jesus! Surely not! It was! They had actually been in his
company a few seconds earlier — within touching distance,
listening to his voice; and yet he had died the previous Friday!
One moment he was beside them, and the next gone. It was
impossible, incredible — but true!

There was no doubting his presence. Both were witnesses;
they had conversed with him, and he with them. They could
not have imagined it all. In any case, it was not as if the appearance had been fleeting — a flickering silhouette, a shadowy form, or a trick of the light. He had actually been their
companion for a length of time on their sixty furlongs' walk,
and then for that brief spell in the house (Luke 24:13). And
what about that wonderful in-depth Scripture lesson, which
certainly could not have been a figment of their imagination?
It had left their hearts 'burning' for more (Luke 24:32).

The point had been made, their confidence assured, but
now what were they to do? It did not take long for them to
make up their minds — 'the same hour' (Luke 24:33) — they
had to go back to Jerusalem to inform the apostles. How they
had wanted to leave that city, but now how eager they were to
return! Not long before, their tired bodies had told them it

was 'toward evening, and the day is far spent' (Luke 24:29), but the situation had altered dramatically. They must leave Emmaus as quickly as possible and set off once more along that seven-mile stretch.

Apart from general fatigue, this was not quite as simple as it might appear. The mention of its being 'toward evening' had not only referred to their physical tiredness, but to the dangers faced when travelling after dark. No one did unless they had to, or had a retinue to protect them (S. of S. 3:6-8). The solitary road would have meandered through inhospitable territory, hidden in the blackness of the night, where the grunt of a wandering camel, or the bleat of a nearby goat, would stimulate the fertile imagination. Behind large boulders and wild bushes might be thought to lurk men, whose sinister intentions could cause flesh to creep. If the victim who was left 'half dead' by thieves as he travelled from Jerusalem to Jericho (Luke 10:30) had been attacked in broad daylight, as appears likely, those who travelled at night risked a great deal more.

Still, they had to go (cf. 2 Kings 7:9); the triumphant news swept all other thoughts away: 'Jesus is alive!' Exhaustion, lurking terrors — these were nothing compared to the news they had to tell. Besides, if their Lord had accompanied them once along that road, could he not do so again in order to protect them? Into the darkness they went, with the 'brilliance' of their experience providing 'light' for their souls, and his masterly exposition of Scripture a lamp for their feet to lighten the road (Ps. 119:105).

Joyful news — fearful anticipation

They knew where the apostles would be assembled. It seems likely it was the 'upper room' (Mark 14:14-15) — probably a section of Mark's home (Acts 12:12) — where so much drama was experienced. When they arrived, breathless and excited, they discovered that, late though the hour was, there was quite a gathering of equally ecstatic brethren (Luke 24:33). No longer was the news of their Lord's resurrection confined to a small group of joyful women (Luke 24:10), which had been conveyed to tearful and unbelieving men (Mark 16:10-11); now it had spread in all directions among the disciples at large. The house had become a communications centre for news about the resurrection and buzzed with excited chatter. How quickly, but understandably, the scorn poured upon the sisters' tale had been forgotten, and how swiftly did the women step out of the limelight once their brethren believed!

However, the thrill and wonder of it all had not diminished the fear of reprisals from the authorities, the hatred for Jesus and his 'movement' being as intense as ever (John 9:22; 7:13). They had killed him; would the apostles be next? Secrecy had, therefore, to be maintained, the brethren and sisters meeting behind closed, if not barred, doors (John 20:19).

It had been that way since at least the previous Thursday, when Satan's most horrendous opposition had been rising to its crescendo, with the events at Skull Hill only hours away. The task allotted to Peter and John was the preparation of the Last Supper, but coded signals had to be used, Jerusalem's atmosphere being heavy with tension. The 'upper room' was located only after following a man seen doing a woman's job, carrying a water pitcher on his head, and when the owner of the house was approached Jesus' name was not mentioned. The two apostles had been told what to say: 'The Master saith unto thee, Where is the guest-chamber...?' (Luke 22:10-11).

A mysterious encounter

Cleopas and his friend were undoubtedly surprised by what they saw. They had rushed back all the way from Emmaus to tell their story, perhaps rather thrilled that they would be the first of the brethren to substantiate the women's account, only to be told upon their arrival, 'The Lord is risen indeed, and hath appeared to Simon' (Luke 24:34). 'Oh, they know!'

Chronologically Peter's experience was sandwiched between the morning appearances to the women (Mark 16:7) and the one the brethren received that evening (Luke 24:36). Apart from that, only one fact is known: it occurred in the aftermath of Peter's denial, his public disowning of his Lord and the uncontrollable weeping of a broken man (Matt. 26:75).

There had been a mass exit from Gethsemane by the eleven apostles (Matt. 26:56), as the Scriptures had foretold there would be (Zech. 13:7), but Peter's action was particularly unpleasant. He had cursed and even uttered oaths — presumably in God's name, in defiance of Jesus' teaching (Matt. 5:35-37) — that he did not know him (Matt. 26:74). It had been this sin which had separated the incident from the others, and needed to be dealt with quickly. That being so, Peter would not have been asked later by his Lord, 'Lovest thou me?' (John 21:15-17), without having repented first of all. Hence, the need for the first encounter (Luke 24:34). Confession of a supposed 'love' for God can *never* precede genuine repentance for sin, or if it is attempted, the rejection is swift and sharp, as Cain discovered (Gen. 4:3-5).

The words spoken between the Lord and his erring servant in those moments when their eyes met again (cf. Luke 22:61) have not been recorded, but the public rejection was answered by a private repentance, reminding sinners everywhere of the most precious invitation they could hear: 'Come unto me, all ye that labour and are heavy laden, and I will give you rest' (Matt. 11:28). Where else could Peter go — where else would he want to go? — but to the one more ready to forgive him than he was to seek that forgiveness? The scribes were correct: 'Who can forgive sins but God only?' (Mark 2:7).

It was his graciousness that kept Peter's humiliation and embarrassment from the pages of the New Testament, and from succeeding generations of its readers. Certainly, once Christ was 'seen of Cephas' (1 Cor. 15:5), the disciple who was not normally known for being bashful appeared remarkably subdued. That evening his silence was ear-splitting (Luke 24:36-48; John 20:19-25).

Questions and answers

The house guests, numbering more than a dozen by this time (Luke 24:33), would have been eager for news about the resurrection. Needless to say, curiosity being what it is, everyone present was anxious to gain as much information as possible from those who had actually seen the risen Christ for themselves that tremendous day: Mary Magdalene (Mark 16:9), 'the other Mary', Alphaeus' wife and the mother of James 'the less' and probably also of Matthew (Matt. 28:1); Zebedee's wife Salome, the mother of John and the other James (Mark 16:1); Joanna, the wife of Chuza, and perhaps other women (Luke 24:10); and now Peter, Cleopas and his friend (Luke 24:31-34).

Seven, at least, had seen him, but there were so many present *without* a story to relate. The room would, surely, have been filled with eager faces, ears straining to catch every word, as answers were given to questions which must have tumbled one upon another: 'Where did it happen? What did he look like? What did he say? Did you also see angels?' Now it was the turn of the latest two to testify of their experience (Luke 24:35), which was in some ways even more wonderful, because they seem to have spent longer in his company than the others. Theirs was no brief meeting, but a full-scale Scripture class, followed by the beginnings of a meal. There was so much to tell, awe and wonder expressed by sheer excited joy, and an audience hanging upon every word. History has not known a night like it.

The guest appearance

Then it happened. Those present would not have been capable of describing the moment, the finite mind not having been created to evaluate such experiences. All eyes were upon the two travellers from Emmaus as they earnestly told their story (Luke 24:35), surrounded as they were by their excited companions, when without warning they were interrupted.

Above their voices another was heard, a familiar greeting: 'Peace be unto you!' (Luke 24:36). John, who was present, later wrote, with a vague and quaint simplicity, 'Then ... came Jesus and stood in the midst' (John 20:19). That was all. There was no trumpet blast, or flash of dazzling light, no halo surrounding his head, or heavenly choirs to announce his presence. He just 'came' and stood among them. The miraculous moment excluded explanations, beyond merely reporting the fact that the person who had died on the cross two days before was now alive and in the room.

A stunned silence surely descended upon it, the once chattering occupants frozen into immobility, and such was their shock that they spoke no more that evening (Luke 24:37-41; John 20:19-23). They just listened, floating in a sea of mixed emotions; incredulity coupled with awe, unbelief with wonder, hesitant belief with exquisite joy (Luke 24:41). 'Could it be...? Is it a dream? Is it true? How did it happen?' Then, when reality had emerged into sharp focus once more, bewilderment gave way to fright and trembling. It must be a ghost! (Luke 24:37). So shocked were they all, that even those for

(John 19:34). The wound was still clearly visible. This too was examined closely.

Thomas, for some unknown reason, was absent (John 20:24), and Judas had committed suicide (Matt. 27:5), but the number in that room was not few. There were ten apostles (Matt. 10:2-4) — Peter and Andrew, James and John, Matthew and James 'the less', Philip, Bartholomew (Nathanael), Jude (Lebbaeus/Thaddaeus), Simon the Canaanite (or 'Zelotes', Luke 6:15) — and also others (Luke 24:33), including Cleopas and the other man. This meant that there were more than a dozen official witnesses of Christ's bodily resurrection, the miraculous and historical event unrelated to anything mystical or merely philosophical. This was no apparition on a mission to haunt, no dream draped in gossamer, but flesh and bones (Luke 24:39).

They stepped back from their examination of the evidence. There was no doubting it was Jesus, the one most of them had known personally for three years, so that they knew better than anyone what he looked like. True, mysterious changes had obviously taken place in his body, but they knew who it was. The eyes, the hair, the features and those nail-prints — who could overlook them? The witnesses were not liars. Their testimony is genuine, rooted in historical fact and a personal encounter: they had 'handled' the Word 'made flesh' (1 John 1:1; John 1:14). In that, they have a distinct advantage over the sceptics.

How precious this body was to them, and to all the redeemed everywhere. 'For thou wast slain, and hast redeemed us to God by thy blood,' is the triumphant heavenly cry (Rev. 5:9). It was through his sacrifice at Calvary that salvation was wonderfully accomplished. But privileged though they were, they were now even more amazed and awestruck than before, a plethora of emotions rising to the surface, along with a number of apparently insoluble questions. They had been fearful when he had first appeared (Luke 24:37), but an apparition was more readily understood. Everyone knew a ghost had no difficulty in entering a locked room, but a man, made of solid flesh and bones? It was a story no one would invent and hope to be believed. How could it happen? What did it all mean? They were about to find out, although without understanding it.

Then, as joy and incredulity vied with each other for mastery over them, Jesus astonished them still further. He requested food (Luke 24:41). Food? It was a gesture completely foreign to the circumstances, as if the weekend had been erased, with all its blackness and despair, its noise and clamour. He wanted to eat! Confused, baffled and in a quandary, the assembly hastily placed on the table a frugal meal: 'a piece of a broiled fish, and of an honeycomb' (Luke 24:42).

They watched in fascinated silence, like those who had never before seen food. Just think, the one whose crumpled and lifeless body had been removed from Skull Hill on its journey to the garden tomb now sat at the table eating (Luke 24:43). The simplicity of the request had been breathtaking, hurtling in an instance from the sublime to the mundane. The reasons for it, though, were threefold: the practical, the psychological and the theological.

As Jesus began to eat, the tension in the room would have eased considerably. The assembly had proved for themselves that he was not an apparition when they handled his hands and feet, but the sight of him sitting at a table eating, like ordinary mortals do every day, might have somewhat calmed their troubled minds (Luke 24:38). They remained puzzled, the entire proceedings beyond their understanding, but at least they now possessed the joy of knowing it really *was* Jesus.

But that had been the psychology of requesting something to eat — not only to demonstrate conclusively that he was 'flesh and bone', but to build a bridge between heaven and earth. Clearly, what had taken place during an extraordinary weekend was at the time understood only in eternity. The paradoxes were too profound for these unsophisticated men and women, whose entire lives had been spent alongside Galilee's lake, where the dead remained buried. Now they were confronted with death, resurrection, sudden appearances and disappearances, and their minds were spinning. The sight of Jesus eating food adjusted the balances in their thinking. How often they had seen him enjoying a meal with them! It was like old times again!

Food for the soul

But was it really like old times? They did not appreciate it, but in fact, rather than returning to *their* world, he had brought them part-way into *his*. They saw him eating food, and that appears to have satisfied them; he was back, but during that momentous first evening after his resurrection such was their bewilderment that one astonishing matter escaped them. Christ's followers in modern times still overlook it and are just as hazy in their understanding, although with less excuse. Seated at the table calmly eating, without saying a word, he was giving the most exciting theological lecture known to man. In fact, so profound was it that he was answering some of the metaphysical questions the greatest minds in history, whose books occupy the libraries of the world, have debated.

These are very largely summed up by Hamlet when contemplating suicide. What happens 'when we have shuffled off this mortal coil'? Is there a realm of the spirit — a heaven to enter, or a hell to fear? Is man in possession of a soul in need of redeeming? There, indeed, is the 'rub'! According to the prince, the hardships of this 'weary life' could easily be terminated by suicide, but for one thought: the dread of something after death, 'the undiscovered country from whose bourn no traveller returns,' puzzles the will. But Shakespeare had evidently overlooked, or rejected, the figure seated at the table eating. Here was the most expert of all 'travellers' returning with his evidence, but as usual the world was looking in the wrong direction, and it still is. It hankers after a life beyond this one, perhaps upon some planet far away, and amuses itself with talk about 'extra-terrestrial' beings and unusual sightings in the sky, but the truth is much closer than is generally supposed.

That resurrection night no 'unidentified flying object' had landed in the courtyard of the house; no weird monstrosity from deep space confronted the amazed onlookers. On the contrary, life descended not from the furthest outreaches of the cosmos, but through the thinnest of veils near at hand (John 11:25; 14:6). But how does one know this? The answer lies not in mathematical genius, or obscure equations typed into a computer system, but in a mere gesture and a simple request: 'He showed them his hands and his feet... Have ye here any meat?' (Luke 24:40-41).

Of course he was not hungry, but quietly demonstrating a glorious fact. A ghost would have been incapable of eating — certainly of eating actual food — but he was doing so. A real slice of broiled fish and a piece of honeycomb were at that moment being digested. Nevertheless he had no need of food. Something more remarkable than the numerous mysteries found in nature had taken place, and if man is unable to fathom these, he is in no position to deny the realm of grace its miracles (1 Cor. 2:14).

The friends were rejoicing to have their Master back with them, but in fact he was already removed from them, having undergone the resurrection transformation of the human form; the preparation for a more glorious dimension of experience having begun (John 20:17), enabling him to straddle both the realm of time and that of the spirit and be equally at home in both. He who walked the Emmaus road could also vanish in a wink, as befits one whose second advent will prove just as shocking (1 Cor. 15:51-52). And likewise, that which was solid flesh and bone (Luke 24:39) materialized unhindered by walls and locked doors, passing through them at will. As Elihu once stated within Job's hearing, 'Touching the Almighty, we cannot find him out: he is excellent in power...' (Job 37:23).

But such 'mysteries of godliness' (1 Tim. 3:16) should not surprise anyone, least of all those to whom they have been revealed (Matt. 13:11). Were not Abraham and Sarah visited by three unusual 'men', one of whom was 'the LORD' and the other two angels? (Gen.18; 19). Did not Jacob, on his journey to Haran, 'behold the LORD' in a dream in which God's covenant with Abraham was ratified (Gen. 28:12-13), and was he not later, in another dream, reminded of that experience by 'the angel of God', who introduced himself with the words: 'I am the God of Bethel'? (Gen. 31:11,13). In any case, who was 'the man' wrestling with Jacob throughout the night over whom he 'prevailed', causing the patriarch to exclaim that he had seen the face of God? (Hosea 12:2-4; Gen. 32:24-32).

Moses (Exod. 3:1-5) and Joshua (Josh. 5:13-15) could also testify of mysterious 'theophanic' appearances, and who was that figure sitting under an oak tree in Ophrah seeking to encourage Gideon? (Judg. 6:11-12). Surely, the same being with the angelic face ('very terrible') whose name was wonderfully 'secret' and who announced the forthcoming birth of Samson (Judg. 13; cf. Isa. 9:6).

He it is who sometimes stretched out his hand in judgement, as in the days of David (2 Sam. 24:16), and never fails to protect the people of God from their enemies (2 Kings 19:35; Isa. 37:36), surrounding them with divine security (Ps. 34:7). Walking the Emmaus road, suddenly standing amidst his friends, eating a meal, appearing, vanishing — these resurrection experiences of the Son of God could not be remarkable to

God the Son, history's Angel of the LORD, the vanguard of the Israelite nation in its wilderness wanderings (Exod. 14:19).

Watching him eat could have introduced the assembly to another aspect of the mystery they were privileged to witness — a marvel likely to be overlooked. They had already been overwhelmed by the fact that the one sitting at the table had lain in a tomb shortly before, but now this astonishment must be taken a step further. How precious the human form must be to its Creator — so much so that even after the mighty atonement had been accomplished through the full and sufficient offering of himself upon the cross (John 19:30), it was Christ's *body* which arose from the dead. That is vital to remember, and must be insisted upon when confronted by doubters.

He did not discard it, appearing only in theophanies as in Old Testament times, but identified with his people by returning to them in the body that had brought them redemption and glory. It was 'in the body of his flesh' that he was able to present his people 'holy and unblameable' (Col. 1:22). Their sins had crucified him, but his *physical* resurrection assured them that his sacrifice had been willingly accepted in heaven (Rom. 4:25).

In other words, the initial terror upon seeing their Lord and Redeemer that evening (Luke 24:37), which in turn had led to amazement, had every reason to develop into a deeper love for him than they had known before. It is this fervent love for Christ, even to martyrdom, which puzzles those not in possession of it. Simon Peter saw his Lord and loved him, but what of those believers who have never seen him? (John 20:29). The apostle understood the mystery of new birth when he wrote to such brethren and sisters, 'Whom having not seen, ye love; in whom, though now ye see him not, yet believing, ye rejoice with joy unspeakable and full of glory' (1 Peter 1:8).

Christ had not only identified with them in the death and resurrection of his body, but in doing so, had directed their attention to the uniqueness of their own bodies in the sight of God, something which is invariably taken for granted. They were not run off an assembly line, planks in a builder's yard, or identical bricks piled high on his site, but 'chosen ... precious' (1 Peter 2:4). As their Lord's body was unique (how else could they have recognized him?), so each blood-bought child of his is also unique (even 'identical' twins are not clones of each other) and their names — not numbers — have always been known in heaven, written in the Lamb's book of life (Rev. 20:12,15). How devilish and obscene, therefore, is the concept of cloning humans!

Then, at the appointed time, that uniquely precious individual entered the world in flesh and, such was Christ's love, it was poured out for him or her at Golgotha and in the significance of the empty tomb. As John was later to write to these precious people called Christians, the 'sheep' for whom the Good Shepherd had died (John 10:11), 'Herein is love, not that we loved God, but that he loved us, and sent his Son to be the propitiation for our sins' (1 John 4:10).

But even at that point the mighty gospel is not complete. He ascended to glory bodily (Luke 24:51), taking the nail-prints with him — something for which everlasting rejoicing will be heard (Rev. 5:6,9). He will also return in majesty to earth physically, with the same body seen in the 'upper room' that evening. Then the human form will be seen at its most glorious: the 'vile' body of each redeemed sinner, after years of struggling against the 'flesh' (Gal. 5:17), transformed into the likeness of Christ's own body (Phil. 3:21; 1 John 3:2).

God will never forsake the human form, created as it is in the image of the Creator (Gen. 1:26). It is most precious to him, the Son having sanctified it when he assumed 'the likeness of men' (Phil. 2:7-8). The body, 'fearfully and wonderfully made' (Ps. 139:14), with all its component parts (1Cor. 12:14-26), is 'for the Lord; and the Lord for the body' (1 Cor.

6:13) — a fact which even the unsaved will one day appreciate, but to their cost, as they in bodily form bow before Christ
(Phil. 2:9-11).

But the request for food, while demonstrating the fact that
the welcomed Guest was not a mere apparition (Luke 24:39),
also opened two more vistas of understanding for those searching for Hamlet's 'undiscovered country'. First of all, the figure calmly eating his meal was a reminder of how close it is,
not a spacecraft's flight of 'light years' away, but as near as
one deep breath. Nor is it the imagined journey often sung by
children, 'above the bright blue sky' (What a long way away!),
but only a whispered gasp. The young Samuel heard his name,
not from afar, but from near at hand (1 Sam. 3:3-4). Likewise,
was this not the experience of those who shared such wonderful moments in ancient times? (Deut. 5:24-26).

The fact is, to almighty God the Spirit Being (John 4:24),
distance, like time itself, possesses no limiting powers. He
moves effortlessly through all boundaries — geographic,
national and linguistic. To which destination could David travel,
whether vertically or horizontally, and lose the presence of his
Lord? Could he wing his way towards the sky, soaring through
'the blue', or plummet to the lowest regions, and fail to exult
in the divine omnipresence? From the womb to the throne
David had been watched over, both in encouraging moments
and through dismal experiences (1 Sam. 16; 2 Sam. 12); every
thought, word and deed known and analysed by one who is
omniscient (Ps. 139).

It must then be said of God that, if he is 'afar off' in his
magnificence within the spirit realm (Ps. 139:2), then equally
he must be intimately close to each individual in his beneficence (Acts 17:27-28); on the one hand Ruler over infinity
(Deut. 10:14; 1 Kings 8:27), yet on the other stooping to the
lowly (Isa. 40:28-31). He who has stretched the firmament far
and wide like an awning to cover the earth (Isa. 40:22), and

will one day sweep it aside to reveal the glory of Christ (Isa. 34:4; Rev. 6:14), also takes note of lilies in a field (Matt. 6:28).

When therefore the first witnesses to Christ's resurrection shared accounts of their experiences, it would have proved evident that wherever he went when he vanished from sight, it could not have been far away. One moment he was close to the tomb (John 20:16), the next along the road from the garden (Matt. 28:9), then striding the Emmaus road (Luke 24:15) and, in a remarkably short space of time, there he was standing in their midst (Luke 24:36). By contrast, how long the journey from deep space! If only the eye of the astronomer was as penetrating as the eye of faith (Heb. 11:1).

But what of mankind as a whole? Each individual must one day die and, said Jesus, rise again from the realm of death. In fact, he taught that no one should 'marvel' at such a thought (John 5:28). His sudden appearances and disappearances bring us closer to the reality of this profound matter, as does the meal he requested and ate in front of his friends. Not only must it have reminded the group that the veil between life and death is frail, but that souls pass from one to the other as speedily as their Lord appeared and vanished; in fact, with the suddenness of his second advent — like lightning (Matt. 24:27). That brief moment when the door shuts tight against the past, when the individual is confined to history, is the most swift he will ever experience. There will be no drifting or soaring, no uncertainties as to one's eternal destination; the soul's transformation from time to timelessness is immediate.

It is this immediacy which Jesus emphasized in his account of the rich man and Lazarus, the beggar who sat at his gate (Luke 16:22-23). The latter died and straight away entered 'Abraham's bosom', the eternal domain for those sharing the patriarch's saving faith (Gal. 3:26-29). True, he was 'carried' there by angels, but this denotes not distance but triumph: 'absent from the body ... present with the Lord' (2 Cor. 5:8).

By contrast, the ungodly rich man 'also died, and was buried', and then Jesus continued without pausing, 'and in hell...'. Nothing could be more certain, or swifter. The witnesses of Christ's resurrection must have been extremely aware of man's fragile hold upon mortality and of the fact that, as Jesus appeared or disappeared with great suddenness and ease, likewise at any time of day or night one can be summoned to appear before God (Luke 12:20). The prophet had already reminded the Jewish nation of the need to be prepared (Amos 4:12).

But is it possible to tread still further into the mystery of an individual's passing from the earthly scene, to learn as much about his death as is known about his birth? The sight of the Lord at the table, where the mysterious and the mundane overlapped, appears to suggest that it is. Was this really the man who had hung so helplessly upon the cross, and yet minutes before had entered a locked room and, having done so, to the astonishment of everyone present, ate food as if nothing untoward had occurred? There he is, now no more; the nail-prints, the fish and the honeycomb: two opposing worlds colliding (John 3:6), yet in the risen Christ embracing. The lesson had been learned that he was not a ghost (Luke 24:39), but was there not one other point to be noted? What of the rest of us whose bodies must die, and whose souls will enter the spirit realm? (John 5:28-29). Do not these paradoxes have something vital to teach us?

First, what happens to *the Christian* when he at last 'falls asleep' in the blessed hope of the resurrection? (1 Cor. 15:6). Before the request for food, terror had filled the room when without warning the spirit realm confronted the friends. The unknown can be a frightening foe to encounter, like 'falling' unredeemed into the hands of the living God, who is a 'consuming fire' (Heb. 10:31; 12:29). But this can never be the position of the Christian, nor should fear have been permitted to clasp those first witnesses by the throat, for had they not heard Jesus' gracious introduction when he made his dramatic appearance? Only to his people would he say, 'Peace be unto you' (Luke 24:36; John 20:21), and had this precious gift of peace not already been promised them? (John 14:27). It is a covenant of peace (Ezek. 34:25; 37:26).

At their final meeting together just prior to his arrest they had heard him say, 'Let not your heart be troubled, neither let it be afraid.' On what grounds? Those which the angels had sung about when they announced his birth: '... on earth peace, goodwill toward men' (Luke 2:14; cf. Isa. 52:7). This is the heavenly peace he provides for all his people as his personal gift to them (John 14:27), peace with God (Rom. 5:1) 'through the blood of his cross' (Col. 1:20), and tranquillity of heart as a result (Isa. 26:3).

Small wonder he particularly asked why they were 'troubled' (Luke 24:38). And yet, what an extraordinary question to ask, as if the sight of a supposedly 'dead' man enjoying a meal was the most normal of experiences. But that was the point: it was, to him, if not to them. What is more simple than for the living God to raise the dead — he has life in himself (John 5:21,26) — or for the spirit realm to feel 'comfortable' with food even though there is no more need of it? In which case, should not the redeemed respond by feeling at ease when contemplating their passing into that world? Certainly, Jesus has given them reason to be. Of course, he was speaking metaphorically and of gospel truths, but it cannot be overlooked that he was also at a table (perhaps the same one) when he referred to wine: 'I will not drink henceforth of this fruit of the vine, until that day when I drink it new with you in my Father's kingdom' (Matt. 26:29). Once more, in him, time and timelessness link arms.

In other words, for those in possession of saving faith there is a sense of being 'at home' about their eventual departure to be with Christ, 'which is far better' (Phil. 1:23). The 'little flock' (such a gentle title!) has no need to fear; entrance into the kingdom of heaven is assured. After all, in the Father's 'good pleasure' it is his gift to them (Luke 12:32). With the closure of the eyes for the final time, will not that pleasant voice be heard again saying, 'Peace be unto you'? (Luke 24:36). As Christ appeared suddenly among his friends, so too will his brethren and sisters appear before him (Mark 3:31-35). He was confronted with frightened faces, but theirs is a welcome with open arms: 'Come, ye blessed of my Father, inherit the kingdom prepared for you from the foundation of the world' (Matt. 25:34).

In any case, he was provided with frugal fare, a slice of fish and a piece of honeycomb (Luke 24:42), but the honour awaits them of sitting at the heavenly 'table' for the marriage supper of the Lamb (Rev. 19:9). He had to ask for food, but 'blessed' indeed are those who have it spread before them without having to request it! They will have been irresistibly brought by grace to the banquet (John 6:44), sheltering beneath 'his banner' of love (S. of S. 2:4). The joy befits the occasion of the marriage: Christ the groom, the church his bride, and faith, as Luther suggests, the 'wedding ring' which unites the two for ever (Isa. 54:5-6; Eph. 5:22-33).

It is a resplendent scene, graphically illustrated in the Scriptures. Are we not therefore entitled to believe that all seated at the 'table' will be aware of each other? (Those who sit at tables usually are!) This will be, not in terms of relationships familiar to the flesh, but 'as the angels of God in heaven' (Matt. 22:30), who although of that realm were nevertheless individuals capable of recognizing each other (Luke 24:4).

Jesus appears to have provided credence for this concept. In a debate with the unbelieving Sadducees (cf. Acts 23:8) 'touching the resurrection of the dead', he astonished his hearers when he chose a very familiar statement from their

Scriptures (the Pentateuch) as a 'proof text' for life beyond death (Matt. 22:31-32). It still astonishes. On that mysterious occasion in Hebrew history when, in the desert, Moses stood at the burning bush, he heard God say, 'I am the God of thy father, the God of Abraham, and the God of Isaac, and the God of Jacob' (Exod. 3:6). When the covenant originally given to Abraham (Gen. 12:1-3) was ratified to Isaac and Jacob, they too heard similar words (Gen. 26:24; 28:13).

It was, of course, an introductory pronouncement, Almighty God offering his 'credentials' as the one whom the patriarchs knew and worshipped but, as Christ revealed, it was much more than that. 'I AM' is his name (Exod. 3:14), but 'I AM' is also the present tense (John 8:58). God, then, in the words of David (Ps. 42:2) and Jeremiah (Jer. 10:10), is 'the living God'. He is *not*, Jesus teaches, 'the God of the dead' (Matt. 22:32). Moses learned that day, in a most extraordinary revelation, that his father Amram and the three patriarchs were all with God *at that moment*! (Exod. 6:18-20). All were long since dead — yet alive! One can imagine how Moses felt — the comfort it brought him, to be told that his father, particularly, was eternally safe and secure. But that being so, were the four in the presence of God in total isolation to each other, or incapable of knowing who the other was? Surely the concept of the 'marriage supper', where both words denote happy fellowship, would exclude such a thought.

The irony behind Jesus' choice of illustration evidently escaped the unbelieving and cynical Sadducees, who denied the existence of the realm of the spirit (Acts 23:8). Their vocabulary therefore had no place for the word 'theophany'. They saw 'only' Jesus of Nazareth standing before them, but as 'the Angel of the LORD' he had also stood in the midst of the bush which appeared on fire, and observed Moses approaching it. The Sadducees thought they heard 'only' the carpenter from Galilee speaking to them; Moses heard the same voice, and it belonged to God (Exod. 3:1-6). He had been comforted in the revelation that there is life beyond the veil of death; the Sadducees were rebuked for their ignorance of the Scriptures, and the power of God (Matt. 22:29).

Food for thought

This truth, coming from Christ himself, is breathtaking. If there is life beyond death, what of those who die unprepared to meet 'the living God'? (Amos 4:12: Heb. 10:31). He considers them 'fools' (Luke 12:20), warning them about the possibility of dying 'in' their sins (John 8:24).

The redeemed pass from spiritual death to everlasting life (John 5:24); the unsaved are immediately transported from physical life to eternal 'death'. Hell is not a 'state of mind', or 'what you make it' here on earth, but an actual place of everlasting torment (Luke 16:23). In fact, so intensely did Jesus feel about the matter that, when appropriately referring to the Ten Commandments (Gal. 3:10), he suddenly broke off and burst into a passionate and moving appeal: far better to pluck out the 'offending' eye or amputate the 'offending' hand, than to be 'cast into hell' (Matt. 5:29-30). Never originally intended for humans, it was 'prepared for the devil and his angels' (Matt. 25:41). Tragically, mankind's fall in Eden changed that. Death, they were warned, would be the penalty for disobedience; 'death' they received when they disobeyed (Gen. 2:17).

Nothing encouraging can be spoken or written about the place — the sinner instantly plummeting into the hands of God, the 'consuming fire' (Heb. 12:29), whose perfection is absolute. The unsaved also 'see' Christ, for he is their Judge (John 5:22), but the 'table' is bare of anything to alleviate their terror (Luke 24:37). No message of peace do they hear (Isa. 48:22), but only one of wrath, the 'cursed' for whom there is no more hope (Matt. 25:41). These are the 'tares' to be pulled up and burned at harvest-time (Matt. 13:30). Fires that are never put out, and never abate, await them (Mark 9:43-48).

Isolated in eternal darkness (Luke 16:23), 'afar off' from God and his mercy, they nevertheless are aware of the glory from which they are for ever excluded (Luke 16:23-26; John 17:24). In never-ceasing torment (Luke 16:28), enduring never-diminishing anguish (Matt. 22:13), these 'weep and wail', waiting in trepidation for Christ's glorious return and the culmination of all things (Eph. 1:10), when the divine ledgers are to be opened (Dan. 7:10; Rev. 20:12). Then heaven's official verdicts will be read out, the redeemed vindicated, the rebels exposed and, above everything, Almighty God seen by his entire creation as being 'all in all' (1 Cor. 15:23-28).

First the body, now the word

The meal was quickly dispensed with (Luke 24:43-44); it was, after all, incidental to the main reason why he had visited them (John 4:31-32). Something vital had to be addressed, which Cleopas and his friend may have had time to mention to the gathered apostles as a warning, for the two had already tasted something of their Lord's disapproval. No doubt to their surprise, he had referred to them as 'fools, and slow of heart' (Luke 24:25). Clearly, the resurrection was not an event to excite mere curiosity, but the opportunity for lessons to be learned in preparation for the future. They had received their joy (Luke 24:41), but now it was time for sober reflection and teaching. The second master-class of the day began (Luke 24:26-27,44-45).

7.
Further causes for astonishment

The Lord set the tone, which was one of earnestness. On his first appearing he had greeted them all generally with the words, 'Peace be unto you' (Luke 24:36), but he made no attempt to address them individually. One suspects that a fictional account would have had him jovially chatting, recounting the experiences of the awful weekend and exchanging stories with them. But no, what mattered to him was the Word of God (Luke 24:25-27), something which his disciples had learned during their three years with him. In fact, on one notable occasion, he provided an insight into his thinking on the subject. Wishing to express her appreciation of him, a certain woman began praising his mother, but Jesus was not impressed. Instead, he quickly retorted, 'Yea rather, blessed are they that hear the word of God, and keep it' (Luke 11:27-28). This is the definitive statement of priorities for all those claiming allegiance to him.

That was typical of him. His attitude was straightforward, and one which needs to be remembered today; the divine record, like God himself (Isa. 42:8), does not tolerate rivals. As Christ originated from the 'bosom' of the Father (John 1:18), the revealed Word (the communication of his heart and mind) issued from his 'mouth' (Deut. 8:3; Matt. 4:4). From boyhood, when he had astonished the scholars with his grasp of the Jewish Scriptures (Luke 2:46-47), the Son of David's approach to them had reflected that of his inspired ancestor: 'Thou hast magnified thy word above all thy name' (Ps. 138:2). So elevated is this view of Holy Writ that it produces gasps of amazement, if not outrage, from those not in tune with the purposes of God.

Here lay the deep chasm between the religious authorities and Jesus: the place of God's Word (John 17:17) in the life of the nation, a conflict he considered so important there was never any question of compromising his stand. If the Pharisees and scribes held the Jewish Scriptures in one hand, the cherished 'Talmud' was clutched in the other. Among the Jews it still is. Divided into two, the oral law (the Mishnah) and its official interpretation (the Gemara), it consists of the scholarly additions to God's Word collated over generations — the one believed to be of equal worth to the other.

As a result of the oral law now encrusted within the very fabric of Judaism, a plethora of rules flooded religious observance, from the practical to the absurd; a maze of detailed regulations weaving their way through Jewish life, bringing in their wake much confusion among the people. Even the great doctors of the law were not always in agreement about its interpretation, or the minutiae of some detail or other. But they agreed on one point: *'Sola Scriptura'* ('Scripture alone' — the motto of the sixteenth-century Reformers) was *not* their motto. To them the 'Talmud' was equally 'of God', with its traditions *('halachoth')* and legends *('hagadoth')*. His 'commandments' and those of men were fused together (Matt. 15:9).

In a famous passage (Mark 7:7-13), Jesus outlined the consequences of the prevailing folly, one which the Pharisees and scribes had committed. They had undermined God's Word. Human nature being what it is (Jer. 17:9), they had set it to one side, preferring irrelevant details unrelated to divine revelation. As a result, in Israel traditional thinking had superseded

its rival, and the 'commandment of God' had been rejected
(Mark 7:8-9). The principle is plain: true worship, that which
is acceptable to God (Isa. 29:13), is impossible unless the
worshippers believe his Word to be without equal (Mark 7:7).
Manufactured appendages to the revelation, then, are not only
an irrelevance, but an obscenity, and a danger to the soul.

Just one example will suffice. Centuries of rabbinical influences have multiplied the Ten Commandments of God's law
(Exod. 20:1-17) to 603! As it is through the correct understanding of the moral law that convicted sinners are brought
to Christ for salvation (John 16:8; Rom. 7; Gal. 3:24), it is
imperative that the Word of God remains free from interfer-
ence. Therefore in the light of the fact that 'Whosoever shall
keep the whole law, and yet offend in one point, he is guilty of
all' (James 2:10), it is not surprising that Jesus condemned the
priests for 'binding' the people with heavy burdens 'grievous
to be borne' (Matt. 23:4). He had observed their pathetic condition, under a legalistic 'yoke' through no fault of their own,
and graciously invited the 'heavy laden' to reach out to him:
'For my yoke is easy, and my burden is light' (Matt.11:30).

But Jesus always practised what he preached, showing by
example what he thought of the intrusive 'commandments of
men'. The apostles had often been present when he had debated this issue. For three years they had watched him publicly apply the principle of *'Sola Scriptura'*, by fearlessly strip-
ping away Talmudic influences which the rabbis taught were
fundamental to Jewish belief. What they considered 'lawful'
he openly challenged (Matt. 12:1-5), comparing traditional
'legality' with their Scriptures (Mark 7:13), and revealing how
far the priests were from the truth. He was also not slow in
pointing out their inconsistencies even when they claimed to
be strict adherents to the Mishnah (Matt. 12:10-11).

That being so, how little the apostles can have understood,
for their Lord to have felt obliged to remind them of his teaching

(Luke 24:44). He was merely repeating what they had heard many times before ('while I was yet with you'), that the gradual unfolding of God's plan of salvation through centuries of Jewish history had to be fulfilled, and now they were privileged to be present during its blossoming. From Eden (Gen. 3:15) to the patriarchs (Gen. 12:1-3; 26:24; 28:13-14), the patriarchs to the prophets (Isa. 7:14; Micah 5:2), the prophets to John the Baptist (Matt. 3:3) — the gospel promise had never wavered or dimmed. The Messianic hope (Isa. 25:8-9), the atoning sacrifice (Ps. 22:1), the glorious resurrection (Hosea 13:14) — these had all been spoken about, hoped for, prayed over (2 Sam 7:16; Job 19:25-26; Hab. 3:17-19) and now fulfilled!

But what of the apostles, who with the prophets were to be the 'foundation' of the truth revealed? (Eph. 2:20). They had sought elevation within the kingdom (Matt. 20:20-21) and greatness among themselves (Luke 9:46), were proud of their loyalty to their Master (Matt. 26:35) but in reality had proved weak and cowardly (Matt. 26:56), as Scripture had foretold that they would be (Zech. 13:7), despondent and unbelieving (Luke 24:11). In fact, while the women had rejoiced in the wake of the resurrection (Matt. 28:8), they had remained weeping! (Mark 16:10). Small wonder that, having hesitated at believing their Scriptures, they had taken little heed to what their Lord had promised — that he would 'be raised again the third day' (Matt. 16:21). It was the third day, but his appearance, far from being eagerly anticipated, had been reduced in their eyes to the level of an apparition! (Luke 24:37).

The fault was theirs in failing to believe 'all that the prophets have spoken' (Luke 24:25), but equally, Jesus would have appreciated that the apostles and their friends had been reared within the confines of Jewish apostasy. Those who are victims of such an influence find themselves enmeshed, not so much by lies, but by half-truths, the more deadly of the two. Truths and errors are tightly intertwined, the task of separating them from each other virtually impossible — that is, without the Instructor who guides the people of God 'into all truth' (John 16:13).

The rebuke having been proffered, the risen Lord embarked upon a favourite subject, launching into his second Scripture class that day (Luke 24:25-27,44-46). Cleopas and his friend had attended the first one, but clearly were thrilled to listen again, as he conducted the guided tour around the treasury of God's grace. Here the Talmud had no say and the traditions of men were swept under his footstool as each section of the Hebrew Scriptures, 'the law of Moses ... the prophets ... the psalms' was given free rein to disclose the beauty and glory of the Messiah (1 Peter 1:10). Those who without reserve accept the Mosaic authorship of the Pentateuch and the revelatory ministry of the prophets (Hab. 3:2) and the psalmists (2 Sam. 23:1-2) have a keen supporter in the Son of God. Conversely, those who trifle with the strict authority of the Scriptures, whether through unbelieving scholarship or personal disregard, have erected a very flimsy house on a great deal of sand (Matt. 7:26-29).

In this fresh master-class, their Lord's objective was quickly appreciated: it was that his avid listeners might 'understand the scriptures' (Luke 24:45), not merely believing that truth could be found somewhere there, but rather that the Word of the living God *is* the truth. They would have noted, and not for the first time, the authoritative expression their Lord employed: 'Thus it is written...' (Luke 24:46; cf. Matt. 4:1-11). That is sufficient. If the Scriptures have it recorded, then it is certainly true. Any other approach is not recognized by Christ.

The subject is known, even if his method is not. It was that 'It behoved Christ to suffer, and to rise from the dead the third day' (Luke 24:46). Many, if not all, of the following references must surely have featured prominently in his exposition.

The ten prophetic Messianic titles

1.	Immanuel	Isa. 7:14; 9:6
2.	The Suffering Servant	Isa. 42:1-4; 49:1-6; 50:4-9; 52:13 - 53:12
3.	The Branch	Isa. 4:2; Jer. 23:5; Zech. 3:8; 6:12
4.	The Son of Man	Dan. 7:13-14
5.	The Son of David	2 Sam. 7:12-13; Jer. 30:9; Ezek. 34:23-24
6.	The Star and Sceptre	Gen. 49:10; Num. 24:15-17; Ps. 45:6
7.	Shiloh (Babylonian: 'Shelu' = 'prince')	Gen. 49:10; Exod. 25:22; Josh. 18:1; Isa. 9:6
8.	The royal Bridegroom	Ps. 45:2,6-8,11,13-15
9.	The Cornerstone	Ps. 118:22-23; Isa. 28:16; Dan. 2:34,44
10.	The Angel of the LORD	Gen. 16:7-13; 18:1-33; 22:15; Exod. 3:2; 14:19; Josh. 5:13-15; Judg. 6:11-24; 13:1-23; Ps. 110:1.

Each Christian is in possession of the Spirit of Christ (1 Cor. 3:16), whose unveiling of the mysteries (Matt. 13:11) and instruction in matters divine (John 16:13) are as valid and remarkable as they were that evening. Nevertheless, honesty would confess the deep desire to have been present, listening spellbound to the one who is truth personified (John 14:6) unfolding truths first heard in eternal ages past (John 18:37). Perhaps questions were asked, but it is more likely that the silence in the room was broken only by the sound of the lone voice, as the risen Christ dipped into his 'treasure' and produced 'things new and old' (Matt. 13:52).

The threefold aspect of the Messiah

1. The divine

Lord	Isa. 40:3; Mal. 4:5-6
Mighty God	Isa. 9:6
Immanuel	Isa. 7:14
Eternal Son	Ps. 2:7
Eternal King	Ps. 45:1,6
Creator	Ps. 102:25-27
Ruler	Ps. 110:1
Ascended Lord	Ps. 68:18

2. The human

The seed	
of the woman	Gen. 3:15
of Abraham	Gen. 12:1-3; 22:18; 26:4
of Isaac	Gen. 21:12; 26:24
of Jacob	Gen. 28:14
of Judah	Gen. 49:10
of Jesse	Isa. 11:1
of David	2 Sam. 7:12-13; 1 Kings 9:5; Ps. 89:3-4,35-37
His birth	Isa. 7:14
His birthplace	Micah 5:2

3. The sufferings of the Messiah

Betrayal	Ps. 41:9; Zech. 13:6
Silence	Isa. 53:7
Scourging	Isa. 50:6; 53:5
Crown of thorns	Isa. 52:14

Crucifixion	Ps. 22:16; Zech. 12:10
Humiliation	Ps. 22:7-8
Divided clothes	Ps. 22:18
Anguish	Ps. 22:1
Thirst	Ps. 69:21
The curse	Deut. 21:23
The Lamb of God	Exod.12:3; 24:8; Isa. 53:7

Stirred to action

Now that the Scriptures were at last understood (Luke 24:45), the haze had lifted. As is the case for everyone born anew (John 3:7), the marvel and beauty of God's epic plan of salvation filled the thoughts of the group with thanksgiving. Their Master, like the true Angel of the LORD (Exod. 14:19), had led his followers through the 'howling wilderness' (Deut. 32:10) of their confusion. Centuries of human meddling in the affairs of God, additions to his Word merely undermining it, had been stripped away. When witnesses had 'seen' the God of Israel for themselves (Exod. 24:9-10), or had heard his 'speech' (Hab. 3:2), why trust the mere notions of those who had not? *'Sola Scriptura'*: it was so simple! Why had they not understood before? But as they would eventually realize, matters 'spiritually discerned' require Christ to unlock them (1 Cor. 2:14). This he had done that unique evening, and by his Spirit still does (John 16:13).

With the unfolding of their Scriptures in such a wonderful way, a breathtaking insight into heaven's progressive revelation, the friends might have been tempted to sit back and enjoy the view. How thrilling to be locked in a room with the risen Christ! Who would desire the experience to end? Heaven had broken in among them, time had evaporated, and all their fears, anxieties and enemies were kept at bay. If only the room, and the house itself, could have remained barred and bolted against the world! (John 20:19).

But mysticism finds no favour with Christ, for whom a 'conversation in heaven' (Phil. 3:20) means feet firmly planted upon earth. There is no one more intensely practical than God, and the carpenter's shop in Nazareth, where Jesus had spent so many years with hammer and nails, had been no place for dreaming! (Mark 6:3). The gospel, correctly understood, enthrals and although initially there may be the temptation to bask in wonderment, it quickly stimulates the believer into action. Christ is the pivot around which everything revolves, the 'finger' pointing in the right and only direction (Matt. 7:14), and the one who provides meaning in a chaotic world brought about by man's ignominious fall in Eden (John 14:6). The realization has suddenly dawned, with the appearance of 'his marvellous light' (1 Peter 2:9), that life's biggest secret has been revealed (John 10:10), its greatest problem solved, and at its heart is reconciliation with God through what took place at Calvary and through the empty tomb (Luke 24:46).

That being so, the world must be told this unique gospel before it is too late, when its inhabitants confront Christ in their sins at the bar of judgement (Acts 17:31; John 8:24; 5:22) and enter hell for ever (Matt. 5:29-30). There is no option; every disciple must proclaim the message by lip and by life and sinners everywhere must repent (Acts 17:30). The doors therefore must be flung wide open, not hidden behind (John 20:19), and the apostles must be busy among the people preaching the exhilarating message of 'repentance toward God, and faith toward our Lord Jesus Christ' (Luke 24:47; Acts 20:21). In him alone is hope (Col. 1:27), and through him alone can salvation be received (Acts 4:12).

There was no mistaking the urgency that evening behind their Lord's words, nor the vital importance of the future role they were to fulfil as apostles (Eph. 2:20). As the Father had 'given' his Son to a lost world whom he created and loved (John 3:16), had 'sent' him (John 17:3) as the Saviour of the 'sheep' for whom he died (John 10:15), so they too would be 'sent' forth *('apostolos')* in his name preaching the Word (John 20:21). The days of personal self-seeking (Luke 9:46), despondency and tears (Mark 16:10) were over; now they were the official witnesses (Luke 24:48), in the sight of heaven and before men (1 Cor. 15:5-8), of the most astounding event known to history: Christ is risen from the dead!

Such news cannot be hidden (and if invented could not last for long) but would spread in ever-widening circles, starting from Jerusalem (Acts 1:8), the city central to every Jewish thought (Ps. 137:5-6). Beyond the city walls the startling realization must penetrate to every remote corner of Israel where the 'lost sheep' were (Matt. 10:6, sweep on through the Judean towns and villages, into hated Samaria (John 4:9), bringing lasting peace in its wake wherever it is believed (Luke 9:52-56).

Then the despised, 'uncircumcised' Gentiles would hear (Eph. 2:11; Gen. 12:3; Isa. 11:10), much to the chagrin of the Sadducees and Pharisees, for whom the 'heathen' were godless and without hope (Eph. 2:12). How daring Simeon was, to speak of so controversial a topic within the very temple precincts (Luke 2:30-32); how, faithful too, in mirroring the Father's eternal promise to the Son! (Ps. 2:7-8). In short, the entire world must hear the proclamation, which will excite the saint (Luke 24:34) and should alarm the sinner (Acts 17:31).

Among all nations

The little group listened to both the Scripture lesson and its application with rapt attention, for it does not appear that any questions were asked (Luke 24:44-48), as they had been the previous Thursday evening (John 14:5,8). They were too much in awe of the occasion, and what had been told them, to express an opinion. How could they have been other than mesmerized by the trauma of gazing at someone they had watched die, seeing him now alive and hearing him talking to them?

But one thought must surely have been uppermost in their minds. He had stated categorically that this wonderful message about his death and resurrection, 'repentance and remission of sins', must be preached 'among all nations' (Luke 24:47). It would not have taken a mere glance around the room to appreciate how puzzled, if not alarmed, the friends must have been to be told they were to be Christ's witnesses not only in their own country (Luke 24:48), but 'unto the uttermost part of the earth' (Acts 1:8). What a task, and the labourers were indeed few! (Luke 10:2).

Their Lord anticipated what was to them a practical problem, by immediately informing them how such a miracle would be accomplished. Once again, he directed their thoughts to the Word of God, 'the promise of my Father' (Luke 24:49). Had not an assurance been given to Israel of future 'blessing' upon the nation's 'offspring', of 'floods upon the dry ground' and the pouring out of the Spirit of God upon its 'seed'? (Isa. 44:3). And did not Ezekiel speak of the sprinkling of 'clean water', and of a 'new heart' being substituted for a 'stony' one through the indwelling Spirit of God? (Ezek. 36:25-26). Joel qualified this, when he revealed the extent of this widespread 'blessing', that every strata of society was to experience it: the elderly, the young, the men, the women, the servants — in fact, 'all flesh' (Joel 2:28-29).

Of course, that evening the apostles had no idea of what the immediate future held, but days later, during the feast of the 'fiftieth day' (Lev. 23:16), the 'Feast of Weeks' (Deut. 16:16), or 'Pentecost', it happened. The apostles had not needed to travel far — in fact, right on their very doorstep crowds gathered 'out of every nation under heaven' to hear the gospel preached in their own languages (Acts 2:5). The purposes of God are never thwarted, and invariably filled with pleasant surprises.

Had the group known what heaven intended to do through them, amazement would not have been their only reaction, but also a great sense of unworthiness. How the situation had been transformed in a short time! Only a day or so before they had demonstrated their weakness, both of faith and character (Matt. 26:56), and now suddenly Christ was entrusting them with great responsibilities. Perhaps passing through their minds were thoughts which Moses and Jeremiah would have recognized (Exod. 4:10; Jer. 1:6).

Knowing their hearts, and anticipating their thoughts, Christ did something which may have surprised them. In a symbolic gesture he simply blew (cf. John 3:8), and then made a solemn pronouncement, 'Receive ye the Holy Ghost' (John 20:22). There could be no misunderstanding of the wonderful truth that was being taught, one which they had heard at the Last Supper but had probably failed to grasp: namely, that Christ is of the same essence as the Father, and therefore the Holy Spirit proceeds authoritatively from both the Father (John 14:26) and the Son (John 15:26).

In other words, the apostles were uniquely being set aside for office, and in anticipation of both the mighty ministry they were to exercise (John 20:23) and the forthcoming ungodly reactions to it (Matt. 10), were being provided with a fore-taste of Ascension Day triumph (Luke 24:50-53). God the Spirit would alight upon them with such awesome authority, and invincible power, that they would be transformed above the ordinary (Luke 24:49). These 'unlearned and ignorant' men (Acts 4:13) would speak languages they had never learned (Acts 2:6), miraculously heal (Acts 3:6-7), and even pronounce judgements (Acts 5:1-10) — all in Christ's name (John 20:23). Such would be the intensity of God's presence and power (Acts

1:8), it would be said of them that they had 'turned the world upside down' (Acts 17:6).

The late arrival

How long the occasion lasted is unknown. The appearance had been followed by the meal, the Scripture lesson and the application; one thing is certain, it could not have been brief. Judas was dead (Matt. 27:5), but during that time another of the apostles was noticeably absent from the room. What a great deal Thomas missed! Why he was not present, or where he had been, is not known. His experience, though, has re- minded every Christian since that to be absent from the means of grace is to have missed the blessing. However, it is unfair to refer to Thomas as merely 'the doubter'. There was very much more to him than that: he was a man of a complex character.

Christ must have vanished as swiftly as he had done at Emmaus (Luke 24:31), and probably Thomas turned up shortly afterwards, because his friends' excitement still danced upon their lips: 'We have seen the Lord' (John 20:25). But knowing Thomas so well, they would not have expected him to jump for joy. He was not the type. Besides, he had already been confronted that day with similar emotional outbursts (Luke 24:10-11) and, being an intensely practical man, he was not satisfied with mere 'hearsay'. So his retort may well have been expected: 'Except I shall see...' (John 20:25). He had been present when his Lord had raised Lazarus from the grave (John 11), had seen it happen, and therefore must surely have be- lieved it possible for Jesus to raise himself, yet for him practi- cality placed sight before faith.

However, despite his stubborn reticence, Thomas appears to have been a well-respected member of the group, especially by John, who mentions him four times in his Gospel. The first was that memorable occasion when Lazarus was raised. The news of their friend's death at Bethany had come when Thomas and the other apostles were in the desert with their Lord, who after two days told them he intended returning to Judea (John 11:6-7). They were horrified, suggesting it was far too dangerous, as not long before the Jews had sought to stone him (John 8:58-59). But Jesus was in possession of a secret agenda, the raising of Lazarus (John 11:11), and knew he had to go. He obviously recognized the dangers, and for that reason did not encourage the others to accompany him. It was at this point that Thomas's love for his Master appeared from behind the down-to-earth exterior. Without hesitation, he urged the others on. There was no pretence; everyone knew Jerusalem and the surrounding areas (Bethany was only two miles away) seethed with hostility towards Jesus fomented by the Sanhedrin. Nevertheless, Thomas was insistent: 'Let us also go, that we may die with him' (John 11:16). They went.

In other words, Thomas was the person often seen among the people of God, never likely to wear his devotion on his sleeve, and for most of the time remaining in the background. However, when his pastor needs encouraging, no one more loyal can be found. As Thomas was his Lord's unostentatious but true friend, a pastor has often thanked God for such a person in his church.

Yet Thomas had his 'Achilles heel'; heels so firmly planted on the earth, spiritual issues were difficult for him to grasp. John remembered that his friend's problem was exposed during that last evening together before Jesus' arrest, but even then a positive aspect of Thomas' character came to the fore. Jesus had been speaking about heaven, a place where there 'are many mansions' (John 14:2), a topic not likely to prove simple for Thomas to accept without question! All the apostles were ordinary working men, not theologically trained, and therefore at that stage none of them would have grasped the implications of what Jesus was saying. People in that situation are invariably too embarrassed to reveal their ignorance and uncertainty, and remain silent, but not Thomas. He really wanted to learn, and was not prepared to remain ignorant, or not too proud to reveal how little he knew and understood. Practical as ever, he was dissatisfied with words and wanted something tangible to hold on to: 'Lord, we know not whither thou goest; and how can we know the way?' (John 14:5).

Thomas, in fact, was addressing his question to one who was also intensely practical, there being nobody more practical than the one who in the flesh was a carpenter, but Jesus did not encourage the apostle to remain bound by his temperament. Rather, he elevated his thinking, even if at first the apostle continued to be mystified. As a response to a practical question, 'How can we know the way?', Jesus' reply would at first have mystified Thomas even more. He received a profound answer, and one which could never be bettered: 'I am the way, the truth, and the life: no man cometh unto the Father, but by me' (John 14:6). What his Lord wanted from the apostle was simple trust. There cannot be a more straightforward demonstration of love. As Jesus stated, when his teaching was clearly above and beyond the apostles' grasp at the time, 'Believe me that I am in the Father, and the Father in me: or else believe me for the very works' sake' (John 14:11).

His friends, then, would not have been surprised by Thomas's reaction to their insistence that they had actually seen the Lord. The fact was that he had not! John noted how vehement was his reply to their excitement, 'Except I shall see...' (John 20:25), as if the events throughout the hectic weekend, which had followed so fast one upon another, had affected him more than the others. Perhaps that was the reason why he was absent, having separated himself from the rest to spend time alone in thought.

There was no doubting how let down the apostles felt following the death of their Master (Luke 24:21); the women discovered them so low in spirit they were overcome with grief (Mark 16:10). They had lost a loved one, the most charismatic leader known to history, from whom so much had been expected. And this expectation was enhanced by the teaching in which they had been reared. Surely, after seeing for themselves the blind receiving their sight, the lame walking, the lepers cleansed, the deaf hearing and even the dead raised up (Matt. 11:5), they believed they had a right to expect the overthrow of Roman oppression. In fact, so strong was this expectation, that when confronted by their risen Lord they still persisted in asking, not as one would expect, about the resurrection and the life to come, but 'Lord, wilt thou at this time restore again the kingdom to Israel?' (Acts 1:6). The subject just would not go away.

For a man of Thomas' temperament then, the weekend would have proved too much. For three years he had followed Jesus, a 'working man' like himself to whom he could relate. He had heard wonderful teaching of a 'relevant' nature which he could easily understand (Matt. 5-7), and seen many remarkable miracles with his own eyes (John 21:25). Jesus was surely the Messiah! Then it was all over, the hopes and dreams splintering into pieces, and entombed with him in cold darkness. Everything had run away from Thomas as quickly as he had from the garden of Gethsemane (Matt. 26:56). Unable as he was at that time to appreciate the theological backcloth to the crucifixion, nothing appeared to make sense any more. He may well have sought solitude to think things over, and it would certainly not have been surprising had he done so. His response to the news that the others had seen the Lord suggests this.

John particularly noted it in his third reference to Thomas. To begin with, the reply was lengthy (John 20:25), a sign that there was much thought behind it. After all, that morning he had heard the women report that they had seen the Lord (Luke 24:10-11), and therefore he would have had the entire day to think about what they had said. By the time he heard the account again, now from a different source, his reply had obviously been worked out in advance — hence its length. Someone who had not been contemplating the matter, and was therefore taken completely by surprise by what he was told, would have said something like, 'What — Jesus alive? Are you sure?' But Thomas's complex response had been honed especially for such an occasion. It was conditional ('Except... '), practical ('I shall *see* in his hands ... and *put* my finger into the print...'), and vehement ('I will *not* believe').

His use of the word 'except' denotes a response which has to be viewed from more than one angle. First it reveals how insistent he was, determined not to be drawn into giving an emotional response to the news upon mere hearsay. By the very nature of what had occurred, the weekend had been filled with trauma. The crucifixion itself had been more than enough to cope with, as Thomas and the others found themselves quietly standing by while Jesus suffered torment, unable to do anything about it and believing the previous three years had come to nothing. This in turn was followed by the gloom of anticlimax. Then to be told by the women the Lord was alive after all — what a heart-stopping moment that had been! Now, once again, he was hearing the same story. His feelings had been trampled on, and he was not tolerating it any more unless he saw the evidence for himself; he was stepping aside from involvement in the entire matter. He had had enough.

Then again, the word might well have reflected a bitterness of spirit, resulting from Thomas's anxiety at the final supper. Such was the dependence upon their Lord throughout his three-year companionship, the pronouncement of his intended departure had come as a shock. They had just learned their time together was soon to be terminated, that they had 'yet a little while' (John 14:19) with him, and then he would be leaving them. The thought of crucifixion and death had been overlooked; like children their minds were occupied with the prospect of being without him, but making matters worse were his ominous words that where he was going, 'Ye cannot come' (John 13:33). Why not? They loved Jesus, and had expected to accompany him wherever he was going. The rest kept their disappointment to themselves, but not Thomas. He blurted out, as if in panic, what the others were no doubt thinking — that they had no idea where he was going; in which case, how could they find their way there? (John 14:5). The fact was, however, that Jesus had left, and done so without them. Was Thomas's separation from the others due to dismay and bitterness, a desire for a solitary sulk?

If Thomas had been unsure then about Jesus' departure, he was determined now to be absolutely sure about his return. Had he really returned? Oh, that it might be true! Trusting was not a virtue Thomas possessed, whether in his friends' news, which to him was merely second-hand (John 20:25), or even in his Master's promise (Matt. 16:21). Nor, strangely enough, coming as the words did from one who loved Jesus, would it apparently have been sufficient just to have seen the Lord for himself. Yet could there have been any doubting who it was, once their eyes had met each other? One would have thought that the moment for Thomas to make his confession of Christ's deity would have been that of seeing Christ's face once more, replete with resurrection grace (Num. 6:25-26). Apparently not. He had not said, 'Except I shall see Jesus...', because even that blessed experience would not have satisfied his yearning. When a soul's delight is not found in Christ alone, there is evidently something seriously wrong.

Rather he wanted to see for himself the actual wounds received at Calvary: 'Except I shall see in his hands the print of the nails ... and thrust my hand into his side...' (John 20:25). A condition was stipulated, not from an idle curiosity, but because of an inability on his part to recognize that true faith is the 'evidence' of the eternal (Heb. 11:1). Mary Magdalene

only had to hear the 'gardener' mention her name to respond
in a fully committed way, believing without hesitation who it
was that was speaking to her (John 20:16). It would not have
entered her mind to ask to see his 'credentials' before believing — the nail-prints and the wounded side. What an insult
that would have been, and how hurtful to the one she loved!

Thomas's reaction, on the other hand, his insistence upon
seeing the results of the violence involved in his Lord's crucifixion, revealed how bitter had been the experience for him.
He was irresistibly drawn to the prints and the gash in Christ's
hands and side — so much so, he actually wanted to touch
them (John 20:25). Evidently, the significance of the nails and
the spear meant more to him than his friends might have supposed. Those fearful nails driven ruthlessly into Jesus' flesh
(Ps. 22:16) and the viciousness of the spear-thrust into his
body (John 19:34) had been the tools, it would appear, which
had undermined Thomas's fervour. In short, his life had
crumbled with the death of his Master.

In which case, his 'faith' had too, or at least what he considered it to have been. There are many like Thomas, in possession of preconceived ideas about Christ, and expecting him
to fit neatly into them. When it is discovered he is not doing
so, disillusionment closes in, and trust evaporates. In the crucifixion, personal assumptions harboured among the disciples
had taken a nasty blow. With the others, Thomas had 'trusted
that it had been he which should have redeemed Israel' (Luke
24:21), and now his trust had spiralled downwards. He was
therefore adamant. Not even seeing Jesus again would suffice. Unless he was in the position of handling that which had
done him and his Lord so much harm, he would refuse to
believe in the resurrection. By his vehement and stubborn response, 'I will not believe' (John 20:25), there appeared no
possibility of persuading him otherwise.

A week of anguish

The period must have seemed much longer than it was — eight days in fact (John 20:26) — during which time Thomas kept company with his thoughts. They were poor companions. His refusal to believe that Jesus had risen, when the many witnesses among his friends were crying out to be heard, could only have weighed heavily upon him. Mixed were his emotions, and numerous the questions, but pride manacled him to his stance. He understandably wanted to believe, and those surrounding him had good reason for urging him on to do so, but he had chosen a lonely road and the way back was too humiliating. His threat, 'I will not believe' (John 20:25), was capable of causing too much pain should it fail to be carried out.

For eight long days then, Thomas was isolated in his misery, absent from his Lord and surely out of sorts with his friends. The fellowship they had all formerly enjoyed must have been marred in the circumstances, as he remained glum while the others rejoiced together. There was surely only one topic of conversation among the latter, their remarkable meeting with Jesus, and no one could blame them. They were confidently overjoyed as every moment of that evening's events was discussed (and no doubt from every conceivable angle), and presumably attempts were made to persuade the single doubter to accept the truth. Thomas, though, was unable to contribute anything of worth, as he had chosen to sit in shadows.

He was resolute in his refusal to accept that his Lord had risen from the dead; he would not believe (John 20:25), and yet common sense reminded him of at least twelve testimonies from trustworthy close companions which contradicted his morose assumptions. He knew that ten apostles had certainly been present in the room, as well as Cleopas and his friend who also claimed to have seen Jesus earlier in the day, and there may well have been others (Luke 24:35-36). All of them without exception shared the experience, and equally the same joy. Had he forgotten so quickly how distressed they had all been, weeping with him? (Mark 16:10). Now look at them! Then what about the women, whose original accounts had been arrogantly dismissed as 'idle tales'? (Luke 24:11). Could they all be so mistaken, trusting in an illusion or, worse, liars?

In other words, in his many solemn moments that desolate week, Thomas must surely have asked himself why he so stubbornly discounted the assurances given him by such good people. Had his love and respect for them diminished so rapidly that he was no longer prepared to accept their word? The isolated apostle must have realized — a fact which would have hurt his pride still further — the extent of his departure not only from rationality, but from his Lord. If that was so, he would have ruminated despondently upon why he had wanted to examine Jesus' hands, and not his face also (John 20:25). As Peter had discovered, guilt finds it impossible to look into his eyes without breaking down (Luke 22:61-62).

Throughout those eight days the scene was being quietly observed by the one capable of appearing and vanishing at will, as the close-knit community of his disciples huddled together in Jerusalem. How strange was their situation, fearful of the Sanhedrin's opposition, yet in possession of the most remarkable 'secret' known to man. Heaven was on their side, triumphant with resurrection power, but such was their apprehension, they appear to have spent most of their time 'within' doors (John 20:19,26). They had been instructed to remain in the city, in anticipation of the promised event (Acts 1:4,8), but it would have proved unwise to wander its streets too often.

If hatred for Jesus and his followers had lurked in every corner prior to 'the third day', it had intensified since the tomb had been vacated. The Jewish authorities had arrested and condemned their leader to death, but now his disciples had to be rounded up. After all, according to the widespread rumour (Matt. 28:13), they had removed his body from the tomb. The general feeling was that, wherever Jesus' friends were, his corpse would not be far away. In which case, there could have been few in Jerusalem disinterested in the affair; in fact the apostles and their friends were prey to all and sundry. They therefore lived surreptitiously and behind closed doors (for the time at least), in a kind of underground situation (John 20:19,26).

Living in such close proximity for those weeks between Calvary and Pentecost (Acts 1:3), under constant threat, could not have been easy for the disciples. They knew the Lord might suddenly appear at any moment, a wonderful encouragement, but they had only 'received' the Spirit symbolically then (John 20:22) and not actually (Acts 2:4). They were still the same men who had sought grandeur and greatness (Matt. 20:20-21; Luke 22:24), and had run from Gethsemane (Matt. 26:56). The rivalry between them was sometimes so intense that strife lingered among them, even if only in the shadows (Mark 9:34), and now within the limited radius in which they lived Thomas was proving 'awkward'!

The waiting process

In retrospect, when he reflected upon the matter, Thomas would have realized why his Lord had kept him waiting an entire week and more before compassionately reaching out to him (John 20:26). He had already witnessed this principle at work in Jesus' ministry — the delayed response to an urgent need — on the occasion when news reached the Master that his friend Lazarus was sick. Instead of travelling immediately to Bethany to see him, to the apostles' surprise, Jesus remained where he was for two days. The reason was soon made clear: the raising of Lazarus from the dead was 'for the glory of God, that the Son of God might be glorified thereby' (John 11:4). Patient and submissive waiting is what God often requires as a test of faithfulness, a lesson King Saul failed to learn to his cost (1 Sam. 13:8-14).

Thomas was also obliged to wait. He had defiantly declared, 'Except I shall see...' (John 20:25), and eight lonely days were to pass before his insistence was gratified. During that time, his qualities as an apostle were under scrutiny by the one who observed unseen from close at hand. The 'silent listener to every conversation' had heard much from Thomas to grieve him — a wealth of words (John 20:25), but accompanied by a paucity of faith — always an indication of an unhealthy soul.

Seeing and believing

As had by this time come to be expected, the appearance was sudden, without warning (1 Cor. 15:52), and once again took place in the secret hideaway behind 'shut' doors (John 20:26). What happened was without any preparation, the Lord possessing no visiting cards (Matt. 24:42-44), and therefore one is left wondering what atmosphere greeted the risen Christ as he entered the room. Certainly Thomas's sullen mood would have spread a 'cold blanket' over the general rejoicing, as he persisted in his unbelief.

Swiftly he arrived, as before, unhindered by material considerations — one moment not there, and the next, standing in the centre of the room. Such a phenomenon could never be experienced without startling those involved, but the warm and cheery greeting (John 20:19,26), the welcoming reminder that 'peace' did indeed now exist between his friends and heaven (Luke 2:14), would have comforted them. Whatever was the general reaction to his appearance, or whether Christ spoke to the joyful majority, is not mentioned by John. His main concern, in his fourth reference to Thomas, is to point out that the doubting apostle was the prime consideration for the visit.

How Thomas reacted upon seeing his Lord, and only a few feet away from him, can best be intelligently imagined. How jumbled must have been his thoughts. His fearful flight from Gethsemane (Matt. 26:56), the raucous sounds of excited crowds, Calvary's gruesome reputation, the public humiliation of the one he believed to be the Messiah — the weekend's miserable memories must surely have come flooding back. Then when the wonderful news of the resurrection had first poured out from the empty tomb, far from being thrilled, he had with the others insulted the ladies by scorning the notion (Luke 24:10-11). Even when their accounts had been corroborated by his fellow apostles, and others, Thomas remained dismissive (John 20:25). Now, here was the 'evidence' standing in front of him!

He had got his way; his condition had been met ('Except I shall see...'), but his satisfaction was tinged with shame. Eight days earlier, the others had been invited by Jesus to examine his hands and feet in order to calm their understandable fears, and to demonstrate that he was not the apparition they assumed he was (Luke 24:39). But Thomas was commanded to study the evidence from a different standpoint — not to quell the alarm, but to convict the sinner. As he observed at close quarters his Lord's wounded hands and side, the rebuke he heard overshadowed the rejoicing at what he saw. Thomas's delight was at the expense of hearing himself described as 'faithless' by the Son of God (John 20:27). It was a stern reminder of the importance he places upon faith and faithfulness, the primary delight of everyone who loves, to trust the one loved and illustrate it by being in turn trustworthy (Prov. 18:24).

Everyone in the room must have watched Thomas, as the dawn broke over his understanding of what had happened on that resurrection morning. There was no more doubting; his Lord had certainly risen from the dead. It was impossible, seen from a human point of view, but true! Every objection he could think of had suddenly been swept to one side, the practical being the final obstacle to bow to the truth. Those hideous wounds had proved their point. He was convinced.

How vital had been that moment, occupying thoughts for many centuries to come, when sight was permitted for a brief while to take precedence over faith. Thomas, though, would have preferred it otherwise had he known the assessment of history, that he would always be known, not as the down-to-earth, 'no-nonsense' apostle who loved his Lord enough to be willing to die with him (John 11:16), but merely as 'Doubting Thomas'. Even within the church during succeeding generations, his name has always been synonymous with uncertainty at best and unbelief at worst. How tragic that a single undesirable incident in one's life is capable of burning its imprint in the memory of others, while at the same time blurring the rest of the picture!

Believing and adoring

Standing before Christ, Thomas was overcome as few others have been, both with shame as well as with awe. He surely felt like Isaiah had done, who when he beheld the glory of God and heard the adulation of the angels, was moved profoundly to acknowledge his own unworthiness: 'Woe is me! For I am undone, because I am a man of unclean lips ... for mine eyes have seen the King, the Lord of hosts' (Isa. 6:5).

That small room was by no means Jerusalem's temple, where the prophet had stood, but the apostles were also able to say they had 'seen the King, the Lord of hosts' (Heb. 1:6). There was something more to do, although John leaves it unsaid, but one cannot imagine Thomas remaining on his feet in such circumstances. Instead, like Moses when 'the Lord descended in the cloud and stood with him' on Mount Sinai (Exod. 34:5-8), surely Thomas must have sunk to his knees adoringly. What words were fitting to describe how he felt — indeed, how they all felt? In later years, one is not surprised that even Paul's vocabulary was almost stretched to its limits in the attempt to express the splendour of Christ's resurrection and the wonder of his everlasting glory (Eph.1:20-23). As for Thomas, only five words sprang to his mind: 'My Lord and my God' (John 20:28).

It was the briefest of testimonies, and one which the entire world should note, but the more effective because it issued from one who had been resolute in his disbelief in the resurrection of Christ. Within that room and witnessed by others, he not only saw his Lord face to face, but proved who it was by closely examining the wounds inflicted at Calvary. He also heard him speak to him, though his words were words of rebuke. The result of this very close encounter was that Thomas concluded not only that he had been visited by his Lord, but that he was confronted by God himself 'manifest in the flesh' (John 20:28; 1 Tim. 3:16).

8.
Breakfast on the beach

One week had passed (John 20:26) — that was all — and in that time a small group within the crowded city of Jerusalem claimed to have experienced the most astonishing event known to mankind. At least seventeen people, thirteen men and four women, could testify that they had actually seen the crucified prophet from Galilee who had risen from the dead. As yet though, they and their friends retained the secret; the authorities had heard only that the tomb was empty and the body of Jesus missing.

To recap, there was Mary Magdalene, who maintained she had conversed with him in the garden where the tomb was located (John 20:16). Her women friends were also in no doubt they had met him, and that he had spoken to them (Matt. 28:9). Then there were the men. Cleopas and his travelling companion said they had been accompanied by a 'stranger' who had spoken to them at some length as they walked the seven miles to Emmaus and on their arrival had joined them for a meal. Then, believe it or not, he had literally vanished in front of them while at the table, but not before they had been in a position to see the nail-prints in his hands (Luke 24:30-31). In the meantime, as they later discovered, Peter had also seen him (Luke 24:34; 1 Cor. 15:5).

The two men had rushed back to Jerusalem to report the incident to the disciples, and were in the process of doing so, when he suddenly appeared in the room. On that occasion, no fewer than twelve were present and witnessed the amazing spectacle of Jesus of Nazareth displaying his wounds to illustrate who he was. He even ate food in front of them (Luke 24:36-43). After another few days it happened again, with eleven present this time, including Thomas, who had been absent on the previous visit (John 20:26-28).

Had all these people fallen victim to hallucinations? Were they suffering from stress disorders? Or were they perhaps liars? It seems extremely unlikely, especially in the light of what occurred shortly afterwards at the annual Feast of Pentecost, when an extraordinary phenomenon hit Jerusalem that is still commemorated 2,000 years later (Acts 2). Then the city witnessed an amazing transformation in these apostles, men whose courage and powerful preaching on the day in question belied the confusion and weakness they had revealed not long before (Matt. 26:56).

They recognized the change that had taken place in them, and also its source (Acts 4:1-2; 3:15); in fact the resurrection was, with the crucifixion of Christ, the major theme in the missionary endeavours which followed (Acts 13:30; 17:18, 31,32). Soon it was said of the apostolic ministry that it had 'turned the world upside down' (Acts 17:6). Clearly, whatever happened during that week in Jerusalem was a phenomenon of giant proportions and the testimonies of the apostles and their friends are worthy of acceptance: 'The Lord is risen indeed' (Luke 24:34).

A strange affair

But then suddenly something happened which has since caused a frown to appear on many a brow, and scholars to put fingers to computer keys. The scene changes dramatically from Jerusalem in the south to Galilee in the north, and from the victorious climax of Thomas's 'My Lord and my God' (John 20:28) to Peter's more mundane 'I go a fishing' (John 21:3). In other words, the glorious assurances which bring John 20 to its triumphant close (vv. 30-31) are immediately followed in John 21 by the sight of seven of the disciples returning to secular employment far removed from where they had seen their risen Lord (vv. 1-3). The two incidents are linked by the significant phrase, 'after these things' (John 21:1), one which implies that a period had elapsed during which time changes had taken place.

John, who openly records the apparent change of direction, also has no hesitation in naming most of his companions: his brother James, Peter, Thomas, Nathanael (Bartholomew) and 'two other of his disciples' (John 21:2). Perhaps, by not mentioning the latter two by name, he means us to infer that they were not apostles. Whatever the reason, most, if not all, of them had only recently experienced something so astonishing that words are inadequate to describe its uniqueness. They had been dramatically confronted by eternal power breaking into time, by the extraordinary sight of the spiritual and material realms melting into each other, and of the finality of death being joyously overcome. To put it another way, they had been in the immediate presence of a corpse restored to life, who had no need of a door to walk through, and yet could eat a meal in front of them! (Luke 24:36-43).

Having seen such things for oneself — surely a topic of conversation guaranteed to last for a lifetime — who would want to do anything else but talk about it, or would be capable of overlooking it? Could the mundane affairs of everyday life ever satisfy again, or enough reserves of concentration be mustered to think of other matters? Yet when Peter said he was going back to his old job, the other six agreed they would too (John 21:3). Who wants to go fishing, when one could spend many hours discussing the resurrection of Christ, especially when the 'eye' of this supreme event had been looked into at extremely close quarters? Apparently, they did.

It could, of course, be argued that, so many had been the miraculous events they had witnessed in the previous three years, once the initial shock had subsided, the resurrection of their Lord had been taken for granted. After all, on at least two occasions the apostles had been present when the dead had been raised (Luke 7:14-15), the most memorable being the raising of Lazarus (John 11). Then again Peter, James and John had seen even more 'miracles and wonders and signs' (Acts 2:22) than the others: for example, the 'transfiguration' of Christ (Matt. 17:1-5) and the raising of Jairus' daughter (Mark 5:35-43), to name but two.

On the other hand, the seven might have considered they were in need of a respite from the trauma suffered throughout a lengthy period. There had not only been the events of recent days, but one can estimate that the pressure had been deepening ever since that significant moment when Jesus had 'steadfastly set his face to go to Jerusalem' (Luke 9:51). That is a key verse and marks a turning-point in his ministry among sinners, one which there was no possibility of shunning, as his Father's will drew him irresistibly to a beckoning Calvary.

For those who accompanied Jesus at such a time, a great deal of the oppressive solemnity overshadowing them must have been exhausting as well as alarming (Matt. 26:43). No one could hope to fathom what effect the experience had upon the disciples: the ominous sense of expectancy within the upper room as they heard their Master declare, 'The hour is come' (John 17:1); the satanic stirrings of Gethsemane, when they saw him 'sorrowful and very heavy' (Matt. 26:37); the clamour of the crowds shouting, 'His blood be on us, and on our children' (Matt. 27:25); the stamp of imperial Rome put on the proceedings as Pilate presented Jesus to the crowds with the words, 'Behold the man!' (John 19:5); the dreadful Golgotha, 'the place of a skull' (John 19:17); the hammer and the nails. The emotional strain must have been immense, even before the staggering experience of meeting their Lord again alive and well. It is possible, it was all too much for them, and the desire to cling to their old way of life had proved too strong.

The hankering to return

It would not last for long. Once the divine finger points towards the future, there is no returning to the past. Lot's wife discovered that principle the hard way, when fleeing from God's judgement upon Sodom and Gomorrah. She hesitated and looked back and 'became a pillar of salt' (Gen. 19:26). Moses learned the lesson in a split second when, at one of the most dramatic moments in history, he stood on the brink of the Red Sea with Pharaoh's mighty army in hot pursuit. As he prayed, waiting for God to intervene, God answered in an unexpected way: 'Wherefore criest thou unto me? Speak unto the children of Israel, that they go forward' (Exod. 14:15). Forward with God is always a worthwhile adventure into the unknown (Exod. 40:34-38), but walking backwards into the future hankering after the past can only lead to dryness of soul, as the Hebrews soon discovered (Num. 11:5-6).

The seven were about to learn the lesson too. Back in Galilee, with fishing on their minds, they seem to have wanted to recapture something of the more peaceful times of their youth. Life had been uncomplicated in those days among the bustling communities who lived alongside Galilee's lake, in such small towns as Capernaum (Luke 4:31), Magdala (Luke 8:2) and Bethsaida (John 1:44). Each busy day was like the one which preceded it: loyalty to the local synagogue, domestic responsibilities, trading in fish and mending the nets. It was all plain and simple. Most were poor, although a few were not

(Mark 1:20), but for all life was straightforward. The big city of Jerusalem, with its grandeur and social graces, must have seemed very far away indeed.

Then one day Jesus visited them (Mark 1:16-17). Off they went with him, dropping everything (Mark 1:18), and for three years travelled the land and beyond (Matt. 4:20-25). True, there were many times when his ministry was in the vicinity of their homes (Luke 7:1), but their boats were more likely to be used for other purposes now (Luke 5:3; Mark 4:35-36). In other words, the small circle in which they had spent their lives was broken. They no longer searched the lake for fish, but the land for men (Mark 1:17), and in doing so were introduced to the Sanhedrin's sophisticated guile and the aggression of religious intolerance (John 8:59).

But that was not all. The longer these chosen men spent in Jesus' company, the more they realized their role was by no means passive; they were not merely to be an audience for his teaching (Matt. 5:1), or witnesses of his miraculous powers (Matt. 11:5). Eventually, he provided them with a ministry of their own as those 'sent forth' ('apostles'), as both preachers and healers in his name (Matt. 10:1). How far removed they were from their roots now! In fact, they rather enjoyed the situation, and in no time were squabbling among themselves as to which of them would be the greatest in the kingdom (Mark 9:34). Even at the Last Supper, when the Lord's mind was so obviously occupied with solemn thoughts, the subject was not dropped and we read of 'strife' breaking out within the insensitive group (Luke 22:24). They had clearly lost sight of their humble beginnings.

There is no doubt that the immediate events prior to the crucifixion took their toll upon this pride, one born of a marriage between immaturity and naïveté. That black occasion in the upper room, with Calvary's silhouette looming large, was the last time they swaggered before their world splintered around them. Jesus prepared them for it, quoting the Scriptures in doing so (Zech. 13:7), warning them of what was shortly to happen in Gethsemane (Matt. 26:31-35). These men, who sought greatness for themselves, would scatter from the garden in all directions at the first glint of steel in the moonlight. But they were proud men; so proud, they even contradicted their Lord. They — be ashamed of him, and run away? Never! Peter, who would soon openly deny Christ (Matt. 26:69-75), even placed himself above 'all men' in this respect. They might prove disloyal, but certainly not he; in fact Jesus could count on him to pay the ultimate price! (Matt. 26:33-35). Had the circumstances not been so tragic, their boastings might have been amusing, but at least the old proverb was proved to be correct: 'A man's pride shall bring him low' (Prov. 29:23).

Still, in the evening of that special 'third day', and probably in the very room where the pride had reached its zenith (John 20:19), Christ stood before a band of greatly chastened disciples. Another proverb could have sprung to mind: 'Before honour is humility' (Prov. 18:12), because despite their public failings and inadequacy their Lord not only forgave but honoured them. As apostles they were set apart, symbolically breathed upon in anticipation of the Spirit's generous outpouring on the Day of Pentecost. Then they heard words of great moment, revealing the importance of preaching the gospel: 'Whose soever sins ye remit, they are remitted unto them; and whose soever sins ye retain, they are retained' (John 20:22-23; cf. Rom.10:14-15).

Earlier, the bestowal of such a blessing would have stirred latent pride to fresh vigour, but events had humbled them. They were in no position to boast; in fact, the departure by a few of them to Galilee seems to reveal how much they were aware of the privileged responsibility thrust upon them. The transition from the lowly landscape of the north to the breathtaking heights of apostleship, from being ordinary working men to judging the twelve tribes of Israel (Matt.19:28), could not have been undertaken easily! The seven, therefore, went back to Galilee's lake in an attempt at clinging to the past.

A troubled crew

It was impossible. On the surface everything was as it had been before — the lake, the boat, the nets, the toil — yet, even as they sought to function as fishermen, they obviously knew it was hopeless. Try as hard as they could through an exhausting night (John 21:3), casting the net and dragging it back to the boat again, nothing was the same as in former times. The resurrection had confronted them, each man having his own account to relate, and yet here they were pretending that glorious fact made no difference. By the very nature of their experience *everything* was now different, because what they had seen for themselves transcended all else. It is something every Christian since has understood, but far beyond the sight of 'Christless eyes'.

John records what happened with meticulous care for detail, evidently believing it important to do so, and although there were 'two other' disciples, identifies the apostles involved (John 21:2): five men, each with his private thoughts, as he struggled vainly in the darkness to net fish. Could the minds of the five have been on the job?

There was Peter, for example, whose idea it had been to return to the old life. He had claimed so much for himself, yet proved so weak (Matt. 26:33,75). How unusually silent he had been the evening his Lord had made his appearance. It is always a shocking experience confronting painful truth about oneself, a humiliation which must have continued to sting that night in the boat.

Thomas must also have been troubled in spirit. His weaknesses had been exposed, too, discovering things about himself of which he was probably unaware: for instance, that his love for Christ was not as deep as he had supposed, and in fact was largely governed by ulterior motives. It had obviously come as a terrible realization to him, and should do to many today in a similar situation, that his had not been a submissive devotion, a true love, which remains constant whatever the circumstances. Rather, like the tide, it ebbed and flowed, in accordance with how far his Lord lived up to his expectations. When Jesus strode the land, energetically engaged in his remarkable and widespread ministry (Matt. 4:24), Thomas expressed a genuine willingness to die with him (John 11:16). However, with the arrest and crucifixion, although he remained devoted to his Master, it was tempered by disappointment. Yet unreserved love, bearing, believing, hoping and enduring all things (1 Cor. 13:7), would have been satisfied, as David was, with a mere glimpse of the Lord's face (Ps. 27:8). Nothing else would have been needed.

As he toiled through the night, Thomas had cause to muse upon the fact that, although he had been given much more than just a quick glance at Christ's features when he knelt before him, yet still this had not satisfied him. His acknowledgement, 'My Lord and my God' (John 20:28), was therefore more the establishment of proof than a declaration of love. Thomas might well have wondered whether, in reality, it possessed the depth and the warmth of the waters which splashed against the side of the boat. It could not have been a happy few hours for him, with such thoughts chasing each other.

Then there was Nathanael, or Bartholomew. Why was he in the boat? This disciple, who is introduced to the reader in such an encouraging way in the first chapter of the Gospel (John 1:45-51), has clearly changed by the time he makes his departure in the final one (John 21:2). In fact, an interesting comparison with Thomas is not out of place. The latter believed when he saw (John 20:25); Nathanael believed as a result of having been 'seen' (John 1:50). Again, whereas it took five wounds and a miraculous resurrection to bend Thomas's knee and cause him to say, 'My Lord and my God', and that at the close of Christ's three-year ministry, a mere casual utterance at its start had caused Nathanael to exclaim, 'Thou art the Son of God; thou art the King of Israel' (John 1:49). Thomas was rebuked (John 20:29) and Nathanael recommended (John 1:47-51), yet now they literally shared the same boat, preferring to fish than contemplate.

Nathanael's first appearance in the Gospel story is extremely heartening. During a period of spiritual dearth, following the 400 years of inter-testamental 'silence' — the mighty prophetic ministry having been terminated by the hand of God (Zech. 13:2-5) — here was someone whose anchorage was in the Scriptures. One day Nathanael was approached by an extremely excited Philip, who could hardly wait to pass on his news: 'We have found him, of whom Moses in the law, and the prophets, did write, Jesus of Nazareth, the son of Joseph' (John 1:45). But to Philip's undoubted surprise, Nathanael refused to share his friend's glee; he remained unimpressed.

So enthusiastic was Philip in spreading his news, his account of what had happened was incorrect — a subtle but extremely important detail which many Christians since have overlooked. He claimed, with others, to have 'found' the long-awaited Messiah; in fact, Jesus had found him! (John 1:43,45). Far from the splitting of a hair, theologically, quite a chasm exists between the two (John 6:44,65), as Nathanael was to learn shortly afterwards (John 1:48).

In his excitement Philip also overlooked another vital point, which Nathanael was quick to note: the coupling of the Messianic hope with the town of Nazareth. It is true, 'the law and the prophets', indeed the entire Old Testament, cannot be understood without a reference to Christ — but Nazareth? Philip had added to his initial statement that the one he had met was 'Jesus of Nazareth' (John 1:45), but Nathanael's response was that of a student of the Scriptures. The long-awaited Messiah would spring from the south of Israel (Gen. 49:10), not the north, from Bethlehem (Micah 5:2) and not Nazareth. No 'good thing' was likely to come from there (John 1:46). In which case, Philip was evidently wrong. He was, however, insistent that Nathanael should 'come and see'.

When they met, Jesus immediately complimented Nathanael for his scepticism: 'Behold an Israelite indeed, in whom is no guile!' (John 1:47). The patriarch Jacob had been full of guile, securing for himself his brother Esau's birthright and blessing (Gen. 25:33; 27:35), until that remarkable occasion when he was forced to wrestle with the 'angel' (Gen. 32:24). And who had that 'angel' in fact been? If Nathanael addressed Jesus as 'the Son of God' (John 1:49), Jacob's realization was equally thrilling: 'I have seen God face to face' (Gen. 32:30). Nathanael's astonishment may have shared Jacob's understanding (John 1:49).

On that mysterious night (Hosea 12:3-4), Jacob's name and character were changed. Guile had been replaced by grace, and he was no longer Jacob, but 'Israel' (Gen. 32:28-30). Philip would not have understood what Jesus meant, and three years later little had changed: 'Lord, show us the Father, and it sufficeth us' (John 14:8). But Nathanael was a man after Jesus' own heart, conversant with the Word of God (Luke 11:28). He was not gullible enough to accept teaching unless it had its roots in Scripture. He was a true child of 'Israel' indeed.

For some unknown reason, Nathanael never figures prominently in any discussion about the apostles, yet he and Jesus shared an immediate rapport from this first meeting — more so than with any of the others at that early period, because of their shared love for the Scriptures (see Luke 2:46) — even casually introducing subjects which at that time would have been way beyond the grasp of the others: omniscience and the deity of Christ.

For example, Nathanael's surprise at Jesus' welcoming greeting, rooted as it was in Scripture ('Behold an Israelite indeed...'), intrigued him into enquiring how this stranger knew him. Jesus replied that he had 'seen' Nathanael before Philip had called him. Whichever way that statement is read today, there is no mistaking Nathanael's understanding of it. In an instant — reminiscent of Peter's blurted declaration at a later date: 'Thou art the Christ, the Son of the living God' (Matt. 16:16) — Nathanael recognized Jesus as the Messiah. It was an extraordinary moment, which can only be understood not in terms of 'flesh and blood', but as a revelation from the Father (Matt. 16:17).

Jesus was evidently enjoying this encouraging first encounter, with Philip presumably standing by nonplussed, because he immediately continued his use of the biblical metaphor. Was Nathanael impressed so quickly? There would be much more to come. Then, returning to the patriarch, who in a dream had seen angels ascending and descending on a ladder which reached to heaven (Gen. 28:12), Jesus further astonished Nathanael by applying Jacob's experience, deep within Jewish history, to himself. As the ladder which Jacob saw was the connecting link between heaven and earth, so Christ (and he alone) is the mediator between God and man (1 Tim. 2:5). Knowing Nathanael was capable of understanding these 'deep things of God' (1 Cor. 2:10), he went further, referring to himself so early on in his ministry as Daniel's 'Son of Man' (Dan. 7:13), that sacred and significant phrase which three years later, at his trial before the high priest, would cause such furore (Matt. 26:63-64). All this in one brief conversation!

Now, for reasons unknown, Nathanael too was on board the boat toiling vainly for fish. It is perhaps helpful to place

Breakfast on the beach

one's feet in his sandals, to try to fathom his thoughts that night. As a student of the Scriptures, Nathanael would have been particularly moved by what had occurred, and in his lifetime too!

For thousands of years the promise of God had been circulating through history that he would send the seed of the woman to bruise the serpent's head (Gen. 3:15) — an expectation which can be found in many world cultures, even though in a perverted form.

Gradually over centuries there blossomed within Judaism the revelation from God of a glorious era beyond the horizon, 'the day of the Lord' (Joel 1:15), bringing with it the fulfilment of Israel's hopes and dreams. From this 'golden age' would arise the mighty Messianic kingdom, and the reign of its King the Messiah, the hero David and his kingdom idealized (Jer. 23:5-6; 2 Sam. 7:16), when God's righteous judgement upon his enemies and unmerited mercy towards his people would be displayed throughout the earth (Obad. 15,17; Ps. 98:1-3). Entire nations were to be brought to heel (Isa. 2:2-5), and subdued within the circumference of a universal peace (Micah 4:1-7).

It is a vast canvas upon which the Messiah's picture was painted, stretching from that sublime moment in Eden (Gen. 3:15) to the patriarchs (e.g. Deut. 18:15-22) and reaching the zenith of its beauty in the mighty prophetic ministries (e.g. Isa. 9:6). Not only is he portrayed as the King (Ps. 2:6), but also as the Prophet (Isa. 61:1) and the Priest (Zech. 6:13), who would arise as a 'Branch' (Jer. 33:15) with roots in Jesse's family (Isa. 11:1), as promised to his famous son by the prophet Nathan (2 Sam. 7:16-17). That son was David, King of Israel (1 Sam. 16:11-13); the Messianic King (Jer. 30:9), prophetically considered, is spoken of in terms of 'David' (Isa. 55:3), the 'Son' (Ps. 2:7-8) and 'Servant' (Ezek. 34:23-24; 37:24). He would enter the world from a virgin's womb (Isa. 7:14), be born in Bethlehem (Micah 5:2), David's birthplace (1 Sam. 16), and reared as 'a tender plant' in the 'dry ground' (Isa. 53:2) of what we now know was Nazareth (Luke 1:26-27).

With his exclamation, 'Thou art the Son of God; thou art the King of Israel' (John 1:49), it seems more than likely Nathanael was familiar with the rich tapestry of truth as outlined above. Three years had passed since that first meeting with Jesus, and certainly everything he had heard and witnessed during that period could only have strengthened his initial belief (Matt. 11:5). From the outset he had been 'astonished' at the teaching (Matt. 7:28), and with the others had exclaimed, 'What manner of man is this, that even the wind and the sea obey him?' (Mark 4:41). He had witnessed, on the one hand, the fearful overpowering of the demonic (Luke 8:35), and in sharp contrast the tender compassion towards the 'broken-hearted' (Mark 1:41); clearly, in Jesus, the Messianic hope was fulfilled (Isa. 61:1).

The crucifixion, the Lamb 'bruised for our iniquities' (Isa. 53:5), and now the resurrection had surely served to enhance the wonder of it all. Perhaps, then, when Peter suggested returning to the old lake (John 21:3), filled not only with fish but with memories, Nathanael was happy to go along with the idea. He too needed to step aside from the vortex of extraordinary and astonishing events, and what better way to do it than in the tranquil setting so familiar to him, against the backcloth of a black sky filled with myriads of stars?

The seven were probably not alone on the waters, the night being considered a profitable time for fishing (Luke 5:5), but it might have seemed like it. How peaceful it all was! In the distance the flaming torches of Safad twinkled on the skyline, as they always did (Matt. 5:14), watching over the small communities which hugged the shoreline as they slumbered. The familiar sights and sounds were welcome: the chill breezes sweeping across the lake from the surrounding hills, the evocative tang in the air, the gentle lapping of the water, the boat bobbing from side to side and creaking as it did so, and the occasional grunts of the friends heaving on the nets. It all seemed far removed from the world's hatred and its evil, which they had heard Jesus mention in his prayer on that solemn evening prior to his arrest (John 17:14-15) and something of which they had already tasted (Matt. 10:22-25).

John records that he and his brother James were also in the group, although he significantly fails to mention their names, merely referring to 'the sons of Zebedee' (John 21:2). But as the two laboured through the night, the irony of their situation could not have eluded them: this was a far cry from the heights of grandeur they had coveted (Matt. 20:20-21). They did not even have their father's 'hired servants' to assist them! (cf. Mark 1:19-20).

The brothers might have wondered how they came to be in the boat, and why they had succumbed to Peter's invitation to return to their old trade, if only for one last occasion. Perhaps when they clambered aboard they also wanted to experience the death-throes of their past life (2 Cor. 5:17), knowing they were soon to step forward into an unknown future. There would be no turning back. Shortly, the apostles were to be drawn by God the Spirit into a unique intimacy with heaven (John 14-16), and endued with even mightier powers than they had already received (John 20:22-23; Matt. 10:1).

A great 'temple' was in the process of being erected (Prov. 9:1; John 2:20), each 'brick' a redeemed child of God (Rev. 21). It would far surpass in beauty and size the giant edifice in Jerusalem, which was the envy of the known world (Matt. 24:1). Christ is its chief cornerstone (Ps. 118:22), and these unsophisticated apostles were about to be united with the mighty prophets as its foundation (Eph. 2:20-22). It is indeed 'the Lord's doing', and marvellous to the people of God (Matt. 21:42). Perhaps by contrast a little fishing back home, in quiet waters under cover of darkness, proved a comforting balm when contemplating such awesome responsibilities.

But as the brothers worked alongside each other, there were lesser mysteries about which they knew nothing, and it was just as well. Jesus' cousins, John and James, were very close. Jesus recognized this, and always included them both when, with Peter, they shared together as 'eyewitnesses' (2 Peter 1:16) of remarkable moments (Matt. 17:1; Matt. 26:37; Luke 8:51). In fact they appeared inseparable — that is, until Jesus' arrest. Then James sheltered in shadows, as his brother accompanied Peter to the high priest's palace (John 18:15) and afterwards stood with the courageous women at the foot of the cross (John 19:25-26).

Now though, unknown to them, their time together was rapidly drawing to a close. Soon, in a twist of providential irony, they would suffer a separation of a sadder nature, with James the first of the apostles to be martyred (Acts 12:2) and John living to such a great age the early church wondered if he would ever die (John 21:23). However, in the boat together they were blissfully unaware of what lay in store for them both.

Through the morning mist

Dawn broke. The sun's rays appeared slowly but steadily over the skyline, as they had done each new day for thousands of years, swathing the hillsides which skirted 'the lake of Gennesaret' (Luke 5:1) with increasing warmth after the coolness of the night. It was time for the little fishing vessels to head for the shore with their catches, through the early morning mist which ascended from the glistening water. A night's fishing had been completed, another day begun.

The boat containing the seven tired men drew within a short distance from the shore (John 21:8), observed by a solitary figure awaiting their arrival. How forlorn they looked. They were exhausted, hungry and frustrated, their craft more full of fishermen than fish. In fact, the cold light of day had revealed the embarrassment of empty nets, and a long and wasted night. Just a few years earlier, at least three of them on that very coastline had unhesitatingly discarded their search for fish to hunt for souls (Mark 1:17-20). Now they were back where it all began, but with less success, although that moment was not the time to remind them. In another context, he had informed them of the futility of attempting anything without him, and this occasion was certainly a case in point (John 15:5).

Suddenly a voice was heard calling to them, enquiring whether they had caught anything, but the early morning haze provided them only with the outline of a man standing on the shingle. They shouted back their discouragement (John 21:5), without expecting a response, for there were few who understood the lake better than they did, but to their astonishment the quiet bystander proffered some advice. He not only suggested they should cast the net in one final attempt, but also in which direction it should be flung. He even assured them of a catch if they did as he suggested (John 21:6).

For an unknown reason nobody queried it. Did the seven instinctively suspect from whom the unusual advice had come, recognizing the voice, or did they believe they might as well have one last attempt at succeeding? Whatever the reason, the net was cast, and to the very area pointed out to them, a task which proved much easier than when they attempted to drag it back to the boat again. The shock they received far outweighed their expectation of any catch being made; in fact they could scarcely believe their eyes. The net was squirming with feverish activity as fish fought to enter it. Peter, the brothers John and James, Nathanael, Thomas and their two companions — fourteen muscular arms wrestled with the net as they heaved and pulled, but to no avail (John 21:6). The craft must have been close to capsizing.

The contrast between a sea apparently devoid of fish and a net bulging with them was so sharp, and the surprise so great, it must have taken some moments before the significance of what had happened alerted them. Besides, they were too busily occupied in practical matters for contemplation. But as they struggled, a particular thought entered John's mind, which may also have been shared by his brother James and Peter, but John was the one whose conclusion was first reached. The figure standing yards from them on the shore (John 21:8), bathed in dawn's early mist like a silhouette of haze and unrecognizable to them, could only be one person: 'It's the Lord!', he cried out to the others. For a moment, they all forgot the fish and looked towards the spot from where they had heard the voice. Peter jumped overboard (John 21:7).

John's good memory had prompted his exclamation. The scene that morning was very similar to one he had shared with James and Peter several years earlier, shortly after their discipleship began. Jesus had borrowed Peter's boat as a 'pulpit' from which to address the crowds, and having done so, suggested he should return to his fishing and 'launch out into the deep'. Jesus must surely have known, but Peter explained anyway, that he and his partners John and James had fished in vain throughout the night. However, if Jesus wanted him to try again, he would. He did, and there had been so many fish that, not only had the net broken but the boats involved in bringing the fish to shore had been in danger of sinking. The astonished Peter on that occasion fell at his Master's feet in awe: 'Depart from me; for I am a sinful man, O Lord' (Luke 5:1-11).

How different it all was now! A similar miracle had occurred, but Peter's reaction was not to revere his Lord, but to jump overboard (John 21:7). Some have intimated he did so because he wanted to get to Jesus as quickly as possible, but in the light of the fact that it had been Peter who had encouraged the others to think more of fish than the resurrection (John 21:3), it appears his was the action of an embarrassed man. Jesus' challenge to him shortly afterwards seems to confirm this: 'Lovest thou me?' (John 21:15-17). Besides, Peter would not have felt comfortable at his Lord's side, if it meant leaving his friends to heave the mound of fish ashore without his assistance (Matt. 7:12). One could imagine him in the circumstances sheltering behind the boat, as he waded through the water pushing it the final few feet to the shingle.

Either that day, or more likely in retrospect, the seven would have mused upon the miracle they had witnessed, which as professional fishermen they would have appreciated more than most. A former carpenter had much to teach them! They knew the Sea of Galilee as experts, had spent their lives fishing its waters, and on those two occasions it so happened they had failed to catch anything. Yet, by merely standing on the shore, Jesus had known where the fish were to be located. Even more remarkably, the creatures congregated 'on the right side of the ship' (John 21:6), like metal filings drawn irresistibly to a giant magnet, as if commanded to do so. It was reminiscent of Noah's day, when the animals entered the ark 'two and two'; for who had assembled the creatures (even 'every creeping thing') but God himself? (Gen. 7:9,14). What 'manner of man' (Mark 4:41) could command the unruly elements, or exercise authority over fish, except the Lord of creation? (Col. 1:16).

The sublime paradox

Exhausted, bewildered, amazed and humbled, the men reached the shore, securing the boat, no longer in any doubt as to who was awaiting them. Their thoughts were surely mixed, not knowing the reception they would receive. After all, the resurrection of their Lord had so far not been without its censure. Had he not rebuked Cleopas and his friend, calling them 'fools, and slow of heart'? (Luke 24:25). And what about Thomas? (John 20:29). Now, here they were caught unawares hankering after the old life (2 Cor. 5:17), when they should have been joyfully anticipating the wonder of what was shortly to happen (John 20:22-23). It was not only tiredness after a night's fishing which had silenced them.

Whatever their feelings as they dragged the loaded net to the water's edge (John 21:8), the first thing they saw was not a stern face, but a curl of smoke. A welcoming breakfast had been lovingly prepared (John 21:9). Fish were frying, some bread laid alongside ready for use, and he who delighted in ministering to others was as a servant standing nearby (John 21:13), not to rebuke, but to wait upon them (Matt. 20:26-28). They learned, and not for the first time, what Christians since have been constantly discovering, that the triune God so delights in the elect, his gracious generosity far surpasses not only their deserving but also all expectation. He loves them 'freely' (Hosea 14:4), and therefore gives unreservedly (Acts 20:35). So contrary is this behaviour to what Christians experience in the world that, like the seven that morning, they remain puzzled, God's ways being so unlike the ways of man (Isa. 55:8).

In short, what confronted them was a paradox the world could never hope to understand, and one which is almost beyond the grasp of most Christians. The one who is the glory of heaven (Ps. 110:1), eternally served by angelic hosts (Heb. 1:6), knelt humbly on the beach to light a fire; the one who is Judge of mankind (John 5:22) supplied a simple meal for hungry men; the one who was disappointed by his friends considered only their welfare (John 15:12-13). In place of sternness was love, and instead of impatience was tender care and divine humility. The recipients of this graciousness were so surprised they remained silent, bewildered by the display of immeasurable love (Jer. 31:3).

Perhaps he felt guilty at not having assisted the others (as appears likely) in pulling the bulky net from the sea (John 21:7-8), but upon his Lord's suggestion, it was Peter who dragged it further inland. The fish were counted: 153 large ones, and he noted that unlike the previous occasion, the net had not broken (John 21:11; cf. Luke 5:6). What a catch! But before a fisherman's tale could be told, and despite his Lord's generous suggestion that it was theirs (John 21:10), Peter knew who had really been responsible for the haul (John 21:6). In fact without him, how useless they had been, unsuccessful even in a task at which they were experts (John 15:5).

It was a strange scene, a group of eight seated around a small fire silently and solemnly sharing a breakfast on the shingle, the waters gently lapping close by. In another context, the occasion might have been idyllic, a tranquil setting; the sun rising over the hills and spreading its rays across the beautiful landscape, yet a gentle breeze wafting in from across the lake. But social intercourse around the fire was at a low premium; in fact at any table in the land, the situation would have proved unbearable and the guests would never have been invited again.

The invitation had been proffered, the victuals obtained, cooked and served all by the host (John 21:9-13). In turn his guests sat silently eating, leaving him to break the silences, without any gratitude being shown for the generous hospitality. No other host or hostess would have tolerated the discourtesy, but this was no ordinary host, but a Servant to the servants of God (2 Cor. 8:9). However, their fellowship together would not always be so frail, as he had once told them (Matt. 26:29), because a 'banquet' awaited them all at which the elect from every generation since the dawn of time would be warmly welcomed: the marriage supper of the Lamb (Rev. 19:6-9). But on that very early morning — though late enough for the world in those parts to have awoken — a passer-by would have noticed something unusual about the little group seated on the shore.

In truth, the seven were at a loss to know what to do. Their awkwardness in the situation was the result of various emotions: guilt at having been caught unawares, embarrassment by the display of unmerited love, uncertainty of what to do in the circumstances, and no doubt hesitancy in wondering which of them would reveal that they knew who he was. In the event none of them did. They had been caught between several 'stools', and had fallen between them all.

More than these

The breakfast could not have lasted long — if there had been no other reason, the lengthy silences would have seen to that — and then an opportunity arose for the 'ringleader' to be taken to one side (John 21:15), probably beyond the hearing of the others (John 21:20-22). If that was the case, Peter evidently told John at a later date what had transpired during this memorable meeting, when he, whose idea it had been to return to the old familiar waters (John 21:3), had to look his Lord in the face. On a previous occasion, a mere glance in his direction had produced copious tears (Luke 22:61-62), but now the gaze was close at hand and unavoidable. From his throne in heaven, or on a beach, the Lord's 'eyes behold, his eyelids try, the children of men' (Ps. 11:4). There could be no walking off, turning away, or remaining silent.

John's account makes no mention of a reconciliation between the risen Christ and his wayward apostle on this occasion and his public denial is not mentioned (Mark 14:71);

that had presumably already taken place shortly before when in a quiet moment Peter had 'seen' him (Luke 24:34; 1 Cor. 15:5). The question asked was not, 'Have you repented?', but 'Do you love me?' (John 21:15-17). As mentioned before, loving God can never precede repentance and forgiveness, as Cain discovered to his cost (Gen. 4:5).

The approach was direct, with no time wasted. Peter was asked an apparently simple question which he knew only too well was far from being so. His Lord provided clear warning of this fact when he addressed the apostle merely as 'Simon, son of Jonas' (John 21:15). For Peter, the expression conjured up memories of the day they first met, when Jesus had referred to him as 'Simon the son of Jona', before adding, 'Thou shalt be called Cephas' ('a stone'). (John 1:42). Now on the beach it was no longer 'Cephas' or 'Peter' (Matt. 16:15-16) but just 'Simon, son of Jonas', the 'stone' having somewhat crumbled! The message was plain: Peter was not as he had formerly been, Satan having 'desired' him, as Jesus had warned he would (Luke 22:31-32).

Still, his Lord having prayed for him, Peter's faith could not fail completely, as he later taught Christians everywhere. The elect are enabled to 'persevere' to the end of their days, redeemed by God's Son (Heb. 6:18-20), but also 'kept' by God's power (1 Peter 1:5). But there was an important issue still unresolved: did 'Simon' love his Lord 'more than these'? (John 21:15). It was an uncomfortable moment, and Peter knew what his Lord meant when he mentioned 'these'. It would have been easier for him had it referred to his boat and tackle, and his refusal to resist the temptation to return to them (John 21:3), but the issue was much more significant than that.

It is always embarrassing to be reminded of past follies, because 'these' were his brethren, some of whom were close by. Had it only been recently — so much had happened — that Peter had not only boasted he would never be ashamed of

Jesus, but had implied his fellow apostles might be? (Matt. 26:33). In other words, what had lain dormant within had been exposed in a brief moment: Peter's secret belief that his love for the Master (and his Master's for him?) exceeded the others. That was hardly a way to encourage good fellowship among the brethren! Little wonder they had spent so much time seeking prominence for themselves (Luke 22:24).

In a declaration of love and loyalty, though, one looks for reality, not mere words, and on the beach that morning Peter knew he was under the microscope of Christ's gaze. The apostle's eyes could not be averted, but upon being asked the straightforward question, his reply was glib. Of course he loved his Lord (John 21:15). But not far away, perhaps reflected in Christ's eyes, was a charcoal fire, the sight of which diminished the ardour of his declaration and painfully stirred his conscience. Had not 'a fire of coals' witnessed his treachery only a short time before (John 18:18), burning his boast to a cinder, and exposing his show of affection as an affectation? How could he, a strong man, forget his reaction when challenged by the servant girl, cursing and swearing (probably in God's name) that he did not know Jesus? So, the question was asked once more, did 'Simon' *really* love him? (John 21:16). Theirs was a meeting of eyes, but not of minds.

The swagger that evening in the upper room, although possibly excused as an act of impetuous immaturity, was nevertheless an obscenity within the shadow of the cross. Divine, sinless humility was confronted by sinful arrogance. Peter's words, although insulting to his brethren, appeared impressive on the surface. Even if everyone else proved disloyal, he alone would be the exception, never denying his Lord and even dying with him if need be (Matt. 26:33-35). It sounded an impressive testimony. But Jesus knew the reality, and for the one who is truth personified (John 14:6) that is always the only consideration; anything else is a lie (John 8:44).

When confronted by naked purity, what complexities of the soul are exposed. Even as Peter professed such devotion, he little realized what he was revealing about his inner self. There was no doubt he loved Jesus, having 'forsaken all' for him (Matt. 19:27). Once the call came to follow, Peter and his brother Andrew discovered it was irresistible, leaving everything behind them (Matt. 4:18-20). But during the three years between his calling and his boasting something had happened to Peter: a secret pride had taken possession of his devotion, leading him to believe his love for the Master was so great it exceeded that of anyone else. In other words, it was revealed that night in the upper room that his love for himself outweighed his affection for Jesus. So did he really love his Master?

Had he done so, at least to the degree he claimed, with the close proximity of Calvary that Thursday night his thoughts should have focused upon the Saviour. Reality demanded it. Instead, Peter's outburst showed he was primarily interested in himself, not even listening to what Jesus was saying. Over forty words were spoken by his Lord, but Peter appeared to hear only one: 'offended' (Matt. 26:31-33). He overlooked four extremely important references — to Christ himself, to the infallible Word of God (Zech. 13:7), to the miraculous resurrection and the location where he would meet them again. Even as his Lord was speaking Peter was thinking of himself. In short, self was seeking the spotlight, preventing everyone in the room from concentrating upon the vital issues. So whom did Peter really love?

The question cut to the quick (John 21:15). Perhaps the phrase 'more than these', a reference to his friends, had taken him by surprise, because in his reply he overlooked it. Instead, he passed the issue back to his Lord. He, who knows all things, is aware of how deeply or otherwise he is loved. Peter therefore was hurt — 'Thou knowest that I love thee' — but there was much more to the brief conversation than appeared on the surface. Both understood, but the matter was not openly mentioned, that they were talking at cross purposes. The question asked, 'Lovest thou me...?', referred to the most profound kind of love. Did Peter's love consist of that depth which the apostle Paul, in his beautiful eulogy on the subject, later attributed to divine love? (1 Cor. 13). Peter's reply, 'Thou knowest that I love thee', failed to measure up. His 'love' was of a lesser kind — 'brotherly affection'. So the attempt was made again in a most solemn and repeated question: 'Simon, son of Jonas, lovest thou me?', and once more Peter's response was disappointing as he spoke only of his 'affection' for the Lord (John 21:16).

As 'Simon, son of Jonas' had denied Jesus three times (Mark 14:72), the prickly question 'Lovest thou me?' was repeated three times (John 21:17), but on this third occasion Peter must have been surprised. In place of 'love' at its highest and deepest, Jesus descended to Peter's level, using the word for 'affection'; to which he replied '...Thou knowest that I love thee' (again speaking in terms of 'affection'). Prior to the Day of Pentecost and the Spirit's phenomenal anointing (Acts 2:3), Peter was always likely to disappoint, as his Lord realized only too well. For that reason new birth is essential (John 3:6-7), for who can breathe out heaven's grace, except those indwelt by the Holy Spirit of love? (Rom. 5:5).

However, it has to be admitted, the significance in the brief conversation of the use of the two Greek verbs, *'agapao'* and *'phileo'*, can be overstated. Elsewhere in his Gospel, John employs them interchangeably — for example, in his reference to the Father 'loving' the Son (3:35; 5:20), or to Jesus 'loving' Lazarus (11:5,36), but it does seem unusual that within the space of a limited conversation covering a mere three verses both verbs are used in the Greek translation of the Aramaic originally spoken unless the reader is being encouraged to observe something of significance.

Feeding lambs and sheep

We have presumed that when the risen Christ was 'seen' by
Peter (Luke 24:34;1 Cor. 15:5), the backslidden apostle repented and was forgiven by the one he had so wilfully denied
(Mark 14:71); that there could be no restoration such as took
place beside Galilee's lake (John 21:15-17) without contrition
preceding it. That being so, Peter now received his instructions from the Head of the church (Col. 1:18). He was to 'feed'
Christ's lambs and sheep.

The first thing Peter would surely have noticed was that his
Lord did not speak vaguely, or collectively, about his flock.
He did not even speak on this occasion in general terms of
'sheep', but such is the Good Shepherd's concern for the ones
for whom he died (John 10:11) that he has a particular interest
in them, protecting and caring for each member of the flock,
the young of the faith as well as those who are older and more
mature. After all, was not 'the flock' sought by him until triumphantly found? (Luke 15:4-6).

Then again, the words of the Shepherd were very plain: the
flock belonged to him. '*My* lambs ... *my* sheep', he distinctly
said. They did not belong to Peter, or anyone else. He knew
them from eternity (Rev. 20:15), having loved them everlastingly (Jer. 31:3), was actively obedient to the law's demands
on their behalf (Rom. 8:1 4), and passively laid down his life
for them (John 10:11), becoming accursed under the divine
wrath (Deut. 21:22-23) because of the broken law for which
they were guilty (2 Cor. 5:21). Drawn irresistibly to his side
(Hosea 11:4) by the will of the Father (John 6:44,65), they
possess his 'mind' (1 Cor. 2:16), and are indwelt by his Spirit
(1 Cor. 3:16; Rom. 8:9). They are his 'body' (Eph. 5:30); he
their head (Col. 1:18). They are his 'bride' (Rev. 19:9), and he
the 'bridegroom'. They are his church, against which hell itself

cannot prevail (Matt. 16:18). How the Shepherd has loved his flock, each one of them known to him (2 Thess. 2:13) like the stars in the heavens! (Ps. 147:4). How precious, and therefore important, they are to him.

That morning on the beach, as he conversed with the Lord, Peter's grasp of these great truths was limited; his anointing with the Spirit had yet to take place (Acts 2). However, Jesus' agricultural metaphor would have been fully understood, as shepherds with their flocks were a familiar sight in the land. Peter would have seen these strong men at their most gentle, as they with great care tended the lambs, sometimes carrying one in weather-beaten arms. How safe and secure it looked (Deut. 33:27). Was not this a prophetic insight into the Messianic hope, that the Messiah would act as graciously, and had Peter not witnessed it in Jesus? (Isa. 40:11).

The fisherman was about to become a shepherd — 'Feed my lambs' (John 21:15) — and was expected to reflect the 'Chief Shepherd's' graciousness (1 Peter 5:1-4). Peter evidently had much to learn, his record up to that moment having been far from promising. The shepherd is sensitive to the needs of his flock, especially the lambs, but the fisherman had revealed his insensitivity, actually boasting in front of the others that he was more faithful than they (Matt. 26:33). Of the 'Chief Shepherd' it was said, 'A bruised reed shall he not break, and the smoking flax shall he not quench' (Isa. 42:3), but he who was shortly to 'feed' the lambs had publicly illustrated his rough-and-ready character by cursing and swearing oaths in a moment of crisis (Mark 14:71). A radical change was required if 'the lambs' in the flock were not to be harmed.

Fishermen handle fish roughly and without consideration, but shepherds behave differently towards those in their care. Peter must have noted their gentleness, but he would also have known how at times they needed to be willing to sacrifice their own lives if necessary, like the shepherd-boy David having to ward off wild animals which threatened the flock (1 Sam. 17:34-37). In the isolated stretches of the land such dangers were never far away, but sheepfolds were without gates. At night-time the shepherd lay across the opening. He knew the sheep would not jump over him to escape, nor would intruders risk doing so to enter. Hence Jesus' reference to himself as 'the door of the sheep' (John 10:7).

How self-sacrificing had Peter been until that moment on the beach, how willing to place others before himself? His record had not been an encouraging one. Far from wanting to 'feed' others, earlier he had been more likely to 'feed' himself, so concerned was he with his own interests. Having sought to lord it over the other apostles (Matt. 26:33), was he a 'shepherd' likely to risk his life for any one of them, or for anyone else for that matter? (Luke 15:1-5).

How like a shepherd had he been when, in front of those who sought to harm his Lord, he had considered only his own safety? (Matt. 26:74). The fisherman considers the catch, not each individual fish, but the shepherd not only watches over the entire flock, but the welfare of each sheep and lamb. That takes love and its offshoots, patience and compassion. So, 'Feed *my* sheep,' Peter heard his forgiving Lord say to him (John 21:16-17). Having learned his lesson, many years later he was able to instruct the 'sheep' to add to their faith 'brotherly kindness [affection], and to brotherly kindness charity [divine love]' (2 Peter 1:7).

His hands stretched forth

How often Peter had heard Jesus say, 'Verily, verily, I say unto you…' When he heard that phrase, he knew the gravity and importance of what was about to be spoken (e.g. Matt. 5:26).

Suddenly, he heard it again (John 21:18). He must have been shaken as his Lord's eyes gazed steadily into his. Having been challenged as to the reality of his love, and having had his motives probed (John 21:15), Peter obviously wondered what was coming next. His surprise was therefore warranted when reference was made, not to the immediate circumstances, but to his past as well as his future. First, the Lord spoke of his youth: 'when thou wast young' (John 21:18). It had been a long time before; what relevance, then, could it have to their conversation on the beach? Much more than Peter realized.

His youth had been similar to that of most young men, but his days were going to end in a unique way, and for that reason Jesus contrasted the one with the other. As a young man, Peter had been confident and carefree, preparing himself each new day to face the world (John 21:18). Off he went, in whichever direction he wished, relishing his independent spirit, his good health and his strength. No doubt these qualities accompanied him to the lake of Galilee, as he and Andrew his brother earned their living fishing it (Mark 1:16) — experts in understanding the waters, in seamanship, in catching and selling fish.

Certainly, this was the character Jesus met when he entered Peter's life. Whether blurting out his belief in Christ's deity (Matt.16:16), scrambling over the side of the boat in an attempt at walking on the water (Matt. 14:29), or even revealing the darker side of his nature when he boasted (Matt. 26:33) or sliced off Malchus' ear (John 18:10), Peter's self-confidence was always in evidence. But was he not also fickle? He who on behalf of the twelve had sought to encourage Jesus, asking, 'Lord, to whom shall we go...?' and assuring him of their certainty that he was 'that Christ' (John 6:68-69), did not hesitate to disown him when cornered (Mark 14:71).

But then Jesus' tone darkened, when he turned from Peter's youth and spoke of the distant future, and did so in an unusual manner: 'when thou shalt be old...' (John 21:18). Like

everyone else, no doubt Peter was intrigued by talk of events
yet to be realized in his life, but his excited curiosity was
tempered by the way his Lord described them. It did not take
much imagining to recognize that danger lay ahead, as the
Lord went on, 'Thou shalt stretch forth thy hands, and another
shall gird thee...', and that he would one day lose the inde-
pendence he had always enjoyed. 'Another' was going to rob
him of it, one at whose mercy he would find himself.

That was all. His Lord's words had been few, but pregnant
with meaning. There was no enlargement upon the theme, no
explanation as to why Peter's hands would be outstretched,
or who this 'other' was. But then, nothing more needed to be
said; the apostle understood. Had he not seen Jesus' hands
outstretched on a cross by 'another'— that is, by the Gentile
Romans? The impetuous fisherman, transformed into an
apostle, would eventually be martyred (John 21:19). As the
realization dawned, Peter may have suddenly appreciated the
reason why Jesus had been so concerned for him in the upper
room, promising prayer support (Luke 22:32). He not only
had that night's events in mind — Jesus' arrest and Peter's
denial — but his apostle's future ministry and martyrdom. In
the hours, and years, that lay ahead it was vital that Peter's
faith did not fail.

From that moment, beside the lake where he had spent his
entire life, it was a question of waiting for the inevitable to
happen. This time there could be no running away (Matt.
26:56), or denying he had anything to do with Christ (Mark
14:71). He was fully committed, and the irony of his boast
shortly before, 'I am ready to go with thee, both into prison,
and to death' (Luke 22:33), would eventually be realized.

Peter's feelings are best imagined, but one thought had been
made clear: he now understood the reason why his character
would have to change. Apart from his 'feeding' Christ's flock,

how could he confront martyrdom behaving as he had? Self-ishness, pride, fickleness — these were not qualities of any use to God. What is required is his grace and graciousness, and the spirit of self-sacrifice, as Peter was later to remind the Christian church (1 Peter 2:20-25).

Whether he was tempted to ask further questions about his future is not known, although it would have been natural for him to enquire further; but his Lord prevented it and did so in a way Peter would have recognized. He merely said to the new 'shepherd', 'Follow me' (John 21:19), the authoritative command the fisherman had heard on that same seashore three years earlier (Matt. 4:19).

There can be no greater privilege than following in Christ's footsteps, but for Peter it was different (2 Peter 1:14). He was not being instructed to walk the beach; rather, like Jesus to glorify God in laying down his life (1 Peter 4:16; cf. John 12:27-28). But it was a mark of the sufficiency of God's grace (2 Cor. 12:9-10), that Peter lived for about another thirty years with the expected prospect of martyrdom overshadowing him each hour of every day.

However, he was unable to remain silent. Who could, when told news of that sort, and from such a source? There may have been a hint of alarm in his voice when, seeing John nearby, he asked what his friend's future was going to be. The reply was swift: it had nothing to do with Peter (John 21:21-22). Each individual is responsible for his own obedience to God's will and faithfulness to every command. That is discipleship (Luke 14:26-27). As it happened, both men had been 'eyewit-nesses' of Christ's majesty (Matt. 17:1-8; 2 Peter 1:16) and were to experience it in its fulness many years later: Peter in martyrdom (2 Peter 1:14), and John as a very elderly prisoner on the isle of Patmos (John 21:23; Rev. 1:9).

Another day

The early breakfast over, with the vicinity bursting into activity as the new day began, presumably Christ vanished from sight leaving the seven disciples alone once more. The were to see him again, in Galilee (Matt. 28:16-20) and Judea (Luke 24:50-53) and, unlike this occasion at the lakeside, 'great joy' would be their experience on those occasions.

9.
One without equal[1]

Shortly afterwards, a number of excited men in various parts of the country — several hundreds in fact — could be seen leaving their homes in a hurry. Their excitement must surely have been noted by curious neighbours, but had these enquired about it, they would not have been told the reason for the haste. It was a wonderful secret known only to a small minority. In any case, would the majority have believed it, if they had been informed that a rendezvous was expected with Jesus of Nazareth, who had risen from the dead?

To compound the mystery, the summons had come from heaven, an angel having heralded it to the women he encountered within the tomb: 'He goeth before you into Galilee' (Matt. 28:7). They in turn spread the news to the disciples as instructed. That presumably meant the brethren of their acquaintance; for if in the event there were 'above five hundred' at the venue (1 Cor. 15:6), the apostles cannot have been the only ones intended to hear it, although they were the first to do so. 'I will go before you into Galilee,' Jesus had told them prior to his arrest (Matt. 26:32).

Until then, only a few people had seen the risen Lord, most of them more than once — eleven apostles, Mary Magdalene and her friends and the two men travelling to Emmaus — but now, the privileged group was about to widen considerably.

That is, it was not just confined to Jesus' inner circle of friends (John 15:15), or for that matter to the disciples living in Jerusalem or Judea as a whole (Luke 10:1), but included several hundreds more (1 Cor. 15:6), and perhaps some from as far away as Syria (Matt. 4:25). The brethren of the embryonic New Testament church, soon to blossom triumphantly during the forthcoming festival of Pentecost (Acts 2), had been summoned to gather to meet its Head (Col. 1:18) — the officers and the male members (Matt. 28:16; 1 Cor. 15:6). Evidently the summons was to the men, and not the women, because they were to receive instructions about their role as missionaries in that church, teachers of the mighty gospel as representatives of the one to whom 'all power' had been given (Matt. 28:18-20; cf. 1 Tim. 2:12).

The undercover grapevine, through which the call came, must have been widespread and, at a time when the apostles were in hiding 'for fear of the Jews' (John 20:19), the message would have arrived secretly. Such was the prevailing antipathy towards Jesus and his followers, no doubt they all kept their heads below the parapet.

In fact, so secret was the message received that nobody knows to this day the exact location where the meeting took place, except that it was on a mountain somewhere in Galilee (Matt. 28:16).

Was it the beautiful Mount Hermon (Deut. 3:9), rising snow-capped over Galilee's north-eastern corner, or could it have been Mount Tabor, with its historical associations (Jer. 46:18; Judg. 4-8), the presence of which was such a familiar sight to the boy Jesus as he gazed out from Nazareth? Both mountains will rejoice in the name of the Lord, according to the psalmist (Ps. 89:12). It is for that reason they are cited as possible venues (traditionally Tabor) for the transfiguration (Matt. 17:1-2). Either could therefore well have been the actual location towards which the faithful were heading to meet their Lord.

Of the two, surely Tabor was the most likely, situated as it was within a small radius of the scenes of so many memorable events in the life of Jesus and his apostles. A mere six miles from Nazareth, it was the noted landmark for all who were raised in the small communities alongside Galilee's lake, as some of the apostles were (Mark 1:28-31). Tabor was therefore more easily accessible to the Galilean disciples than Hermon. Besides, it was situated very near to where the first of the apostles had been called (Matt. 4:12-23), and to the area where Jesus' ministry had begun (Luke 4:16-31).

The gathering

The five hundred and more must surely have arrived intermittently in ones, twos and small groups, some having further to travel than others. One thing was certain: it would not have been wise for too many at a time to be seen ascending the mountain, lest the unusual activity attracted attention. However, as in the days of the Hebrews' exodus from Egypt, the gathered church was sheltered by the sovereign hand of God (Exod. 14:19-20). But in any case, this was no occasion for the merely curious, or those opposed to the faith, and they who gathered could hardly have forcibly turned people away. Whether Hermon or Tabor, neither mountain was private property!

But who were these hundreds of men? Apart from the apostles, we do not know, Matthew's record understandably being concerned with the Speaker rather than the listeners (Matt. 28:16-20). Nevertheless, a fascinating collection of believers had surely been assembled from the various strata of Jewish society across the land (and beyond?), who understood how vital it was to be present. Would they have wished to absent themselves from such an awesome occasion? Hardly!

Their lives had been wonderfully transformed, their souls awakened, their sins forgiven. What differences nature had set between them — the city man and the countryman, the religious leader and the humble labourer, the educated and the poor — yet now through grace, they mingled freely together on that mountain, sharing the deepest of bonds, their devotion to Christ (Gal. 3:26-29). That is true fellowship (Rev. 5:9).

One is tempted to speculate about which well-known New Testament figures might have been present that day — perhaps Nicodemus (John 3:1-13), Joseph of Arimathea (John 19:38-40), Zacchaeus (Luke 19:1-10), or the priests who had at last nailed their 'colours' to Christ's 'mast' (John 12:42-43), among others — but there is a need to refrain. Matthew and Paul (Matt. 28:16-17; 1 Cor.15:6) do and so, therefore, should we.

However, if speculation about personalities is pointless, another question related to the gathering requires answering: why were there so few on the mountainside? True, only the 'brethren' had received the call, but 'above five hundred' was a small congregation of men when compared with the 'great multitudes' which often followed in Jesus' wake (Matt. 13:2). For example, on one memorable occasion, 'the multitude being very great', 4,000 were fed miraculously (Mark 8:1-9); then again on another, 'a great company' of 5,000 (John 6:1-10). Such encouragements were not unusual during Jesus' three years of ministry. Now, though, the numbers had sadly diminished.

The reason is easily discovered. Unlike his followers of succeeding generations, Jesus had only a minimal interest in drawing vast crowds. He understood mankind better than anyone (John 2:25); after all, he had not only created the human race, but had observed its downfall (Col. 1:16; Gen. 3:23-24). One moment the people wanted Jesus to be their king; the next, many who had claimed to be disciples 'walked no more with him' (John 6:15,66). The euphoria from the 'very great multitude' when he rode into Jerusalem was followed, within days, by the raucous cries of denunciation (Matt. 21:8; 27:25). Even his most trusted inner circle, whose promises of loyalty had been sincerely meant, 'forsook him, and fled' once danger appeared (Matt. 26:35,56).

Needless to say, Jesus has never been interested in the superficial — 'converts' desiring only short-term gains for themselves, or those who latch on to paradise as a kind of insurance policy (John 6:26-27). The work of grace within the soul is always profound, an experience which requires constant measuring (2 Peter 1:10), the delightful confidence behind the 'perseverance of the saints' (1 Peter 1:5) being too precious a revelation to be taken for granted. Therefore those claiming allegiance to Christ quickly discover the 'sieve' awaiting them, in which they are vigorously 'shaken' by sharp truth (John 6:44,65) and hard experiences (Luke 14:26), the genuine swiftly separated from the false (Matt. 13:5-8).

Saving faith, like a plant reaching for the sun, instinctively knows its destination and cries out to the one who is light, 'Lord, to whom shall we go? Thou hast the words of eternal life' (John 6:68; cf. 12:35-36). Those who merely 'make a decision for Christ' trail far behind, their eagerness waning with each faltering step, until they eventually drop in their tracks and never rise again (Heb. 6:4-6). Endurance to the end is the proof of electing mercy (Mark 13:13).

The hundreds assembled that day on the mountainside were 'his disciples' (Matt. 28:7), a most privileged company whose spiritual descendants can still be observed worldwide. Falling short of the standard though they often must have done (Luke 14:25-27), nevertheless, theirs was a commitment to Christ which surpassed everything else in life. Parents, wives, close relatives, even their own children — love them all dearly though they did, they recognized in their hearts an even more profound devotion for their Lord and Redeemer. This in turn cut deeper:

their lives were laid at Christ's feet, desiring only to exalt him, whatever the consequences to themselves.

The 'cross' they carried daily was his too, the unreserved and uncomplaining obedience to the will of God (Matt. 26:42). The experience of discipleship was once summed up by probably its greatest master, the apostle Paul: 'I am crucified with Christ: nevertheless I live, yet not I, but Christ liveth in me: and the life which I now live in the flesh I live by the faith of the Son of God, who loved me, and gave himself for me' (Gal. 2:20). Not for the mere 'convert', but for the disciple, Christ is all — lived, breathed, served, constantly in one's thoughts and prayers, and died for if necessary (Luke 14:33).

In another context, the poet and essayist Ralph Waldo Emerson once stated, 'Life consists of what a man is thinking of all day', and Christ's disciples would agree. Like Paul they think of him — in a lesser sense of other matters too, of course — but they live for Christ their Lord (Phil. 1:21). For this reason, Martin Luther prayed that he should be ready to lay down his life as a lamb for his Saviour, and John Calvin's personal emblem was a heart lying on the palm of a hand being offered to God. That is discipleship, the conditions needing to be read daily by those claiming allegiance to Christianity, and clearly for Christ nothing less is sufficient. As a warning, notice should be taken of his threefold insistence, '... cannot be my disciple' (Luke 14:26,27,33). The hundreds of men on the mountain that day were those described as 'his disciples' (Matt. 28:7), a blessed compliment from heaven itself. Who will not envy them?

Every knee bowed

The atmosphere must have been electric. The eleven apostles were already experienced at coping with the shock of being confronted by resurrection, but for the several hundred others, this was the first time. The one who, they knew, had died just beyond the city walls of Jerusalem was about to appear dozens of miles away in Galilee. How their hearts must have thumped with excitement as they ascended the slope to where the apostles were waiting, but by the time the assembly had gathered, the tension must have become unbearable. Heads no doubt jerked in all directions as they wondered how, and from where, their Lord would come. Not even the apostles knew.

Suddenly, there he was — Jesus! A thousand eyes, and more, turned as one man to the spot. Families would hear this moment recalled at many hearths for years to come (1 Cor. 15:6). Nobody knows what they were expecting to see, and perhaps they had no idea themselves, but on this occasion at least he was not accompanied by 'ten thousands of his saints' (Jude 14). In fact, so undramatic was the event that 'some doubted' whether it was Jesus at all (Matt. 28:17), perhaps expecting 'thunders and lightnings, and a thick cloud upon the mount', as when Almighty God memorably appeared at Sinai (Exod. 19:16). In fact, no soft lighting bathed the scene, nor was a heavenly chorus singing, as in a Hollywood film. Sentiment had nothing to do with the occasion. What the men saw, standing, it would appear, some distance from them (Matt. 28:18), was the solitary figure of a man. That was all.

The whole gathering surely fell silent, and every knee was bent, as each mind was transfixed with wonder. Difficult though it had been to grasp the news that Jesus had risen from the dead, despite his having openly spoken of it beforehand (John 2:19-22), the experience of assimilating the news was less complex than that of actually seeing him for oneself. A grotesque montage of fleeting images would have passed before their eyes — scenes which were either witnessed by these men, or were related to them by others: the arrest, the crowds clamouring for his crucifixion, the scourging, the faltering progress to Golgotha, the penetrating nails and heart-rending cries from the cross. This kaleidoscope of unpleasantness appeared in sharp contrast to the sight that now met their gaze.

He had returned to them! The solemn removal of his lifeless body from Skull Hill had appeared so final, symbolizing the dismal outlook of all who loved him. The act of placing it within the tomb, behind the 'very great' stone (Mark 16:4), beyond their reach, had only served to underline the apparent hopelessness of it all. While the Sanhedrin exulted in their victory over its enemy (Matt. 27:40-43), they wallowed in their distress (Mark 16:10). But now suddenly, while the authorities were hunting for his corpse, there he stood! The tomb was empty; Joseph of Arimathea could have it back (Matt. 27:59-60); and tears would never be applicable again. Apparent defeat had been swept aside by certain triumph.

Moses had also been confronted by 'the Lord God', and had immediately discovered that in that situation there was only one thing he could do: he 'bowed his head toward the earth, and worshipped' (Exod. 34:8). Would the brethren on another mountain, and in the presence of the same glorious person, have behaved otherwise? (Matt. 28:17).

But, wait! Was it really Jesus? Previously, through the grapevine, they would have heard how, without warning, he had actually walked and talked with Cleopas and a friend before they realized who he was and, with equal suddenness, had stood among the apostles as they conversed with each other (Luke 24). But here on the mountainside, where there were so many wanting to see him, Jesus stood apart from them — far enough, as already noted, to make some doubt whether it was he at all (Matt. 28:17).

The doors flung wide open

The doubts were quickly dispelled, though, as the distant figure drew nearer to the worshipping throng (Matt. 28:18). It was the Lord all right! But it was plain the occasion was not one for informalities, such as the privileged few had experienced. It was not a time for the whispered affirmation of his presence (John 20:16), or for a study of the Scriptures (Luke 24:26-27,45), nor even for a disclosure of his wounds (Luke 24:39; John 20:27). Those had been startling, but precious, moments of intimacy which had comforted his nearest and dearest. Within the empty garden, behind locked doors, and perhaps in a deserted alleyway (Matt. 28:9-10), the glorious miracle of resurrection had been contained within limits, known only to the circle of Jesus' followers scattered through the land — that is, until this gathering on the mountain (Matt. 28:16; 1 Cor.15:6).

Now the secrecy was over, the doors flung wide open. The believers in Christ no longer needed to whisper the news to each other, and those of succeeding generations be embarrassed by it, but rather they could unashamedly proclaim to everyone within hearing, 'The Lord is risen indeed!' (Luke 24:34). They recognized their Lord, 'flesh and bones' (Luke 24:39), and were about to hear his voice. This was no figment of the collective imagination, nor a phantom enshrouded in a mirage. Rather, the assembly of more than five hundred men 'at once' (1 Cor. 15:6) could all testify as witnesses, in a specific moment in time, not only to the resurrection as a historic fact, but equally to its being a *physical* resurrection. They would not have appreciated being called liars by those who were not there but who would subsequently have the audacity to deny it.

The supreme authority

The audience was entranced as the strong voice, with undeniable authority, rang out with its extraordinary message. It was brief, and startlingly to the point. Nor did it contain a prelude, or a hint of reservation in what it proclaimed. Those in the Judean south were still asking questions about the empty tomb and the missing corpse, but here in the Galilean north, the answers had been discovered. Christ was delivering a declaration, without equal in the annals of history (Matt. 28:18-20). It began simply, yet devastatingly: 'All power is given unto me in heaven and in earth.'

True, only a select minority were the first to hear it, but when the hillside echoed with the sound of his voice, the speaker knew he was not merely addressing a relatively few followers, but the entire church until the end of time, with future generations of unbelievers listening in. Nobody could ever have been in any doubt about the significance of what Christ was stating (he was a stranger to ambivalence): that of all the inhabitants this planet has harboured in its history, to him alone belongs ultimate authority. Alexander, Napoleon, Hitler and other men have sought to rule the world; they may have arrived with a blare of trumpets, but they vanished in the sands of time. Christ Jesus appeared in a filthy stable, but now in resurrection and ascension triumph sits astride both heaven and earth in glory. All do not necessarily believe it — vast multitudes never have done so — but the claim is still heard from the voice which is as loud and persistent as ever (Rev. 1:15).

The declaration was not new; the apostles had heard it before. During that last evening together before the crucifixion Jesus had stated many remarkable truths which had both puzzled and amazed them (John 13-17), but none had surely been so startling as when he prayed in front of them and they heard him remind the Father that he had given his Son 'power over all flesh' (John 17:2). What a staggering confession! A charlatan would have secreted the claim, limiting it to his followers, lest his dignity be lost in the howls of laughter resulting from the publicity. Christ Jesus, on the other hand, was one who everyone, even his enemies, realized had to be taken very seriously indeed. At his so-called trial before the high priest and the members of the Sanhedrin, anger was heard, but no laughter, when their prisoner openly admitted, under the most solemn of oaths (Caiaphas had said, 'I adjure thee by the living God'), that he was indeed the Son of God. The scriptural truth was graphically illustrated: 'Hereafter shall ye see the Son of man sitting on the right hand of power, and coming in the clouds of heaven' (Matt. 26:64). The courtroom exploded in fury at what was considered appalling blasphemy.

The apostles had heard that amazing truth much earlier on, but their reaction to it is unknown (Matt. 16:27). Perhaps at that stage, and not being theologians, they had been too bemused by the constant stream of extraordinary events to say anything at all. At any rate, this astonishing confession had never been an afterthought, reserved only for the Galilean mountain, but had been openly taught by Jesus intermittently throughout the previous three years (e.g. Mark 13:26). To the question, 'Who did he think he was?', the reply is obvious. He knew himself to be Daniel's 'Son of man', a figure who in a thrilling prophecy is pictured receiving the greatest of rewards from the mightiest of beings, the 'Ancient of days': 'dominion, and glory, and a kingdom', and the servitude of everyone who has lived on this planet (Dan. 7:9-14). 'Multi-faith' religion is not recognized in this glorious scenario. Every other religious leader, however vast his following at present, will be obscured in the multitudes submitting to Christ, the Son of man (Phil. 2:9-11). Truly, the Father has promised 'all power' to the Son, and when at the Judgement 'the books' are opened

(Dan. 7:10; Rev. 20:12-15), his will be the hands turning the pages, and his alone (2 Cor. 5:10).

Onward, Christian soldiers!

The assembly, consisting of brethren from a variety of backgrounds and occupations, without doubt listened in silence to their Lord's confident proclamation. It must surely have taken some time before their minds registered the implications of what they had heard, if indeed the finite mind is capable of grasping the concept of 'all power' this side of eternity. However, when they learnt that 'all power' had been entrusted to the one they knew, and before whom they now knelt, what thoughts must have swirled around in their minds. In the uncanny stillness which awe creates, the words of the patriarch Jacob in a similar situation might well have been remembered: 'How dreadful is this place! This is none other but the house of God, and this is the gate of heaven' (Gen. 28:17).

But the men had been summoned to the mountain, not only to savour the spirit of ultimate victory, but to receive commands for the future. Nobody can be more practical than the Lord; therefore past glories were not only to be reflected upon, but employed as a springboard from which to leap forward. They were not to remain kneeling, except in their hearts (1 Thess. 5:17), but to 'go' (Matt. 28:19). There was a work to do as a result of what they had just heard: to circulate from that spot, their 'banners' of truth unfurled, a zealous 'army' proclaiming the crucified, risen, ascended and all-powerful Christ and the infallibility of his teaching (S. of S. 6:4,10).

When the brief and solemn occasion was over, it must be presumed the Lord of glory vanished as swiftly as he had arrived, leaving 'his disciples' to make their way down the side of the mountain homeward bound. Indelibly etched upon their minds were his authoritative words, with encouragement imprinted upon their hearts. Gone was the fear of men (Acts 7:51-53), even those of the Sanhedrin who sought their arrest (Acts 4:12-13), and, instead, a sense of being 'more than conquerors' (Rom. 8:37) and a fresh vigour lightened their step. After all, had not the gathering ended with the most sublime of benedictions, 'Lo, I am with you alway, even unto the end of the world'? (Matt. 28:20). How inseparable are he and his church, whose redemption he has purchased with his own blood (Rom. 8:39; 1 Peter 1:18-21).

At the time they would not have known how it could be accomplished (see Acts 2:9-11), but they had been commanded to influence 'all nations', and they believed it would be done because the triune God was behind the ministry (Matt. 28:19). Off they went, first the apostles, whose teaching, with that of the prophets, would form the foundation of the New Testament church (Eph. 2:20-22), their purpose and privilege not just to seek 'converts' but to 'make disciples', who would enlist in Christ's army (Luke 14:31-33). They went forth preaching his 'good news' of 'repentance toward God, and faith toward our Lord Jesus Christ' (Acts 20:21), baptizing and instructing believers (Acts 2:41-42); everything carried out in the mightiest of all names, that of the Father, and of the Son, and of the Holy Spirit (Matt. 28:19). How could they fail? God the Son, in person, had provided assurance of his presence within the church for time's longest duration — 'unto the end of the world', no less (Matt. 28:20).

In another age and another place, and bearing these things in mind, these hundreds of brethren would have descended the mountain slopes to confront a hostile world singing a doxology:

Praise God from whom all blessings flow;
Praise him, all creatures here below;

Praise him above, ye heavenly host;
Praise Father, Son and Holy Ghost.

The true church, that which Christ owns as his (Matt. 16:18),
cannot possibly do other than prosper (Rom. 8:28-39).

Brothers united

'After that, he was seen of James' (1 Cor. 15:7), but how,
and when? Nobody knows. Perhaps the silence is due to
the intimacy of the occasion, because it was a joyful one
for a reason other than that of the resurrection. This James
was not the son of Zebedee or Alphaeus (Matt. 10:2,3),
but of Mary from Nazareth, and therefore Jesus' younger
brother in the flesh. They had other brothers, sisters too
(Mark 6:3), in what was a divided family. Jesus had spoken
from the heart when, speaking to the apostles, he quoted
the prophet Micah: 'A man's foes shall be they of his own
household' (Matt. 10:36; cf. Micah 7:6). In short, Jesus
experienced what many of his followers have suffered since,
the loneliness felt within the home when outnumbered by
unbelievers. His 'friends' and relatives were so opposed to
his teaching and lifestyle that they openly suggested he was
'beside himself' (Mark 3:21). The accusation was, at the
very least, insulting and hurtful.

Even his mother was not the person she had once been.
With the passing of Joseph (his final appearance in the Scriptures was an incident which had taken place twenty years earlier
— Luke 2:43) and of time itself, she had witnessed severe
changes in her life. Over thirty years earlier, when she was still
a young woman, the angel Gabriel had spoken to her at some
length — not an everyday occurrence — and how eagerly,
like Hannah, she had been full of praise of God! (Luke 1:26-55;

cf. 1 Sam. 2:1-10). But time had elapsed, and her remembrances of that ecstatic experience had faded, if not grown jaded. Since then her marriage to Joseph had produced other children, this time by natural means (Mark 6:3), who in adult life were alienated from their eldest brother and that for which he stood (Ps. 69:8).

Like numerous mothers since, Mary appears to have been influenced by her unbelieving offspring, mellowed by the majority viewpoint. Understandably in one way, at that period of her life she shared a closer fellowship with them than with her eldest son. An illustration of this is the famous occasion when the 'multitude sat about' him, but she and his brothers were on the periphery of the crowd, and not from a desire to learn, but only because they were looking for him. When informed about this, Jesus hinted at the distance between himself and his mother in his response: 'Who is my mother, or my brethren?' Then, scanning the crowds in front of him he added, 'Behold my mother and my brethren! For whosoever shall do the will of God, the same is my brother, and my sister, and mother' (Mark 3:32-35). It was a necessary, but hard lesson, which would have hurt a mother's heart.

But she at least, although apparently influenced by others, was nevertheless a godly soul (Luke 1:46). The same could not have been said of the brothers. The chasm was wide, as is 'flesh' from 'spirit' (John 3:6); in fact seemingly unbridgeable — so much so that at the Feast of Tabernacles (Lev. 23:34-44), a time when families delighted to unite in worship, Jesus cut a solitary figure. He refused to accompany his brothers to Jerusalem. Their unrequested and worldly advice that he should at that time disclose himself to the world was reminiscent of Satan's three years before (Matt. 4:5-9). Instead, he made his way at the appropriate moment —'my time' — (John 7:1-9). Family members though they were, what could his brothers have known about such spiritual matters?

In fact, how embarrassed they must have been, when to their astonishment at the climax of the solemnity ('the last day'), with the temple filled to capacity with worshippers, Jesus intruded into the proceedings. Waiting until the 'great day' of the feast, with its seven processions around the altar and the priests chanting the words of Psalm 118:25, he made his voice distinctly heard. In a reference to the water drawn each day from the pool of Siloam, and symbolically poured out in a reminder of the event recorded in Exodus 17:6-7, Jesus cried out, 'If any man thirst, let him come unto *me*, and drink' (John 7:37). One can imagine how his family must have felt at what to them was an irreverent intrusion (what would the neighbours have said?), resulting in the disgust of the many thousands present and the anger of the authorities. Jesus was undoubtedly 'a stranger unto [his] brethren, and an alien unto [his] mother's children' (Ps. 69:8).

But now, although it appears the family was still 'at variance' (Matt. 10:35), nevertheless two of his brothers, James and Jude (see Jude 1), had been drawn to accept Jesus, no longer merely as their brother, but as the Messiah (James 1:1). Their mother's clarity of godliness was restored too (Acts 1:14), probably as a result of remembering Simeon's solemn words of thirty years earlier (Luke 2:34-35), as she heart-rendingly watched her eldest son suffering at Calvary (John 19: 25).

For whatever reason, the believing brothers were not among the five hundred or so on the mount in Galilee. Had they been present, it would surely have been remembered by those who knew the apostle Paul (1 Cor. 15:6). Besides, if they had been there, Jesus would have been 'seen' by Jude as well as James. But the latter was selected for a sound, not a sentimental, reason. He required encouraging as, shortly, his was to be the onerous task (not Peter's) under the authority of Christ (Col. 1:18) of leading the New Testament church during the early and difficult stages of her development (Gal. 1:18-19; Acts 12:17; 15:1-29).

Was it just over a month since Jesus' crucifixion? (Acts 1:3). How time had flown! So many sudden resurrection appearances had taken place, now experienced by quite literally hundreds of people, that surely it must be irrational to remain unbelieving. And the 'sightings' had not been mirages on the horizon, or the imaginary glimpses of a phantom and silent stranger, but were accompanied by social intercourse. He had spoken to them at length, identified himself by revealing the wounds sustained at Calvary, even eaten a meal in front of them, and provided instructions and encouragements for the future; there was no doubting who he was.

Final instructions

But the moment had arrived for the final meeting, the glorious farewell, not to his mother or the believing brothers, but to the apostles, the appointed custodians of his teaching (Eph. 2:20), who had already been prepared for the great moment. 'Receive ye the Holy Ghost,' he had told them, as in a symbolic gesture he breathed upon the little group on the night of his sudden appearance in the upper room (John 20:22). Sentiment therefore played no part in the departure; nostalgia and tears were out of place and, if the occasion was correctly understood, unnecessary. What mattered was the immediate future: the Son's ascension to the Father's right hand (Heb. 12:2) and the Spirit's descent to the waiting church (John 14:16-17).

The 'Great Commission' (Matt. 28:16-20) had been proclaimed in Israel's northern region, where Christ's ministry had commenced (Luke 4:31-32); it was therefore appropriate that the area of his birth, death and resurrection should witness the climax of it all. Jerusalem, in the south, was therefore where they gathered (Acts 1:4), although in what actual location within the city is unknown. Perhaps in the upper room again? Such was the significance of what was about to take place, overriding every other consideration, it does not matter.

Wherever it was, among the apostles there must have been an extraordinary excitement, coupled with an apprehension born of ignorance of what they were likely to experience. Two things were certain, revealed during their final meal with him before his crucifixion: the mysterious paradox that their Lord standing beside them had to 'go' in order to 'come'. 'I go to prepare... I will come to you' (John 14:2,18).

He was returning home, where he had eternally been his Father's 'delight' (Prov. 8:30), in order to prepare 'a place' for his friends (John 15:15) within this exquisite paradise (John 14:3; Luke 23:43). Nor was the preparation reserved only for the inner circle, but for the elect as a whole. Had the apostles not heard his remarkable prayer that evening in that most sacred of moments (John 17) and been stirred as it drew to its climax? Twice the phrase was used, 'thou hast given me' (John 17:24). The Father had 'given' the Son a people to redeem (1 Peter 2:9-10), and had also given him 'glory' which they were to behold eternally.

But if heaven awaited Christ's arrival — the 'going' — with joyous anticipation (Rev. 5), the apostles also understood that earth was soon to experience the benefits of his 'coming' (John 16:7-11). They knew the resurrection had been the wonderful recognition of the divine acceptance of the atonement, the demands of the broken law satisfied (Rom. 4:24-25), but shortly they would also be able to join in heaven's triumph when the throne on Majesty's right hand was filled by the one who had brought it about (Heb. 12:2).

Jesus had provided the appropriate sign: God the Spirit would arrive at the behest of both the Father and the Son (John 14:26; 15:26), and when he did, not only would the New

Testament church be brought to fruition, but his triumphant victory over Satan and all his forces would be known (although not appreciated — John 16:33) by the world at large (John 14:30-31). Then his people will be able to proclaim, 'Christ the Redeemer has risen and reigns!' (Rev. 7:10), and each individual believer value the experience of being miraculously indwelt by God himself (1 Cor. 3:16; John 14:23).

Their Lord was about to leave them, but how? From the experiences they had had since his resurrection, there was only one way they could have imagined it. He would suddenly, and probably without warning, just vanish from their sight (Luke 24:31). This dramatic event could occur at any minute, a fact which would have served to heighten the acute tension they must have been feeling. But if they believed he would tell them, or paint in glorious colours the scene awaiting him, they were to be disappointed. Instead, they received practical teaching.

On the eve of their Lord's departure, their sights were no longer set in deep waters but upon profound matters; 'the promise of the Father', which they had heard Jesus outline during their final meal together (John 14-16), was about to be fulfilled. They were to be 'baptized' by God the Spirit (Acts 1:5).

But what did that mean? It was left to their imagination when reference was made to John the Baptist. Three years earlier, the 'voice crying in the wilderness' (Isa. 40:3) had spoken of this 'baptism' in terms of fire (Luke 3:16). Fire! The word was sufficient to instil in the apostles' hearts a certain apprehension, being so much a part of the divine vocabulary. The Scriptures speak of God revealed as a 'consuming fire' (Ps. 21:9; Heb. 12:29); of his angels made 'a flaming fire' (Ps. 104:4; Heb. 1:7); of his glory signified by 'devouring fire' (Exod. 24:17); of his fury as being 'poured out' like fire (Nahum 1:6); of valleys melting before his presence like 'wax' before a fire (Micah 1:4); of 'chaff' consumed by 'unquenchable' fire

(Matt. 3:12); and of hell itself, a place of everlasting fire (Matt. 25:41).

Now these apostles, who not long before had been ordinary working men and whose ancestors had been fearful of divine fire (Deut. 5:24-26), were soon to be 'baptized' in heavenly fire (Acts 2:3). Aware as they would have been of what had happened at the inauguration of worship within the tabernacle, when fire from God gushed from the most holy place to the outer courtyard and engulfed the burnt offering upon the altar (Lev. 9:24), with what trepidation they must surely have viewed the immediate future! In the sight of heaven, they too were submissively lying upon that altar and waiting for the flames to arrive, and for God to do with them as he pleased. Like the tabernacle sacrifices, they would also be purged of all uncleanness (Prov. 25:4), and offered up in the 'flames' of holiness for service (Phil. 1:21).

However, it appears the awesome realization was too much to ponder, or perhaps they had not been listening carefully enough to what their Lord had been saying, for when at last they interjected their thoughts, heaven was not uppermost in their minds, as one would have assumed, but Israel! Men, whose Lord was about to leave them, and who would shortly be empowered from on high, were once again asking the old question so familiar to the Jews: 'Lord, wilt thou at this time restore again the kingdom to Israel?' (Acts 1:6). Reared under rabbinical influences and nationalistic fervour, with the Messianic hope in the restored kingdom of David linked to desires for freedom from Roman tyranny, the apostles still had grasped neither Nathan's or Isaiah's famous prophecies (2 Sam. 7:16; Isa. 61:1-3).

The latter passage is a glowing description of the Messiah's gracious ministry, and always worthy of quoting in full: 'The Spirit of the Lord GOD is upon me; because the LORD hath anointed me to preach good tidings unto the meek; he hath sent me to bind up the broken-hearted, to proclaim liberty to the captives, and the opening of the prison to them that are bound; to proclaim the acceptable year of the LORD, and the day of vengeance of our God; to comfort all that mourn; to appoint unto them that mourn in Zion, to give unto them beauty for ashes, the oil of joy for mourning, the garment of praise for the spirit of heaviness; that they might be called trees of righteousness, the planting of the LORD, that he might be glorified.' However, the references in these wonderful verses to liberty, captives and prison stirred in Jewish hearts latent anguish at the Roman occupation of their country.

Early on in his ministry, Jesus had alarmed and angered the citizens of his home town (who had watched him grow to manhood — Mark 6:3-4) when he applied the prophecy to himself; in fact so much so that they tried to kill him (Luke 4:16-30). But from that moment on the belief strengthened among the ordinary people that, in Jesus, they had another Judas Maccabaeus who would eventually drive the legionaries from the land (John 6:15). The crucifixion was therefore a tremendous blow to the prevailing expectancy (Luke 24:21) and now, within moments of his departure, the apostles continued playing the old tune. Truly the sublime had been nudged to one side, to make room for the mundane, for which they received a rebuke (Acts 1:7).

Instead, the original theme was quickly restored. John the Baptist had spoken of fire (Luke 3:16); their Lord now referred to power (Luke 24:49; Acts 1:8). In order to carry out heaven's programme for the evangelization of the entire world, they would need it. On the Galilean mountain the church had received her commission from him to whom 'all power' has been given, to 'teach all nations' and baptize them in the name of the triune God (Matt. 28:18-20). Now in Jerusalem, if Christ's appointed leaders (Eph. 2:20) wondered how such an extensive programme could possibly be carried out (to 'all nations'), they were soon to discover.

Promised a baptism, not of water but of God the Spirit, they would be involved in spreading the good news about Christ in ever-widening circles (Luke 3:16; Acts 1:8): first the immediate city, then the southern half of Israel (Judea) and on towards the north, and from the promised land outwards in all directions until his way is 'known upon earth, [his] saving health among all nations' (Ps. 67:2). Yes, but how? Strong legs, sturdy camels or speedy horses, were no match for jumbo jets! However, the means of transport is never a problem for heaven in whatever age one cares to consider.

Within a very short time, the apostles found themselves publicly exalting Christ and proclaiming the mightiest message known to history, to 'devout men, out of every nation under heaven' (Acts 2:5). The apostles had not needed to visit them, but they were brought by God the Spirit to the apostles, ostensibly to worship at the annual feast of Pentecost, but in fact to hear about 'the wonderful works of God' (Acts 2:11). Failure is never an option if the will of God is being served.

Clearly then, on the eve of the ascension the psalmist's exultation could be loudly heard: 'O let the nations be glad and sing for joy: for thou shalt judge the people righteously, and govern the nations upon earth. Let the people praise thee, O God; let all the people praise thee. Then shall the earth yield her increase; and God, even our own God, shall bless us. God shall bless us; and all the ends of the earth shall fear him' (Ps. 67:4-7).

As far as Bethany

The moment had arrived. The eleven men had no idea what was going to happen, except for the fact that, in the context of the most extraordinary situation, whatever transpired it would be without precedence. They would have remembered he had said, 'I go unto my Father' (John 14:12), but how? Not knowing must surely have only served to enhance the tense yet excited atmosphere among them, and when their Lord suddenly set off for Bethany (Luke 24:50), they followed, wondering what was about to take place.

Presumably, in order to reach the little village two miles away, the group walked through Jerusalem's narrow streets. If so, the numerous passers-by could never have imagined what secret the group harboured as it hurried along. About five weeks had passed since the resurrection (Acts 1:3), and the event must have continued to be the topic of many a conversation in Jerusalem, especially in influential circles. The authorities were still without any further information about the whereabouts of the missing body, and had they been told that the body they sought was walking out of the city at that precise moment, their confusion would have been compounded!

The eleven must surely have shared something of that bewilderment, as centuries of Christians have done since; in fact not to do so is to pay scant attention to the subject at hand. To reiterate the profundity of the mystery, the enormity of what is entailed, the death of Jesus of Nazareth was conclusive — many being capable of testifying to the fact — and yet after 'many infallible proofs' of his resurrection from the dead (Acts 1:3), here he was walking down the street on the way to his ascension. Nobody recognized him even though he was well known in Jerusalem; but then, people would have thought it could not possibly be him, because he was dead. Besides, Mary of Magdala had not done so (John 20:15), nor Cleopas and his friend (Luke 24:16), so why should those who were merely distant acquaintances?

In a steadfast refusal to believe this phenomenon, the world files the account away on the shelf marked 'mythology', but it refuses to remain there. There were too many witnesses to the facts (1 Cor. 15:1-8), too many generations of benefactors resulting from the events, for unbelief to be justified. Once again, with breathtaking astonishment, man, like the prover- bial dish, has been turned upside down by Almighty God (2 Kings 21:13). The second advent will prove a similar experi- ence, with mankind relaxing in its unbelief before plunging into eternal fires (2 Peter 3:1-12; Rev. 20:11-15).

It would not have taken long before the eleven realized where they were heading: Bethany, the 'house of dates', on the south-east of the Mount of Olives (Mark 11:1). So much time had been spent there, in the home of their three friends, Lazarus and his two sisters (John 11:1). For the previous three years it had proved a resting-place for Jesus during a busy schedule, and also in times of distress (Matt. 21:17). It was there Mary had sat at Jesus' feet while Martha was 'troubled about many things' (Luke 10:38-42); in their village, Lazarus had been raised from the dead (John 11).

From the summit of the Mount of Olives, about seven hun- dred feet high, could be seen the Dead Sea, the hills of Moab, the river Jordan and, more especially, Jerusalem's entire net- work of buildings, streets and alleyways, with that focus of Jewish culture, the massive temple, most prominent of all. As he ascended Olivet, King David had wept with thoughts of his son's betrayal in mind (2 Sam. 15:30), and the mountain had witnessed gross idolatry during Solomon's reign, which had led to its being described as this 'mount of corruption' (2 Kings 23:13). Here Christ had sat with four of his apostles and dis- cussed the city's overthrow (which took place forty years later in A.D. 70), and from this teaching emerged that relating to the ending of the world and the warning to 'watch and pray' (Mark 13).

The uplifted hands

But that was the past. It was now appropriate that they should assemble on the Mount of Olives for another reason: it was the location appointed for Christ's feet to stand in 'the day of the Lord' (Zech. 14:4).

There were no more instructions to be given, no 'farewells'; all that remained was surely an unusual silence broken only by the sublimest of benedictions. The words spoken would have been those which were so familiar to the children of Israel. At such a moment, when the old covenant church and the new were united in Christ, they were not likely to be forgotten. In fact, the scene was overlooked by 'so great a cloud of witnesses' (Heb. 12:1), as 'B.C.' joined hands with 'A.D.' at Olivet, as they had done at Calvary and the vacant tomb. With his hands therefore raised in the accustomed manner (Luke 24:50; 1 Tim. 2:8), the nail-prints still visible, eternity's great High Priest, of whom Aaron and his successors were the 'type' (Exod. 28:1; Heb. 5), placed his 'name' upon the eleven (Num. 6:27) as he pronounced the solemn words of the Aaronic blessing: 'The LORD bless thee, and keep thee: the LORD make his face shine upon thee, and be gracious unto thee: the LORD lift up his countenance upon thee, and give thee peace' (Num. 6:24-26).

The men, having spent years with their Lord, were by this time well used to the miraculous. As John was later to testify during the post-resurrection euphoria, 'There are also many other things which Jesus did, the which, if they should be written every one, I suppose that even the world itself could not contain the books that should be written' (John 21:25). Without doubt, what happened that moment on the Mount of Olives was a phenomenon worthy of inclusion among the 'other things', in fact, probably surpassing them all.

It was as unexpected as it was momentous. With the quietness of Olivet disturbed only by the solemn pronouncement, to their amazement they saw his feet leave the ground as he slowly ascended from their midst (Luke 24:51; Acts 1:9). It was impossible! Yet that is what they saw. Being ordinary men caught up in a long series of extraordinary situations, and not classical figures in a stained-glass window, they must have found their thoughts racing in confusion as they sought a rationale for the information their eyes were imparting. First, there had been the rising from the dead, and now this! They would have been too shocked at the time, as they gazed wonderingly towards heaven (Acts 1:11), to appreciate that the two events were intimately linked.

These were not mystics claiming yet another 'vision' for the records, or eccentric mountain cave-dwellers for whom seeking the unusual was 'meat and drink', but down-to-earth working men. Being intensely practical, at heart they all shared Thomas's approach: 'Except I shall see...' (John 20:25). At the Mount of Olives, unquestionably, they saw Christ ascend. So this was his way of returning to the Father! (John 8:21-22).

A pause for thought

Yet, surely, that is absurd! Is one expected to believe that a body was *physically* raised from the dead, and ascended to heaven? In an age of science and technology, such concepts are shown the door. How stubborn is the agnostic spirit; how unwilling to believe the miracles of grace, while at the same time taking for granted the miracles displayed in nature! Resurrection and ascension are no more unusual than creation; to believe the latter is surely sufficient to accept the former.

Nature's miraculous display began with the swiftness of a wink (1 Cor. 15:52); it was at the flick of the finger which would one day write the divine commands on tablets of stone (Exod. 31:18) that from the emptiness of nothing something appeared (Gen. 1:1). Suspended within the blackness of the cosmos' first experience lay chaos, a silent mass, a heap of matter — nothing else. Upon this disorder God breathed, the Spirit brooding over it all like an eagle over her nest, or a hen her chicks (Ps. 33:6; 104:30; cf. Deut. 32:11; Matt. 23:37). Instant transformation was the result: chaotic jumble sprang to order; the inanimate stirred to vigour (cf. Ezek. 37:9).

The canvas was large upon which, with the boldest of brush-strokes, the Creator colourfully dressed the nakedness of the earth. The splash of beauty blotted out the drabness of chaos, while profusion swept it of barrenness, and procreation of impotence; the tender grass, the fruitful trees and the proficient seeds. The Creator is Father, but nature was never a 'mother', or divorced from the divine generosity. Rather it luxuriantly flows freely from it (Hosea 2:9).

Soon, with deft fingers, the Creator garnished the blackness of space with a sparkling array of brilliance (Job 26:13). With colourful planets as their courtiers, two 'great lights' reigned in the firmament (Gen. 1:14-18). A ball of fire burned by day, and through the night the silvery moon appointed for seasons stared down upon the earth like an unblinking eye (Ps. 104:19; 8:3). Accompanying it was a vast retinue of starry galaxies, myriads in number, and each star named by God (Ps. 147:4), signifying with what loving care he fitted each piece of the creative plan into place.

Meticulously attentive to detail, perfectly precise, within those few days of intense activity the Calculator of mathematical laws baffling to human genius had gradually unfolded the symmetric beauty of the universe. If a dome of immense and unmeasured proportions encircled the earth, in which mysterious planets of unending fascination continually spun in the

vast expanse of space, the earth's smallest petal on the minut-
est flower had not received less attention.

Within the animal kingdom variety is 'the spice of life':
from the winsome to the weird, the amazing to the amusing.
Each single creature, from the colossal to the 'creepy-crawly',
is touched with the divine breath, and with tender care — the
gargantuan, the gross, the gauche, the graceful and the gentle.
Screeching, squiggling, swooping, climbing, galloping, jump-
ing and diving, wings flutter in the skies, shoals swarm the
seven seas and creatures great and small prowl the lands (Ps.
8:8; 50:10). Fathoms deep, sky-high, in the mountains, on the
hills, across the plains, up trees, covered under rocks and foliage — they each fit uniquely into the divine scheme of things
(Gen. 1:20). In the light of such a magnificent scenario, why
should Christ's resurrection and ascension be considered un-
reasonable? In fact, everything created is 'of him ... through
him ... to him' (Rom. 11:36).

But what of man himself? He is at the same time the crown-
ing glory of the creative plan (1 Cor. 11:7), a heap of dust
(Gen. 2:7) and a lump of clay in the Potter's hand (Jer. 18:6).
Yet, how 'fearfully and wonderfully' he is 'made'! (Ps. 139:14).
Top to toe, side to side, within, without; from the shapeless
mass emerged a form, ideally proportioned, powerfully muscular and attractively lithe; awesomely designed, intricately
detailed, miraculously primed, wonderfully unique, breathtak-
ingly and evidently divine in origin — Adam!

This was no ordinary creation, no creature of the forests or
seas, but one who stood erect, capable of looking the triune
Potter in the eyes (Eccles. 7:29), a soul upon whom the divine
imprint was indelibly etched (Gen. 2:7). Man was bound to his
Creator uniquely (yet within the shadow cast by the Son —
Heb. 1:3), bearing the nobility of his 'image' and 'likeness'
(Gen. 1:26): reasoning powers, critical faculties, emotional
depths, sagacity, strong convictions and governmental ability

(Ps. 8:6-8). If animal instinct is limited to the horizontal, the human soul can soar vertically to the pinnacle of ecstatic expression (Matt. 22:37) — the worship of 'this glorious and fearful name, THE LORD THY GOD' (Deut. 28:58).

That is not all. The plan unveiled a 'likeness' of another kind: the Maker to the man, the man to his Maker, in a series of gospel paradoxes befitting the divine genius (John 15:1-8). He who was made flesh was created spirit (Gen. 2:7), and he who was Spirit would in Christ be made flesh (John 4:24; 1:14). The one ascended from the dust of life, but fell (Gen. 3:24); the other descended into the dust of death, but arose (Ps. 22:15; 1 Cor. 15:21). The prisoners were freed by the captive who was eternally free (Isa. 61:1; John 18:12; Prov. 8:22-30); the miserably poor made everlastingly wealthy by the one who was eternally rich becoming abysmally poor (2 Cor. 8:9).

When therefore the entire universe testifies to the glory of the Creator (Isa. 40) and the grandeur of his creation (Rom. 1:19-20), to speak disparagingly of Christ's resurrection and ascension, as if a belief in such events is irrational, is to appear somewhat foolish (Ps. 14:1). The eleven apostles possessed no scientific textbook to help them fathom the nature of their environment, or sophisticated technology to conduct them through the solar system but, like ordinary people today, they had cause to marvel at the mysteries which everywhere abound.

How often, during a night on the waters of Galilee, had they, like David, 'considered' the majesty of the heavens, with the moon and stars (Ps. 8:3); or in daylight, like Jesus, 'considered' the lilies of the field more glorious than the golden glitter of Solomon's court? (Matt. 6:28). Did the idea of Christ's resurrection sound impossible? What about seeds buried in the soil and producing wheat? (1 Cor. 15:36-37). That too would have seemed ridiculous, but they knew it was true. Was the idea of Christ ascending to glory absurd? No more so than the concept of an embryo growing in a womb! But unbelief

will counter that the comparisons cannot be measured. Everyone knows what seeds produce and what wombs contain, but
belief in Christ's resurrection and ascension demands faith from
the individual. Of course it does, but faith supported by the
evidence of over five hundred people (1 Cor. 15:1-9). It would
only have taken that number of farmers or midwives, or fewer,
to prove conclusively what emerges from soil and wombs. In
which case, why accept the one and not the other?

Ascent to glory

The group stared upwards in silence. Centuries earlier, the
prophet Elisha in a similar situation spoke twelve words as he
watched Elijah transported to heaven (2 Kings 2:12), but the
apostles' experience, although less overtly dramatic (no chariot
of fire, or a whirlwind!) was much more significantly awe-
inspiring. They were speechless, transfixed by the magnificence
of the scene, the meaning of which they would not have fully
understood at the time. They were merely content to observe
open-mouthed.

The hands raised in blessing provided the clue (Luke 24:50).
The nail-prints were still there. Etched upon his body were the
wounds inflicted at Calvary, when he was 'bruised' for the
iniquity of sinners (Isa. 53:5), and these indelible marks had
been present when he arose from the dead and were now ascending with him to glory. Shouts of acclamation can be heard,
both in heaven and upon earth, when the redeemed realize
what this means. In Christ they too have risen from the dead
(Rom. 6:9-11), and are also assured of ascending to glory as
he promised (2 Cor. 5:8; John 17:24), their 'vile' bodies 'fash-
ioned' like his (Phil. 3:21). 'For thou wast slain', they cry,
'and hast redeemed us to God by thy blood out of every kindred, and tongue, and people, and nation' (Rev. 5:9).

But heaven's mighty 'anthem', it must be remembered, is sung by all the redeemed within the everlasting covenant of grace, the 'new Israel' consisting of both Jews and Gentiles (Eph. 2:16). It was no coincidence, therefore, that the ascension took place on the Mount of Olives, associated so closely with Israel's history. Most important of all, it was within sight of another mount, Moriah, where Abraham enacted a gospel parable when he prepared to offer his son, 'thine only son Isaac, whom thou lovest' (Gen. 22:2; cf. John 3:16). For that reason it was chosen as the site of Jerusalem's temple, built upon orders from Solomon (2 Chron. 3:1), on what was originally the threshing-floor belonging to Araunah (or Ornan), which David had bought from him, with the oxen, for fifty shekels of silver, and upon which he erected an altar to the Lord (2 Sam. 24:18-25).

Time appeared to have stood still as, undisturbed, they watched Christ ascend to a beckoning Father, whose invitation had long been anticipated: 'Sit thou at my right hand, until I make thine enemies thy footstool' (Ps. 110:1; Acts 2:34-35). His mission was accomplished to heaven's satisfaction (John 19:28,30; 17:4); the one who in his person fulfilled all the strict Israelite laws and stern religious observances was approaching the throne of grace as heaven's High Priest (Exod. 28:36). He was about to be seated in regal glory amidst the exquisite splendour of his eternal 'dwelling-place' (Heb. 12:2; 1 Kings 8:30).

He carried no bowl of fresh blood from the animal sacrifices, as the temporal high priests had done when they entered the most holy place on the annual Day of Atonement (Heb. 9:7-14; Lev. 16); rather, he was the Lamb; the precious blood was his own (John 1:36; 1 Peter 1:18-19). Nor was he wearing a jewel-encrusted 'breastplate' with the name of an Israelite tribe written upon each jewel (Exod. 28:29-30); his heart was that 'breastplate', the redeemed for ever secure within it

(Heb. 6:18-20; John 10:28-29) and, as the Father's gift to his beloved Son (John 17:24), they are everlastingly and triumphantly presented before the throne. They are the fruits of his victory and trophies of his grace.

The cloud

Nobody knows for how long the experience had lasted, although long enough for the eleven to have been 'gazing up into heaven' (Acts 1:11), but suddenly the ascended Lord was lost to sight. A cloud had engulfed him (Acts 1:9), no doubt a 'thick' cloud like the one from which he spoke to Moses on Mount Sinai (Exod. 19:9). To meet with the representative of law (John 1:17), the Lord had descended in this cloud (Exod. 34:5), but now on the Mount of Olives, when he was about to leave the apostles to represent grace, he ascended within it (Acts 1:9). It was not weather conditions that had caused the cloud to materialize but, rather, the opening of heaven's door.

Three of them had seen the 'Shekinah' before, the supernatural symbol of God's holy presence, when upon another mount (Tabor or Hermon) with Jesus. He had invited Peter and the two sons of Zebedee to witness an astonishing sight: first his 'transfiguration', when both his face and clothing radiated heaven's glory (Exod. 34:35), and then they observed him holding a conversation with Moses (representing the law — Deut. 34:5-6) and Elijah (the representative of the Prophets — 2 Kings 2:11). At that point the cloud overshadowed them, and from it a voice was distinctly heard: 'This is my beloved Son, in whom I am well pleased; hear ye him' (Matt. 17:1-8). On that occasion, the glory emanating from the cloud had produced such trepidation in the three apostles that they had fallen to the ground (Matt. 17:6), although now on Olivet it filled them all with wonder.

In other words, the knowledge of God's presence among his people can instil in them emotions of varying hues. The 'Shekinah' is likely to be accompanied by 'thunders and lightnings', to underline the dread full purity of the divine, as when the sovereign God manifested his appearance on Sinai (Exod. 19:16). On that 'terrible' occasion, even Moses admitted, 'I exceedingly fear and quake' (Heb. 12:21). When eventually the tabernacle was made and assembled according to the heavenly 'blueprint' (Exod. 25:9), the mysterious cloud often hovered over the 'mercy seat' upon the ark of the covenant within the most holy place.

Such was the glory emanating from it, Moses was unable to approach 'the tent of the congregation' (Exod. 40:34-35). A similar situation occurred on the day the temple in Jerusalem was opened during Solomon's reign, and when the priests were incapable of ministering as 'the glory of the Lord had filled the house of the Lord' (1 Kings 8:10-11). This was 'the smoke' which Isaiah saw in his vision many years later, filling the same temple, as the seraphim proclaimed the majestic purity of the thrice-holy God (Isa. 6:1-4). How fearful must it be to die unsaved (Heb. 10:31; John 8:24).

But the appearance of God through the 'Shekinah' was capable not only of instilling fear, but of providing comfort and protection. When the Israelites commenced their epic journey through the barren deserts, the cloud was seen as a pillar passing before the camp (Num. 14:14). So that it was visible to the entire nation, during the day its appearance could not be mistaken for other clouds, and through the night it shone brilliantly as a flame (Exod. 13:21-22; 40:38). Throughout the forty years of wandering the cloud was always present, God never forsaking his people (Neh. 9:12,19), as the Egyptians quickly discovered at the exodus (Exod. 14:19-20); when it moved forward, the Israelites followed, and they rested when it hovered overhead (Num. 9:17). What comfort this brought the 'holy people' (Deut. 7:6-8), to realize every day that Jehovah was with them, and guiding them through the 'waste howling wilderness' (Deut. 32:10). And is this not the promise from God for the church of the new dispensation? (Isa. 4:5).

But the world has not seen the last of the 'Shekinah', as was intimated that day on the Mount of Olives: 'This same Jesus ... shall so come in like manner...' (Acts 1:11). As already mentioned, the courtroom had rocked with fury when, under a solemn oath ('I adjure thee by the living God'), he had revealed that he was Daniel's long-awaited 'Son of man', depicted as arriving 'with the clouds of heaven' (Dan. 7:13). Amid the astonishment at such an apparent blasphemy, Jesus viewed the future: 'Hereafter shall ye see the Son of man sitting on the right hand of power, and coming in the clouds of heaven' (Matt. 26:64). At that day, the 'Shekinah' will not be a phenomenon seen only by a few, but 'Every eye shall see him, and they also which pierced him: and all kindreds of the earth shall wail because of him.' How? Because 'He cometh with clouds' (Rev. 1:7).

Confidence assured

The eleven remained in total silence, each one staring upwards at the glory which had hidden their Lord from sight, their minds seeking to adjust to the phenomenal situation. What was there to say? The Lord having returned to his 'holy temple', it was wise for those upon earth to be silent before him (Hab. 2:20). God had made foolish the wisdom of this world (1 Cor. 1:20).

The silence, together with their concentration, was suddenly broken by the sound of a voice. The apostles turned and saw two men standing beside them; at least, they had the appearance of men, but their 'white apparel' revealed only too clearly who they were — angels! (Acts 1:10; cf. Mark 16:5). At Christ's incarnation (Luke 1:5-38), when he made his sacrificial atonement (Matt. 26:53), at his resurrection (Matt. 28:2-3) and at now his ascension — during all these mighty events, the Father revealed his close proximity in the appearance of these heavenly messengers (Heb. 1:14).

The tone of the voice was triumphant. Why were they staring upwards? Their faces probably gave them away — astonishment, tinged with sadness at watching their Lord vanish from sight. But they were assured that this moment was not the end; in fact, it was merely the beginning! As the 'Shekinah' had hidden their Lord from them at the ascension (Acts 1:9), it would reveal him to *everyone* at the second advent (Rev. 1:7).

But the angel, perhaps surprisingly to many today, did not speak in such theological terms. This glorious event is not a 'museum piece' to be confined to dusty theological textbooks under the heading of 'eschatology'. Rather, as if to comfort the eleven, he spoke not of 'Christ', or a similar title befitting the Son of man, but of 'Jesus', the name so familiar to them (Acts 1:11). Jesus is returning in glory and in person! (Matt. 25:31).

The message had been heralded, and heaven could not have been more encouraging. The eleven apostles joyfully turned on their heels and hurried back as quickly as possible along the dusty track which led to Jerusalem, to spread the thrilling news to the waiting church (Luke 24:52; Acts 1:12). Within the city many enemies still seethed with rage, but it no longer mattered. The war had been won; the 'foes' merely served as his 'footstool' (Acts 2:34-35; Ps. 110:1). With heaven witnessing the enthronement of the Lord Jesus Christ (Heb. 12:2), and vast multitudes exulting in his glory (Rev. 5:1-9), the threats posed by men upon earth assumed a secondary consideration — so much so that the apostles were no longer afraid to walk

Jerusalem's streets, but even took their joyful thanksgiving into the temple precincts (Luke 24:53), where their Lord's enemies were to be found in great number (Matt. 23). But for that reason spiritual fellowship could not be experienced there; within an upper room (Acts 1:13), probably *the* upper room containing many happy memories, was where the city's true church gathered (Acts 12:12).

120 brethren and sisters, including Jesus' mother, met there. Profound was their fellowship; deep their love for each other; great their rejoicing, and abundant their prayers (Acts 1:14-15). They were waiting patiently for the Father's promise to be fulfilled (Acts 1:4; John 14:16), and when it arrived, they experienced yet another extraordinary event.

10.
The rushing mighty wind

It was 9 in the morning (see Acts 2:15) on a day in the year A.D. 29, or thereabouts, when it happened. It was, without exaggeration, one of the most remarkable experiences in world history, and it took place during a period marked by several such occasions. A certain house in the great city of Jerusalem became, in a moment, the centre of attraction to all its inhabitants. Crowds flocked to it, standing in the street outside, curious to see for themselves what had occurred.

The fact that an ordinary house — and few dwellings in the city were other than that — should attract such attention from so many people only served to underline how phenomenal had been the swift occurrence. But much more astonishing was the fact that the flow of people had dramatically changed its course, away from the direction of the magnificent temple which occupied the central position in the city, to the less opulent quarters of the back streets where the house stood. Something unusual had evidently taken place, and although the history of Jerusalem was full to overflowing with memorable incidents, this one was so different as to outshine them all.

A needful diversion

It was no coincidence, but providential, that Jerusalem was crowded to capacity at the time, a circumstance assuring wide-spread publicity for the event. Jews from all over the known world had arrived in the city and the temple was until that moment the focal point of their attention. From the days of King Solomon, when a temple was first built on the site (1 Kings 6:1), the people had gathered there to celebrate their feasts; that is, they had done so until the seventy years of exile (Jer. 25:11), after which the temple had been rebuilt (Ezra 5:2). Much later Herod the Great had it restored and enlarged in honour of the Caesar in Rome, and did so in so impressive a manner that it became one of the wonders of the known world (Matt. 24:1). It took eighty-six years to complete (B.C. 20 – A.D. 66), although during that period it remained in constant use, as it was on the day under review.

The Feast of Pentecost

The feast which had drawn the crowds was that of Pentecost (Acts 2:1-15); in other words, it was a celebration and thanksgiving for the beginning of wheat harvest (Exod. 23:16). It was also called 'the Feast of the Fiftieth Day', or 'the Feast of Weeks' (Deut. 16:16), because fifty days or seven weeks after the first ripe corn, or barley, had been offered to God, a sacrifice was always made according to the ancient teaching (Lev. 23:15-21).

At Pentecost the Jews also remembered the giving of God's law at Sinai (Exod. 19:1), which had been fifty days after the first Passover and the deliverance from Egypt's bondage (Exod. 12-14). It was therefore a very special occasion (Acts 20:16), one of the three most important events in the Jewish calendar

(Deut. 16:16), and consequently an appropriate opportunity for the sovereign God to make his presence felt.

The breath of God

As with all experiences which are beyond the comprehension of those who share them, the crowds, if asked, would not have been capable of explaining what they had seen or heard. It all happened so suddenly. One moment they were occupied with ordinary affairs; the next, they were aware that something extraordinary had entered their lives. Quite literally 'out of the blue', a deafening sound shuddered Jerusalem. Without warning, what appeared as a fearsome wind gathered in all its power and, travelling unimpeded at great speed, descended upon the city (John 3:8). With unseen intensity, it concentrated overwhelming force upon one single house, screaming its presence as it hurtled towards it (Acts 2:2).

Jerusalem went silent, the solemn feast of Pentecost momentarily forgotten, as everyone incoherently lingered in limbo for a while, until the gigantic army of swishing whips was brought to a halt. 'What was that?' Was it 'the blast of God' (Job 4:9), 'the breath of his nostrils' (2 Sam. 22:16), demonstrating his anger through a natural disaster? Instinctively, as crowds do on such occasions, there would have been a general movement towards the spot from which the strange sound had arisen. Very quickly thousands, far too many for comfort, jammed the narrow streets and alleyways which surrounded the house.

Nobody knew what to expect when he arrived at the scene, except presumably to find havoc had been wreaked and the dwelling no more than a pile of rubble. The fact that the house was not wrecked may well have caused some to ponder the situation, the majority of similar houses being too flimsy to suffer such a 'natural' frenzy and escape unscathed. Now it was the people's turn to create turbulence as they jostled with each other to gain a better view, and the plethora of 'mother tongues', dialects and accents rose in crescendo, seeking answers to the numerous questions being asked (Acts 2:5).

Jerusalem had not experienced such a phenomenon for many generations — in fact not since the miraculous overnight deaths of 185,000 enemy troops just beyond the city walls (2 Kings 19:35; Isa. 37:36), an event which would surely have attracted considerable comment. It had certainly been an astonishing one, but now in A.D. 29 something even more mysterious had visited them, if only for the fact that it took place in broad daylight and in front of thousands of witnesses. But, most significant of all, if Assyria's losses at the hands of an angry God spoke of death, the pouring forth from heaven of the Holy Spirit's power and grace cried aloud of life (John 14:16-17).

Into the sunlight

Suddenly from the house emerged a group of men, twelve in all, the sight of whom must surely have produced a collective gasp of amazement from the crowds. Many would have recognized all but one of them (Mathias having only recently been chosen to replace Judas — Acts 1:26); they had seen them often enough in the city during the previous three years. Then they had accompanied their leader, the prophet from Galilee (Deut. 18:15), living within his massive shadow, but when he had been executed by the Romans at the instigation of the Sanhedrin they had gone into hiding (John 20:19).

Now here they were again, but what a difference! Gone was the trepidation, the spiritual inertia, the ambivalence, the loss of direction. Instead, they fearlessly stood before the vast crowds, among whom there would no doubt have been members of the Sanhedrin, an aura of tongue-shaped holy fire anointing each of them (Acts 2:3; cf. Heb. 12:29). Whatever had taken place within the house, it had provided a startling transformation in the apostles of Jesus of Nazareth (Matt. 10:1). The spectators would not have known it, but that was exactly what he had promised his immediate band of followers (Acts 1:8).

It would also have been clear to most of those assembled there, steeped as they were from childhood in the history of their people, that these men, like Moses, had met with God. Only such an experience could explain the 'charisma', the radiation of the divine presence which could be observed in their bearing (cf. Exod. 34:30). They had evidently been endowed with the Spirit of the Lord, who had conducted them to the 'eye' of heaven's generous outpouring, so that each recipient was now 'turned into another man', like the prophets of antiquity (1 Sam. 10:6) .

Although we cannot be sure of all the details, the following is a possible scenario of what occurred that day.

The initial astonishment of the people, which had been accompanied by a breathtaking silence, was interrupted when the twelve men moved in different directions, preaching as they walked. The seething mass of spectators listened respectfully for a while, but quickly became restless, the vast majority of them unable to understand what was being said. The facetious are present on all such occasions, and they were not in short supply on this one. Ripples of laughter spread through the ranks, as it appeared 'gibberish' was being spoken. 'They're drunk!' (Acts 2:13).

But soon it became clear that in fact twelve sermons were being preached, in as many languages, as each appropriate section of the huge congregation followed the welcome sounds of its mother tongue (Acts 2:9-11). Aramaic was the preachers' own language, with Hebrew that of the synagogue, but how did it come about that they were hearing Coptic, Latin, Arabic, Chaldee, and more besides? After all, Galilee, from where the preachers originated (Acts 2:7), was a poor and barren area of Israel (cf. Isa. 53:2), frowned upon not only by its enemies, but even by those whose home it was (John 7:52; 1:46). The region was certainly not noted for its linguists!

The question on everyone's lips was the obvious one, the Galilean accent being pronounced (see Mark 14:70): how were these ordinary working men from that area in the north capable of such expertise? Little wonder the holy fire hovering over them was tongue-shaped! (Acts 2:3). Providing the answer was just the opportunity the apostle Peter required to proclaim 'the wonderful works of God' (Acts 2:11) to a people seeking solutions to the mysteries which had filled Jerusalem for weeks (Acts 1:3).

Not far away the great Jewish feast of Pentecost was in progress, but few would have noticed. Instead, with supreme irony, those who had been considered of little consequence just seven weeks before, when their leader was crucified outside Jerusalem's walls, now held a large number of its citizens in the palms of their hands. The Spirit of truth had flown, like a swift arrow, direct to the heart of Judaism's unbelief (John 16:13). The axe in God's hands had finally severed the roots from the 'tree' (Luke 3:9); a new covenant had come into being (Ezek. 36:25-27).

Heaven's rebuke

Peter stepped forward. Despite his earlier shame at having openly denied his Lord (John 18:25-27), God the Spirit had driven him from his hiding-place into the street. Therefore, under the tutelage of the most sublime of all teachers (John 14:17), whose linguistic qualifications are impeccable, the apostle boldly proclaimed the good news with remarkable dexterity as he nimbly leapt about among the tongues. All heard, and could understand, what was being declared. In fact, the Jews standing before him might have reflected upon the days of Ezra and Nehemiah. Half a millennium before, the Israelites had assembled in another of Jerusalem's streets to hear the reading of God's Word, when 'The ears of all the people were attentive' (Neh. 8:3). It was like that again, except that this occasion was multi-lingual.

Although the point is invariably overlooked, the first thing an intelligent observer would have noticed about the Spirit's sermon, proclaimed through his anointed vessel, was that it made no concessions to an ecumenical outlook. There was no attempt to appease the Sadducees, in an effort to gain some sympathy for the apostles. Their vociferous enemies (Acts 4:1-3), like Annas and Caiaphas, who were largely responsible for the crucifixion of Christ (John 11:49-53), held only to the Pentateuch as their 'Bible', strongly depreciating the remainder of the 'Old Testament'. Yet Peter's references were only to the prophet Joel and the Psalms (Acts 2:16-36).

To accommodate the Sadducees, the sermon could have been rooted solely in the Pentateuch, although less effectively, because the books of Moses were accepted by the Sanhedrin members as a whole. How Peter would have thrilled to the theme of sacrificial atonement and spoken of Christ fulfilling all the rites and ceremonies of the major offerings laid down by law! (Lev. 1-7). 'It is the blood that maketh an atonement for the soul' (Lev. 17:11). He would have made much of that (1 Peter 1:18-19). Then again, was not Abraham encouraged, like Joel, to learn from God that 'all families of the earth' would one day be blessed? (Gen. 12:3; cf. Joel 2:28). Would it not have been possible for Peter to prove that Jesus of Nazareth was the 'Shiloh' of Jacob's death-bed prophecy (Gen. 49:10), and therefore the victor over death? (Acts 2:24). Could he not have referred to resurrection in general, as revealed by the mysterious 'angel of the LORD' (Exod. 3:2,6; Matt. 22:31-32), and therefore spoken of Christ's resurrection in the same breath; for who was that angel but God the Son? (Josh. 5:13-15; Judg. 13). As for the glorious ascension, and Christ seated at the right hand of the Father (Acts 2:29-36), what more appropriate position could there be for 'the Most High', the 'star out of Jacob' and the 'sceptre' arising from Israel? (Num. 24:16-17).

However, instead, in history's second most famous sermon (the first being, of course, his Master's from the mount — Matt. 5-7), Peter was conducted by God the Spirit to scriptural territory beyond the Pentateuch — in other words, to scriptures unacceptable to Annas and Caiaphas, the nation's high priests (John 18:13). Heaven had bypassed them.

The notable day of the Lord

'The last days...' (Acts 2:17) — that phrase alone revealed how momentous was the occasion, an oration proclaimed on the widest of platforms. Representatives from 'every nation under heaven' (Acts 2:5) stood riveted to the spot, listening to a vindication of the person and work of Christ. If for that reason alone, what occurred at the Feast of Pentecost in A.D. 29 can never lose its relevance; in fact it must rank as one of the major turning-points in the history of mankind.

If proof is required, the spellbound crowds in Jerusalem that morning did not request any. They recognized the poetic alarm in the warning God had provided in his message to the prophet Joel when he spoke of 'blood, and fire, and vapour of smoke' (Acts 2:19; Joel 2:30-31), and knew it was a suitable metaphor for what had happened (Rev. 6:12) — at least, as far as they were concerned. Had they not heard the 'rushing mighty wind' as it swooped to its destination, sweeping every obstacle to one side, and had they not seen for themselves what man becomes when touched by the Spirit of Jehovah? (Acts 2:2,4). And in listening to the apostles, could they not say with the Hebrews of yesteryear, 'We have seen this day that God doth talk with man, and he liveth'? (Deut. 5:24).

And it was upon this theme that the sermon began, not with elevated thoughts about Christ, but leaving the best 'wine' until later (John 2:10). Wisdom dictated that poor sinners should be encouraged first (Prov. 8). He understood their plight, laden down as they were beneath the heavy burden (Matt. 11:28) of God's holy Ten Commandments (Rom. 7:23-24) — a situation made considerably worse by the crushing extra weight of the oral law (the 'Mishnah'), the traditions of men placed unnecessarily upon them by the 'blind guides' (Matt. 15:14) of the Sanhedrin (Matt. 23:4; Mark 7:1-13). In fact the Jews, both at home and abroad, were scattered upon the hills like 'sheep not having a shepherd' (Mark 6:34), as their fore-fathers had been, unattended and forlorn (Jer. 23:1). With the belief that 613 laws were to be obeyed on a daily basis, and the breaking of one of them being sufficient to bring down judgement upon the sinner (James 2:10), it was not surprising!

Later, when the converts sat at the apostles' feet being tutored in the doctrines of grace (Acts 2:41-42), they learned the wonderful news. Their arrival at the house in a state of alarm had not been the catastrophe they had thought, but rather a remarkable blessing (Acts 2:6). After almost 600 years, God's word to Jeremiah had rushed to its fulfilment (Jer. 31:31-32), which included the promise that the hopeless struggle to keep the Mosaic law had been overcome and judgement averted for everyone sheltering within the new covenant that had now been established (Isa. 12:1).

The new believer would have marvelled, reared as he was in the rabbinical school, asking the obvious question: how could

Breakfast on the beach

it be? After all, the Mosaic law is 'holy, and just, and good'
(Rom. 7:12), so much so that, referring just to the law as recorded in Deuteronomy, God's servant had issued an extremely
stern warning: 'If thou wilt not observe to do all the words of
this law that are written in this book, that thou mayest fear this
glorious and fearful name, THE LORD THY GOD...' (Deut. 28:58).
So, how is it possible that a sinner can be commanded to obey
the Decalogue (Exod. 20:1-17), yet have no need to flog himself in the attempt (Matt. 22:36-40), but rather can be at peace
when he does?

It is a good question, but easily answered in the second half
of the covenant promise: 'I will put my law in their inward
parts, and write it in their hearts' (Jer. 31:33). What an amazing statement! Smoke, fire, thunder, lightning, the blaring of a
'trumpet', trembling Israelites, the curious threatened with
death (Exod. 19) and a fearful Moses (Heb. 12:21) — these
were the ingredients which made up the frightening prelude to
the arrival of the 'fiery' law, accompanied by 10,000 holy angels
(Deut. 33:2). Is it possible that sinners can be so intimately
related to Jehovah's unblemished character (Lev. 11:44), reflected in the law, that it could actually be 'written', not just
upon tablets of stone (Exod. 31:18), but upon the human heart?
(2 Cor. 3:3). If so, it is nothing short of a miracle. How would
it be accomplished?

One day, during the time of the exile (Ezek. 1:3), Ezekiel
heard God outline his plan: 'I will put my spirit within you,
and cause you to walk in my statutes, and ye shall keep my
judgements, and do them' (Ezek. 36:27). So that is the secret!
Left to his own devices, the sinner can only fail to do what
God demands, ending his life as a law-breaker and spending
eternity in hell (John 8:24; Matt. 5:27-30). It is an equation
too awful to contemplate, and that is why the majority refuse
to do so, but heaven has graciously supplied an escape from

what would otherwise be inevitable, and it was to take place in 'the last days' (Acts 2:17).

This is that

Those days had arrived. In fact, on the day when the apostle Peter proclaimed his stirring sermon, the world was already about thirty-three years into 'the day of grace', the gates of which were flung wide open at the birth of Christ. The angels understood the significance of this when they cried aloud on that occasion: 'Glory to God in the highest, and on earth peace, good will toward men' (Luke 2:14). Heaven was writing its message upon the wall that, although the pathway to the ultimate bar of judgement had been completed (Matt. 3:2), hope lay in the manger at Bethlehem. In which case, what better time to seek the Lord than now, 'the day of salvation'? (Acts 2:21; 2 Cor. 6:2). The progressively revealed plan of God had moved forward to a new stage.

Before this day, the intimate ministry of God the Spirit had been limited to the imparting of unique gifts to a well-chosen few. It is the story of the Old Testament: epic journeys (Gen. 11:31) led by men of outstanding faith (Exod. 12:31,37); miracles wrought at the raising of a hand (Exod. 14:27); grace given (1 Sam. 16:13); wisdom granted of an unusual kind (Exod. 28:3; 1 Kings 3:12); prophecies proclaimed (Dan. 2:28-45); enormous courage and strength supplied at the point of need (Jer. 7:1-20; Judg. 14:5-6; Heb. 11:32-40). The Israelites benefited from the intrusion of heaven into the life of the nation, a witness to the divine glory and a special people to their God (Deut. 7:6-8), but except on rare occasions (e.g. Exod. 31:1-6), the ordinary citizen could only ever be a spectator.

But now — the contrast is marked — no longer the privileged few, but 'all flesh' (Acts 2:17) is catered for in the provision of the Holy Spirit to grant outpourings of his grace. But long before Joel heard the promise (Joel 2:28-32), Abraham had been encouraged to hear it too. Did not God declare to the mighty patriarch that 'In thee shall all families of the earth be blessed'? (Gen. 12:3). Those 'families' have their source in Noah's three sons (Shem, Ham and Japheth — Gen. 6:10) and their wives, who, following the Flood, journeyed in different directions under God's command to 'multiply and replenish the earth' (Gen. 9:1). In ever-widening circles, therefore, was the divine smile to be radiated.

Not every individual does the Spirit visit: 'Many are called, but few are chosen' (Matt. 22:14). But in seeking the elect he moves across all boundaries and every recess of humanity: the religious, the racial, the social and the linguistic (Rev. 7:9). From among a wide cross-section they are found: the Jews (Rom. 11:1-5) and the Gentiles (Acts 2:39); the greatest and the least (Jer.31:34); the rich and the poor; the sages and the simpletons; employers and employees; men, women and children (Joel 2:28-29). These are now the honoured minority, the 'household of God' (Eph. 2:19), who 'know' him intimately (John 17:3), the law having been 'written' upon their hearts by the Spirit's indwelling (1 Cor. 3:16).

In short, no greater intimacy can there be than that which exists between the citizens of this 'holy nation' and its King, as Peter was to write years later (1 Peter 2:9). They are the treasures in heaven's coffers, jewels in the Sovereign's crown (Mal. 3:17), priests in his temple (Rev. 1:6), members of his family (Mark 3:31-35), a 'bride' for his Son (Eph. 5:22-32); in fact, intertwined with God himself, and he with them (John 14:20). Knowing all this, a confidence the world mistakes for presumption, the recipient of this astonishing beneficence can no more disbelieve or disown it than heaven could cast him and his Redeemer aside (John 10:29). Both are eternally bound by covenant integrity (Heb. 9:15).

The unmistakable presence

Phenomena, not truth, curiosity, not Christ, had summoned the crowds to the house, although behind it all stood the providence of God. How could they have suspected that the raging wind, so unexpectedly exciting their interest as it whistled overhead, had anything to do with Jesus of Nazareth? Besides, he had died weeks before, his presence in the city removed by the intrigues of the Sanhedrin. When the door of the house burst open, therefore, it must have come as a shock to see his apostles streaming into the street, and in such an ecstatic state (Acts 2:12).

It is not surprising, then, that Peter's introduction to the main thrust of his argument was lengthy (Acts 2:14-21) and, wisely, he anchored his audience to the familiar territory of Old Testament prophecy rather than straight away introducing them to something new. There was time enough to soothe jagged nerves, although his listeners were blissfully unaware they were about to witness the preacher leaping headlong into the most controversial oration Jerusalem had ever heard.

At one stage, it must have appeared that the sermon was over as, with the suitable application, 'Whosoever shall call on the name of the Lord shall be saved,' Peter completed his introductory explanation (Acts 2:21). However, there was much more to come. Perhaps the people were on the point of leaving, because they were arrested in their tracks with the words: 'Ye men of Israel, hear these words; Jesus of Nazareth...' (Acts 2:22).

If any had been tempted to leave, the mention of that name would have been enough to prevent them. Judaism was in the

process of observing one of its most important feasts, bringing the 'first-fruits' of harvest to the temple (Lev. 23:10-11),
the priests and people engaged in solemn ceremonies. Now, in
the middle of it all, suddenly and without warning, Israel's
most talked-about figure had been reintroduced to the nation's
conscience and thought-processes. 'Jesus of Nazareth? He's
dead! What's he got to do with all this?', might have been the
instant comment in many minds, and on many lips. Dismay
was writ large across Jerusalem's furrowed brow.

From fear to fearlessness

Under normal circumstances, Peter's stance would have been
heroic, especially when measured by the bleakness of the backcloth against which he preached: the formal religious climate
cold as a corpse, the priestly attitude hostile and aggressive,
the audience ignorant and bewildered. But to a man enjoying
the anointing of the Spirit, the maxim etched upon his soul
was that provided by the pre-incarnate Christ: 'Is anything
too hard for the Lord?' (Gen. 18:14). Nothing can be; nothing
is.

His inspired proclamation was explosive and Jerusalem was
soon to feel its impact (Acts 2-9). A spirit of apparent invinci-
bility (Eph. 6:19) had superseded the fear he had known in
front of the servant girl only a few weeks before (Mark 14:69).
Then he had been afraid to own his Lord, self-preservation
being his main preoccupation (Mark 14:71), but now all that
had dramatically changed.

Under the influence of the euphoric experience received
inside the house, he could have known no greater joy this side
of eternity than to be called upon to proclaim the glory of
Christ Jesus in a public place (John 16:14). Nor could there
have been a better opportunity to engage in such a wonderful

task than before representatives of the entire Jewish world (Acts 2:5) and, through the printed page, ultimately to take the message to the world as a whole (Acts 1:8). The 'axe' was in the sovereign hands of God (Matt. 3:10), but Peter held the 'hammer' of heaven's Word 'that breaketh the rock in pieces' (Jer. 23:29), and he knew it.

His address to the citizens of Jerusalem, and to the world, was an example of gospel preaching at its finest, manifesting expertise provided only by the Spirit of God (John 14:26). As he began his extempore exposition (time would not have allowed for the scribbling of notes!), his authoritative voice rose above the general clamour of excitement and noisy curiosity, with the words: 'Men and brethren...' The temple was beckoning its adherents, but their attention was elsewhere, dead religious observance always having to give way to spiritual life.

How to preach the gospel

The wealth of biblical truth, the certainty of historical evidences and the penetrating conviction of a fearless application (Acts 2:22-36) comprised the 'shaft', from which were taken four 'arrows', aimed in order at the intellect (vv. 23-31), emotion (vv. 32-36), conscience (v. 23) and will (v. 38). Preachers since then have neglected this format at their peril.

Under four distinct headings, each one solemnly introduced, Peter unfolded his major theme and its application, the glory of Christ, to include the entire nation: 'Ye men of Judea' (vv. 14-21); 'Ye men of Israel' (vv. 22-28); 'Men and brethren' (vv. 29-35); 'Therefore let all the house of Israel know assuredly' (vv. 36-39).

The ascent to the highest pinnacle of all was steep, and dangerous as the consciences of the wicked were stirred (v. 23), but the slow climb was made from the level of man to the right hand of God (vv. 22,34). And tempted though Peter must have been, as every preacher is, to touch the most sacred areas of gospel truth as quickly as possible, he refrained from doing so. Calvary and the empty tomb were not his first ports of call; rather, his delight was in reaching out to those who listened. A bridge needed to be built ('a man approved of God among you'), a relationship established between the herald and the hearers; because if a preacher is not united to his congregation and they to him in sharing a common understanding of the subject at hand, he is more likely to bore than to communicate. Before people were led to the abstract (v. 23), they had first to face immediate reality (v. 22).

Approved of God

Many in Peter's position — not only a Galilean outsider (Mark 14:70), but also an uneducated fisherman — being aware that representatives of Jerusalem's influential intelligentsia were listening to them, would have attempted to alter the message for their benefit. When this occurs, and the preacher becomes embarrassed by simplicity and the unsophisticated, his thoughts endeavour to reach heights hitherto unscaled, and in the most untested of vehicles. The result is failure, either to satisfy the few, or to nourish the majority.

However, Peter's anointing lifted him far and above such tactics, pride having no agreement with the Spirit of God. The pleasing of men was not on the agenda, only the passionate proclamation of the gospel. His major concern was that all in the crowds should understand what he had to say — the simple as well as the sage, the young and also the old. He therefore stooped to the lowliest, that they might lift their heads, and in doing so, appealed to all.

What better way could this essential common bond be cemented than by a reference to what everyone had seen for himself, the humanity of Jesus, the prophet from Nazareth? Few would have disputed the fact that he was a man amongst men, 'who went about doing good' (Acts 10:38), as Peter was to express it at a later date. The Spirit's aim, though, through his servant, was the establishing of the wonderful conclusion that 'God hath made that same Jesus, whom ye have crucified, both Lord and Christ' (Acts 2:36).

But first, it had to be noted he was 'a man' (Acts 2:22), capable of 'strong crying and tears' (Heb. 5:7; Matt. 26:38-39), and not an aloof angel. He also possessed a name which was common in Israel. It was likely there were men standing before Peter with the same name — Joshua in Hebrew (Acts 7:45). Hence, this 'Joshua' was identified as the one 'of Nazareth'.

Immediately, everyone was able to identify with him, a man from the 'dry ground' (Isa. 53:2) of the north. Local people and Galilean farmers could testify to how barren it was. There was even a general suggestion that nothing good could come from the town, which was not important enough to be given a mention in the Jewish Bible (John 1:46). Nazareth, and Galilee as a whole, was considered by popular opinion as the poor and inconsequential quarter of the country (John 7:52). So Jesus, the carpenter from a humble background (Mark 6:3) in a lowly area of Israel, was a man of the working-class community and not the establishment. Despite what they had heard their priestly leaders publicly declare (Matt. 27:41-43), Jesus was one who could easily be 'approved' of by the ordinary people.

The facts having been established, it was the moment for consciences to be stirred. Not only had Jesus found favour with the general public, at least for most of his three-year ministry (Matt. 27:22), but by common consent among ordinary

Jews his had been a special anointing. Had they not followed him in droves (Matt. 4:25), and at one point actually sought to make him their king? (John 6:15). Their enthusiasm had stemmed from what they had seen for themselves, 'miracles and wonders and signs' (Acts 2:22); they had been enthralled by seeing the divine manifested through a ministry of gracious compassion (Matt. 11:4-5). The 'God of Israel' was glorified far and wide because of Jesus (Matt. 15:31).

Israel's history had been sprinkled with healers, even 'miracle workers', but who among them had actually raised the dead — and done so more than once? (Luke 7:15; 8:52-56; John 11:43-44). If ever there was someone 'approved of God' (Acts 2:22), with many thousands of witnesses to the fact, it was Jesus of Nazareth. There could hardly have been a household in the land untouched by his ministry, including those in which Gentiles lived (Matt. 15:21-28). So why had they demanded his crucifixion, even at the expense of their children's safety in the sight of God? (Matt. 27:25).

Delivered for crucifixion

The groundwork had been laid, the necessary preparation made, the emphasis placed upon the humanity, yet the divine uniqueness, of Jesus of Nazareth. Now, at length, Peter had arrived at the destination every preacher yearns to reach when uplifting the Redeemer before the people: his sacrificial death and glorious resurrection. The door to the very heart of the gospel had been flung wide open, and he entered without hesitation: 'Him, being delivered...' (Acts 2:23).

The scene had now shifted dramatically. Peter scarcely had time to catch his breath before the majesty of 'signs and wonders' (Heb. 2:4) had given way to the humiliation of 'deliverance', triumph to apparent defeat. And to those who first heard the sermon that is what appeared to be the case, Jesus' magnificent ministry among them (Acts 2:22) having been diminished in their eyes once he had been hammered to the cross (Luke 24:19-21; Matt. 27:42). His finely tuned arguments, during numerous debates with Sanhedrin members (John 5-8; Matt. 23), seemed only to have led to his defeat at their hands (Matt. 27:39-43).

In fact, the awful events on Skull Hill, overshadowed by darkness of many hues, in which the black clouds reflected the agonies and anguish of the suffering and the mood of devilish unbelief (Luke 23:35,45), were to the majority in Israel little more than an exercise in futility. The crucifixion of Jesus of Nazareth to them concerned wood, twine, nails and hammers — nothing more. He had courted the displeasure of Judaism's ruling body, and paid the price. Such a waste of a young man's life!

It was because of this the Holy Spirit did not permit Peter to linger over the theology of substitutionary atonement (the 'deliverance'), which would in any case have been a major theme already preached in numerous languages by all the apostles that day (Acts 2:11). Besides, he enlarged upon the subject shortly afterwards (Acts 3:18-19). Instead, the desire was stirred in him to unfurl the banner of resurrection and ascension glory over Jerusalem, Judea, Samaria and 'the uttermost part of the earth' (Acts 1:8). Without a reference to, and belief in, the latter, the former lacks relevance (Rom. 4:25).

The crowds were about to be shaken, as the Spirit-filled apostle opened the casket of divine mystery (Matt. 13:11), introducing them to concepts at odds with natural thinking. The world, right up to modern times, struggles to oppose them (1 Cor. 2), and only a new-birth experience (John 3:1-8) is capable of penetrating the bulwarks of disbelief.

Jesus of Nazareth had been 'delivered' (Acts 2:23). Of course, everyone knew that the priests had plotted to bring about his arrest, trial and execution (John 11:49-53), but Jerusalem now reverberated with shocking news. The route to Golgotha, from Caiaphas to the cross, had been mapped out by divine decree! All the characters in the drama, both Jewish and Roman (Zech. 11:12-13; John 19:11); every lash he bore in the scourging (Matt. 27:26); each faltering step on the way (Mark 15:21); down to the nails hammered into his hands and feet, the shouts of the priests and the agonized cries from the crucified one (Ps. 22:1-18) — not one detail of the gruesome events had been overlooked. Heaven's chart had registered it all deep within eternal ages past. 'Determined' (Acts 2:23) was the word Peter had heard Jesus use at the Last Supper (Luke 22:22), and the reason why the Son of God knew what awaited him (Matt. 16:21). His 'Father's business' had been known to him from his youth (Luke 2:49).

Peter's unexpected statement surely must have produced an immediate effect. The people, reared in the belief that the Sanhedrin was the custodian of the divine will and its members the élite in God's sight, must have been rocked to their heels. The mask of religious affectation had slipped, exposing the face of corruption. Of course, there was no doubting Jesus' remarkable gifts, 'miracles and wonders and signs' (Acts 2:22), illustrating the fact that he was heaven's delight. Some leading priests recognized it (John 3:2), and all knew deep down that they were dealing with someone of extraordinary qualities and supernatural ability (Mark 2:7). In which case, why had the Sanhedrin conspired to rid the land of him? An air of disgust might well have arisen from the crowds.

But, the 'motes' in the eyes of others having been examined, conscience typically commands the 'beams' in one's own eyes to leap to the fore (Matt. 7:3-5). What about the ordinary people? How enthusiastic had they been in their adherence to Jesus? They had followed him across the plains and over hills for hours on end (Matt. 14:15) and even wanted to make him their king (John 6:15); yet how fickle their devotion had proved! Within a matter of days, from the Sunday to the Friday, their shouts of adulation had turned to blood-curdling screams of detestation: 'Let him be crucified... His blood be on us, and on our children' (Matt. 27:22,25).

What had caused such disloyalty and ungodliness, and in so short a time? Was it not the influence of the guilty men, the chief priests and elders (Matt. 27:20), who were responsible for the death of the man 'approved of God' among them? (Acts 2:22). But they alone were not to be blamed. What about the crowds who now formed Peter's large audience, most of whom allowed themselves to be influenced? Theirs was a case of guilt by association. What excuse could they offer for their shameful and merciless shouts, heard by Rome, and afterwards by the world at large, baying for Jesus' blood and demanding the release of the wicked brigand Barabbas? (Matt. 27:21-26; John 18:40). Calvary had witnessed a few of them mocking him even as he hung upon the cross (Matt. 27:39-40).

In other words, on three levels the convicting message had penetrated the collective conscience of those who first listened to it. First was the fact that they knew their victim was not only innocent — even the pagan Pilate had admitted that (Matt. 27:24) — but the 'miracles and wonders and signs' they had seen for themselves (Acts 2:22) revealed that God knew it too. Yet they still demanded the death by crucifixion of this unique man among them.

But that was not all. Their guilt and corruption had now been underlined still further, not only with the reminder of God's omniscience in the affair, but also in the revealing of his omnipresence over it all. The triune God foreknew throughout eternity past what would transpire when the Son stepped upon earth (Ps. 2); indeed he had 'determined' what should happen (Acts 2:23). That being so, the people, albeit unwittingly, found themselves in the enemy camp. Jehovah was their foe! It was a realization so disturbing that undoubtedly a ripple of unease crossed the faces of the entire gathering.

But Peter, bathed in special anointing, had still not completed the charges levelled by heaven against the Jews. They would have been aghast, the Sanhedrin members seething with anger, at hearing this fisherman's voice as he continued his diatribe against the nation in general, and its leaders in particular. The air was thick with conviction of sin, righteousness and judgement (John 16:8), as God the Spirit ploughed the deepest of furrows through the Jewish conscience.

Attending the festivities of Pentecost, and draped in the appropriate religious fervour considered suitable for the occasion, both priests and people were nevertheless charged with possessing 'wicked hands' (Acts 2:23). A love for sinners had been the motive for Jesus of Nazareth being 'delivered' to the cross (John 3:16), but the rabbis and the rabble had 'taken' him to the same venue because in essence they hated God. Worshippers of Jehovah had killed the one approved by him, the Prince of life put to death! (Acts 3:15).

By this time, the heaviest of burdens weighed down upon the people in an already oppressive atmosphere. There was no hiding-place from the truth's accusing finger, the fact that the sixth commandment in the law had been flagrantly disobeyed (Exod. 20:13), not only in the killing of a man, but of 'a man approved of God' (Acts 2:22). What could they do? (Acts 2:37).

Raised from the tomb

But if they thought the exposure had run dry and the Spirit's penetrating glare was terminated, the preacher's solemn words continued to cascade over them. No sooner had they been charged with having 'crucified and slain' the remarkable Jesus of Nazareth (Acts 2:23), than they blinked in the sunlight with astonishment. Were they hearing correctly? Had their ears deceived them? Did the preacher really say, 'Whom God hath raised up'? (v. 24).

Perhaps at first, before minds had fully caught up with ears, they thought, as every Jew would have done on hearing about a resurrection, of the events to take place 'at the last day', when everyone will rise to judgement (John 5:28-29). Martha did, providing Jesus with the opportunity to make one of the most profound statements known to man: 'I am the resurrection, and the life: he that believeth in me, though he were dead, yet shall he live' (John 11:23-25).

But this was different. The apostle had intimated that Jesus had *already* been raised; the one for whom they had expressed such hatred (Matt. 27:22,25) and whom they had been guilty of condemning to death (Acts 3:15), was alive! Would he return to wreak vengeance upon them all? The fearful thought, and the dawning of the truth, only served to intensify the shame many of the people felt, and there was no hiding-place, even had 'the wings' of that morning taken flight to 'the uttermost parts of the sea' (Ps. 139:9).

For the previous month or so, reports had circulated in Jerusalem that Jesus had not only been seen, both within the city and also as far north as Galilee, but had actually spoken to his followers (Acts 1:3). There was even a suggestion that on one occasion more than five hundred had been present (1 Cor. 15:6). Of course, few believed it, fanciful stories having a tendency to roam freely. Now, however, the crowds that flooded the area where the apostle was preaching were hearing the official version, so authoritatively that there was no questioning what was being said. Like the rose of Sharon itself (S. of S. 2:1), blossoming in a desert place (Isa. 35:1), Peter's message had gradually opened up until at this point at least 3,000 of the listeners were able to appreciate its splendour (Acts 2:41,24-36).

The news which had brought such joy to the disciples for the past weeks could no longer be contained; it had burst forth to the general public at large. Jesus of Nazareth, the man who had so evidently lived at the heart, and in the warmth, of the divine smile, still walked the land at will. His was not a ghostly apparition, unmoved by time, but a physical presence belonging to eternity (Luke 24:37-43). Beyond the reach of his enemies, in touch with his friends, appearing and vanishing, here one moment and there the next — the resurrection had brought with it ultimate freedom.

It was therefore now clear that approval from God was not the only qualification Jesus of Nazareth possessed (Acts 2:22). His resurrection had illustrated the divine power as nothing else could, but also the compassionate relationship between heaven and this 'good shepherd', as well as the flock for which he died (John 10:11).

Unshackled from death

Of all the people who crowded Jerusalem's streets that morning, only the apostles had any idea what 'the pains of death' had meant to their Lord (Acts 2:24), and consequently freedom from it. They had been with him on that last evening together in the upper room, when the atmosphere had been that of a gloomy expectancy, signified in his ominous expression, 'My time is at hand' (Matt. 26:18). Calvary was close by, and the heaviness of spirit accompanying the inevitability of a dreaded event had already taken up residence. Within the garden of Gethsemane, his arrest imminent, it had intensified, as Peter himself had observed. Together with his friends John and James, the privileged few permitted to be with their Lord at such an anguished hour, he had watched death's pangs taking their toll of 'the man of sorrows and acquainted with grief' (Isa. 53:3), a fact which had notably aged him (John 8:57).

The experience ached with a profound solemnity, as the three saw a troubled and restless Lord, one moment urging them to watch and pray, and the next wrestling in prayer to his Father. The conflict between the flesh and the spirit was extreme, despite the comforting presence of an angel (Luke 22:43), yet the filial obedience to the eternal plan was absolute (Matt. 26:38-46). Under an unblinking moon, agonizing tears and 'bloody' sweat could be seen glistening on his face (Heb. 5:7; Luke 22:44). Gethsemane belied its noted tranquillity that night, because the tunnel through which Jesus was called upon to descend was steep, the events in the garden just the beginning.

Death's 'pains' were felt in Gethsemane, but they had their source in another garden long before. In Eden, Adam understood only too well what 'death' is, on two levels, the physical and the theological (Gen. 2:17). He and Eve were driven from the Creator's company because of it (Gen. 3:24). Death is not merely the closing of the eyes for the final time, but the realm into which Adam led mankind (1 Cor. 15:21), and from where there is no possibility of escape except on God's terms (Exod. 33:19). It is a kingdom without gates, the boundaries of which are beyond the reach of man and with walls so high they can never be scaled, although the attempt is often fruitlessly made (John 10:1).

Brave or foolish men, ignorant of what lies ahead, may boast that they do not fear dying, but the realm of death harbours only ultimate terror (Matt. 5:29-30). Nothing worse can be envisaged than to die in one's sins, having rejected, or having been indifferent to, the claims of this extraordinary person, Christ Jesus (John 8:24). Awaiting just beyond time's frontiers is an encasement in everlasting flames, without help of any kind, not even a meagre 'comfort' of knowing many others are in the same situation. The occupant of hell sees no one else, suffering only an eternal and solitary desolation (Luke 16:23-24).

Liberating his chosen people, therefore, from this appalling dilemma was the most sublime expression of love there could be (John 15:13). He, and he alone (Acts 4:12), was in the position to fulfil the task (John 17:4). Calvary was the venue, the appointed trysting-place, where the righteousness of God embraced the peace with him that the situation demanded (Ps. 85:10; Rom. 5:1). There on the mound he suffered the excruciation of his body and soul, more than anyone could. His soul plummeted to the depths of the everlasting fires of divine fury provoked by humanity's sin (Mark 9:44; 1 John 2:2). No greater 'pain' could he have endured, the depth of anguish unimaginable as he lay under the curse of the broken law (Deut. 21:23; Gal. 3:10,13) in the process of proclaiming liberty to his captive people (Isa. 61:1).

Heaven's warrior had invaded the kingdom of death in single combat, stirring his foe to wage its final war, and at first glance appeared to have been overwhelmed — the mighty Lion of Judah no more than a mangled Lamb! (Rev. 5:5-6). But defeat was not the object in view, nor were Satan and his forces permitted a last laugh (John 14:30); rather the noblest of all victories was realized and in the most paradoxical of ways: the Creator arrested by his creatures (Mark 14:53); the Judge of mankind 'tried' before men (John 5:22; Matt. 26:62); the Lord of glory crucified (1 Cor. 2:8); the sinless Prince of life 'made ... sin' and slain (Acts 3:15; 2 Cor. 5:21); not least, the tomb inhabited by the custodian of hell and of death itself (Rev. 1:18), his flesh bruised and bloodied lying in solemn stillness on a cold slab (Matt. 27:59-60).

He was in the place to which death leads all its citizens — something over which they have no control, the grave being the destination least likely to have been chosen by them (1 Cor. 15:32). Yet, in identifying himself with those for whom he laid down his life (John 10:18), the Author of life selected willingly to share their death and its terrors (Acts 3:15; Heb. 2:14-15), that they in return might share his life and its joys. What more reliable proof could they receive that this was so than by his demonstrating his lordship over the darkness of death? (Rom. 4:25; 1 Peter 3:19).

For those hours that Christ's body lay silent in the tomb (Ps. 16:10), Joseph of Arimathea's garden was the centre of the universe, with creation holding its breath in anticipation of the expected glory to be revealed. Resurrection from the realm of the dead was the pivot around which, quite literally, everything, both eternal and temporal, revolved. The integrity and relevance, even the reality, of the Godhead was at stake; the inability to triumph over the 'finality' of death would reduce Jesus, his atonement, the incarnation, the creation by divine fiat and the entire panoply of grace, to a fraudulent level (1 Cor. 15:12-19).

The sepulchre in the quiet corner of the garden was, therefore, heaven's opportunity to illustrate to an unbelieving world that its prince is a liar (John 14:30; 8:44), and the power of darkness by no means invincible (Col. 1:13). The eternal counsel moved then towards the desired aim, operating with the expected harmonious perfection: the Father's glorious power (Rom. 6:42; Cor. 13:4), the Son's resurrection life (John 10:17; 11:25) and the Spirit's life-giving efficiency (Rom. 8:11; 1 Peter 3:18). Had not this been the promise for a thousand years? (Acts 2:25; Ps. 16). The demonstration was conclusive, the debate divinely closed, leaving only blasphemous unbelief to disagree.

For the one who had filled the cosmos with life (Ps. 148), nothing could have been more simple than to empty the tomb of death — any tomb, every grave, and even the smallest pile of human ashes. No one should expect other than that, by the same triune power and grace by which the redeemed are raised from soul-death (Eph. 2:1-3) to eternal life (John 5:24). Nor should anyone 'marvel' when the trumpet-blast of Christ's voice (Rev. 1:10) is eventually heard irresistibly summoning everyone to judgement (John 5:28). Truly, the thoughts of the Highest transcend those of both devils and men (Isa. 55:8-9).

Resting in hope

By this time, Peter was warming to his theme and may well have been astonished that, such was the Spirit's presence, the crowds had made no attempt to halt his flow of words, convicting though they were. Even the priests had not sought to intervene, as they did at a later date (Acts 4:1-2), presumably because the listeners were so riveted to the spot that they were unable to push their way through to where the preacher was standing.

Peter's special anointing had provided him with great wisdom. Despite having been associated with Jesus of Nazareth, he made no mention of himself, apart from testifying very briefly that he and the other apostles had actually seen their risen Lord (Acts 2:32). All that mattered to him was the proclamation of Christ, ascended and exalted, and in unfolding his theme to his vast audience there was no more attractive way of doing it than by referring to national heroes.

Peter could merely have spoken of 'the prophet' and 'the psalmist' (Acts 2:16,25) without mentioning their names; this would have been enough in itself to underline to Jewish ears the solemnity of his words (Luke 24:27), but the mention of

Joel and David immediately brought their messages closer to the listeners' hearts. This was especially so of David, 'the man who was raised up on high, the anointed of the God of Jacob, and the sweet psalmist of Israel' (2 Sam. 23:1). Every recess of the land was proud to call David its own, the legendary warrior and king, hero in each Israelite home and bedtime story. It was therefore fitting that 'David speaketh concerning' the one who answered to the title 'Son of David' (Acts 2:25; Matt. 22:42).

It was not as hero, though, that David was mentioned, but as one to whom a remarkable revelation had been given. One day the king was approached by Nathan the prophet with some astonishing news from heaven, which so staggered David that he 'sat' before God in prayer, unable to stand, overcome by profound unworthiness (2 Sam. 7:18-20). The message was threefold: his 'house' (family tree), his kingdom and his throne would last for ever! (2 Sam. 7:16).

Only monarchs sit on thrones, but what royal figure would grace an eternal throne? Only one could: the King of all kings, the Lord of all lords (Rev. 19:16), God himself 'manifest in flesh' (1 Tim. 3:16), the Messiah (Zech. 6:12-13). Who will not envy the citizen of the everlasting kingdom over which this King rules, before whom all creatures will one day bow? (Phil. 2:10; Dan. 7:14). From then on, David could gaze out over Israel from Jerusalem's bulwarks and his heart would be saying, 'Thine is the kingdom, and the power, and the glory, for ever' (Matt. 6:13).

Heaven's intention, then, was to break through into time and history (2 Sam. 7:26), and it would do so through David's lineage (Ruth 4:17-22). Centuries earlier, the patriarch Jacob understood that 'Shiloh' would be associated with Judah (Gen. 49:10), and many years afterwards Micah the prophet was able to point to the very town in Judea from where the Messiah would arise. It would be in Bethlehem, David's home town

(Micah 5:21; cf. 1 Sam. 16:1). Small wonder that the Queen of Sheba travelled so far to visit his son Solomon, to whom he had passed on the news (1 Kings 8:24-27), his fame 'concerning the name of the LORD' being widespread. The 'hard questions' were of a spiritual nature (Solomon's 'wisdom'), not an economic one, and the queen's joyous testimony at the time was applicable: 'The half was not told me' (1 Kings 10:1-10). That was reason enough for Satan, through the daughter of Ahab and Jezebel, to attempt the destruction of 'all the seed royal' (2 Kings 11:1).

Every Jew in the land was familiar with the account, harboured proudly for a thousand years within Judaism's precious inheritance; this was a good moment, therefore, for Peter to use it as a solid basis for his argument. Nobody — except perhaps the Sadducees whose 'Bible' was limited to the Pentateuch and who cared little about spiritual issues (Acts 23:8) and less about the belief in a Messianic hope — would have dared to dispute that God had 'sworn with an oath' to the heroic patriarch (Acts 2:30). But the Spirit opened up fresh vistas of understanding to those who packed Jerusalem's streets that morning, and to the world as a whole, revealing even more clearly why David had reason to be amazed.

Only an intelligent evaluation of two psalms (Ps. 16; 110), both penned by him, was required to illustrate the point. Great and highly honoured man though he was, declared by Jehovah to be a man after his own heart (Acts 13:22; 1 Sam. 13:14), it could never be said that David 'always' set the Lord before him (Ps. 16:8) Even children were familiar with the stories of the times he turned his head away, most notoriously his conduct towards Bathsheba and her husband Uriah (2 Sam. 11), culminating movingly in tears of repentance (Ps. 32; 51).

However, despite his sins and shortcomings, over the 'sweet psalmist' (2 Sam. 23:1) there was draped the mantle of prophecy, a supernatural clarity of vision, enabling him to see beyond the boundaries of the here and now into eternal mystery. A voice was heard, not for the first time (Ps. 16:8-11; 2:7-9; Acts 4:25), as the Holy One, sent to earth under a covenant arrangement (Ps. 40:7-8; Heb. 10:7) to suffer from the cradle to the cross (Rev. 12:4; Matt. 26:38), nevertheless poetically 'embroidered' a rich tapestry of glorious joy. With Jehovah at his right hand and the 'Shekinah' glory of the Spirit's anointing upon him (Exod. 40:34; Isa. 61:1-2; Luke 4:17-18), his ministry as Prophet, Priest and King (Deut. 18:15; Heb. 9:24-26; Rev. 19:16) can no more fail than God can sin (Acts 2:25).

David understood, as Peter did after him (Acts 2:29), that the poetic scenario contained no place for him. At the age of seventy (2 Sam. 5:4), his years having been spent as a mere fleeting 'shadow' (1 Chron. 29:15), the great king went 'the way of all the earth' (B.C. 972) and was buried in the city named after him (1 Kings 2:1-2,10). Over his corpse was erected a sepulchre, and as it was still in existence a thousand years later when the apostle referred to it (Acts 2:29), it was evidently one worthy of such a hero. There was, however, no doubting the certainty that death would have swiftly consumed the king's frail body (1 Kings 1:1).

The 'Son of David' (Ezek. 34:23), however, was carried to his tomb when only about thirty-three years of age, and at the time of his arrest had been an extremely strong man. His ancestor the King of Israel had been buried with much pomp and ceremony, attended by a large retinue of priests, government officials, high-ranking military men, courtiers, members of his family and numerous servants; the Holy One of Israel, on the other hand, was removed from Calvary to the garden tomb by a handful of men, and watched by two loyal women (Matt. 27:61). The contrast could not have been much sharper; the sinful monarch paraded to his own expensive sepulchre, and the spotless Monarch of all monarchs carried in poverty to another's tomb (2 Cor. 8:9). True 'wealth', however, is measured, not by a standard of living, but by a spiritual confidence in dying. The possession of a crown has worth only if one is a 'jewel' encrusted in it (2 Tim. 4:6-8; Mal. 3:17).

As the king awaited his passing therefore, solemnity would have gripped his thoughts, with past thanksgivings and gospel proclamations more in evidence than the anticipation of future bliss: 'What profit is there in my blood, when I go down to the pit? Shall the dust praise thee? Shall it declare thy truth?' (Ps. 30:9). This attitude was typical of the Jewish mind (Ps. 88:10-11). Another king, Hezekiah was later to declare: 'The grave cannot praise thee, death can not celebrate thee... The living, he shall praise thee...' (Isa. 38:18-19).

Peter's audience would have recognized David's anguish when he wrote, 'In death there is no remembrance of thee: in the grave who shall give thee thanks?' (Ps. 6:5), and would have shared in the gloom surrounding the stealth of death's inevitable approach. The Holy One, however, about whom David wrote, although also of Jewish stock, was clearly not of that ilk. He viewed his death with confidence, actually taking 'hope' with him to his resting-place! (Acts 2:26). This reminder from their Scriptures, particularly from the writings of David (Ps. 16:9), would have stirred the crowds to a fresh fascination. What hope could be found in the cold isolation of death?

What occurred next rocked Jerusalem and, the message not having changed since that morning in A.D. 29, the world as a whole in each generation has received its warning. Temple worship (mere religious formality), which came to an abrupt end forty-one years later, in A.D. 70, when Rome laid siege to the city, had reached the end of the road. The Sadducees seethed with anger (Acts 4:1-3; 5:17), the Pharisees feared for Israel (Acts 5:34-35) and the people were alarmed for their ultimate safety, crying out, 'What shall we do?' (Acts 2:37). The answer was self-evident: 'Repent, and be baptized ... in the name of Jesus Christ for the remission of sins, and ye shall receive the gift of the Holy Ghost' (v. 38).

The entrance to the tomb

As Peter reached the climax of his sermon (Acts 2:29-36), it was clear a major impact had already been made upon everyone within hearing and that mighty truths had been unfolded in relation to Jewish Scripture, contemporary history and eternal doctrine. The Spirit had lighted upon each stage of Jesus' ministry: his blessed life of miracles (v. 22), his pre-determined death by crucifixion (v. 23) and his resurrection through the power of God, which is presented as a statement of fact (v. 24). He was indeed the long-awaited Messiah.

Thus far, the people had been led fascinatingly to the entrance of the tomb, an experience both thrilling and convicting. Now it was time for everyone to look inside, to grapple with mysteries which had baffled Peter himself only a short while before (Luke 24:12), and there were many of them, accompanying the rumours which circulated in the city, and beyond.

From within the tomb

There had been the empty tomb, the corpse which no one could find, the stories about Jesus appearing in various places and holding conversations with those closest to him; now another one was added to the list — his confidence in the face of death, the most dreaded of all enemies. The questions were numerous, each one leading to many more. What did it all mean?

In answering the unspoken queries, Peter pointed in the direction of King David's sepulchre (Acts 2:29), such a popular site that no visitor to Jerusalem would have had any difficulty in finding it. But if David had been buried a thousand years earlier, although his memory was alive and well, there could be no disputing the fact that his 'dust' now mingled freely with the earth. Mighty monarch though he was, there

was no escaping the inevitable, as it affects both king and com-
moner; his body had putrefied, 'dust to dust' (Gen. 2:7).

Over the garden tomb, however, there hovered a solemn
promise first heard in heaven, revealed to David (Acts 2:30;
Ps. 16:10-11) and of which Jesus was aware (Matt. 16:21).
Nothing could hinder it from being fulfilled, however craftily
or viciously it was opposed (Matt. 27:63-64; Luke 13:32).
Confidence was assured; Christ could 'rest in hope' (Ps. 16:9).
His body would not remain in the solitary confinement of the
dark grave. A glorious physical resurrection was implied, a
truth which Jesus had openly taught (Matt. 16:21).

There was also something else. His enemies believed they
had rid themselves of the Galilean when they killed him and
sealed his body in the tomb. Lifeless though it was when removed from Skull Hill, and hopeless though the situation appeared to his disciples as they sat in gloom or scurried around
in alarm, there was nothing to fear. Their Lord carried a secret
with him to his death: he knew his flesh was incapable of de-
composing and his body of failing to rise. How could man
hope to foil the plan of God (Ps. 16:10), imprison the Son of
man in a tomb (Matt. 27:64-65), or believe mere rock could
restrain the Creator of the cosmos? Laughter could be heard
in heaven, and still can be, at such audacity (Ps. 2; Acts
4:23-28).

Exalted to the highest

But the strands of the promise numbered five, not two; three
more were to be fulfilled, and each one more wonderfully positive than its neighbour (Ps. 16:11). While pinioned to the cross
in the throes of death, even when his anguish was at its most
excruciating, the Prince of life and Lord over death (Acts 3:15;
Rev. 1:18) held fast to his secret. Gazing through the blackness
of the skies, he anticipated the brilliance of light. He had no

need to possess David's dismal dread of death (Ps. 30:9). His secret promised more, much more, which he shared with Calvary's most privileged 'guest'. In the briefest and most tender of moments, the whisper was heard by the repentant thief: 'Today shalt thou be with me in paradise' (Luke 23:43). Beyond the bruises and the blood, the tears (Heb. 5:7) and the tomb, he knew there lay a 'pathway' paved with hope upon which he would ride in triumph (S. of S. 3:9-10) towards the brightest of futures — abundance of 'life' (plural), resurrection! (John 5:26; Ps. 16:11).

The 'path' was short, the journey brief, from the vacant tomb to the cloud of glory (Acts 1:9). The Son was returning home to his Father (John 17:24), who was always 'well pleased' with him (Matt. 3:17), and whose 'delight' he had for ever been (Prov. 8:30). There everlasting bliss blossoms (Ps. 16:11), time with its trials cannot venture (Heb. 12:2; 2 Cor. 4:18), and the sounds of thanksgiving resound throughout the heavens: 'Worthy is the Lamb that was slain to receive power, and riches, and wisdom, and strength, and honour, and glory, and blessing' (Rev. 5:12). This was no prodigal setting out to return humbly to a waiting Father (Luke 15:18-20), but a Son whose arduous mission had been triumphantly accomplished (John 17:4). Joy would abound.

But there was still a fifth and final dimension to the promise, the secret buried with the custodian, the impact of which, when unfolded by the apostle Peter, shocked Jerusalem with its grandeur and retains its ability to disturb even more so in modern times within a multi-faith society. It concerned the 'pleasures' to be discovered at the right hand of God (Ps. 16:11): the joyous wonder of everlastingly beholding his face (Acts 2:28), and experiencing its radiation of grace and peace lovingly reciprocated (Num. 6:25-26).

But to whom do these 'pleasures' belong? Clearly to one who in his ascension to glory has the authority to stand on such a sacred spot, and to appear in the exquisite brilliance of

perfect light (Heb. 1:3; 1 John 1:5); the one who shares equally
in the very nature of God himself (John 10:30), is therefore
sinless (John 8:46) and who harbours all truth in his person
(John 1:14; 18:37). Such a one can make the highest claims
upon everyone, without appearing foolish or a figure of fun,
confidently proclaiming himself as the only pathway to God
(John 14:6), whom it is the ultimate folly to reject (John 8:24).

Which, therefore, of all the world's religious leaders could
qualify, being mindful of the 'thieves and robbers' who his-
torically preceded the Galilean carpenter? (John 10:8; 14:6).
Sin clouded their lives, and truth was groped after within the
darkened limitations of the cultural climate of their times. These
were not candidates for such heights; far from it, except as
those who desired the usurpation of heaven's throne. In fact,
their final resting-place will be beneath the foot, and under the
footstool, of the one who sits at the right hand of God (Acts
2:34-35; 1 Cor. 15:25; cf. Josh. 10:24), where everlasting
'pleasures' are to be found (Ps. 16:11). There they will cower,
abjectly submissive, in complete subjection to the one whom
they will at last admit to be 'Lord' over all (Phil. 2:11).

Referred to by David as 'my Lord' *('Adonai')* (Ps. 110:1),
adored by myriads of angelic hosts (Ps. 104:4; Heb. 1:6), and
ushered by Jehovah himself to the highest pinnacle of glory
(Exod. 15:6), this exalted person, resplendent in majesty, is
everlastingly seated upon the great white throne of grace (Rev.
20:11; John 17:24). Who therefore was better qualified than
he to release the 'rushing mighty wind' of the Spirit, as promised by the Father (John 14:26), to the citizens of Jerusalem
and to the entire world? (Acts 2:2,33).

He is creation's Judge (John 5:27), while, as King-Priest
(Zech. 6:12-13), he is also his people's compassionate intercessor (Heb. 7:25). Adorned with the victor's crown, the 'orb'
of world dominion clasped in one hand (Dan. 7:14) and the
'sceptre' of perfect righteousness in the other (Heb. 1:8; Ps.

45:6; Acts 2:34-35), he invites his redeemed elect to share his glory (Rev. 3:21). And, permission having been granted, without reserve they boldly advance upon the throne (Heb. 4:16), a royal nation of holy priests (Rev. 1:6; 1 Peter 2:9); washed in precious blood, dressed in imputed righteousness (2 Cor. 5:21) and bathed in glory (Rev. 19:14-16). No greater honour could heaven have afforded them, and it is one which has its roots profoundly embedded within the eternal counsel of the Godhead (Eph. 1).

So, who is this exalted figure? The one whom they carried to a tomb, and whose secret lay with his body silently within, waiting confidently for the events to follow in accordance with what had been planned before time — resurrection, ascension and glory. How could circumstances, or man, hope to gain a victory over the one who is 'both Lord and Christ'? (Acts 2:36).

Epilogue:
The Visitor

A shimmering haze hovered over the blue Aegean sea towards the distant horizon, the placid water steaming under the blazing sun, solitary in an azure sky. It was likely that, far from shore, sweltering fishermen plied their trade, heaving in the nets, their boats gently swaying from side to side. The scene was picturesque, untroubled, and in sharp contrast to life on the rocky isle of Patmos which overlooked it.

There, just off the coast of Asia Minor, in or around A.D. 96, men suffered in the broiling heat under the Roman lash in one of Emperor Domitian's penal colonies. Claiming deity for himself, the emperor demanded acknowledgement of it from his many subjects throughout the empire, and those brave enough to defy him fell foul of the Roman establishment. This was especially so of those claiming Christ as their Lord and God. If not actually executed, they were banished to uninviting locations, such as this island, where conditions were harsh.

The old man of the island

Among the prisoners was a very old man called John, who was, undoubtedly, the most remarkable person on the island. Even his Roman captors would have thought so. It was not only his great age — there was even a rumour circulating that he would never die (John 21:20-23) — but because he was his Lord's only surviving apostle, nearly seventy years after the events at Calvary. As such, Rome considered John's influence over the Christian communities in Asia Minor far too potent for it to be allowed to continue (Rev. 1:9). Thus he found himself isolated, accepting the fact that he would spend what remained of his life in lonely exile.

If on Patmos John looked forward to glory (John 17:24), he also looked back upon grace (John 1:14), having gazed upon and touched the hem of divine mystery (1 John 1:1). Memories were his constant companion, and Jesus would have been central to them all, the Christ upon whose breast he lay on that last evening together before the horror on Skull Hill and to whose cross he was drawn (John 13:25; 19:26). He, who as a young man searched the water for fish, was later to penetrate the mysteries for truth, a favourite theme of his (3 John 4). At one time a 'son of thunder' and in possession of grandiose notions (Mark 3:17; Matt. 20:20-21), this 'apostle of love' had nevertheless been in close proximity to the majesty of the Son of God (Matt. 17:1-2; 2 Peter 1:16). He little realized he would experience it again, this side of glory (John 17:24).

The astonishment

Later John recalled what happened (Rev. 1:10). There would have been few places on the island, if any, where prisoners would have been permitted to go to enjoy peace and quiet. Perhaps being of great age the apostle was made an exception, and as it was 'the Lord's day', he took advantage of the opportunity. Turning aside from the squalor and hardship of prison life, he found solace where every Christian would in his situation, in prayer and contemplation, and at the safest of venues — 'in the Spirit'. Clearly, his was a prayer life of substance and spiritual intensity, lessons learned at the Master's feet (Luke 11:1).

It was during this precious fellowship that something remarkable occurred and, John being careful about detail, he recorded that it happened behind him. In fact, he mentioned this fact three times (Rev. 1:10,12). From this it can be deduced that he was probably facing out towards the wide-open stretch of sea, which symbolized in its expanse the freedom he yearned after, and beyond which lay his beloved Ephesus and the other six Christian communities of Asia Minor for which he prayed so earnestly (Rev. 2-3).

Suddenly, the aura of meditative silence, which had wrapped itself around him like a cloak, was stripped away by a blast of sound so powerful it must have rivalled that first heard on Sinai (Exod. 19:19). Certainly John felt so, for trumpeting 'voices' were heard on both occasions, and no doubt he 'feared and quaked' as much as Moses had done when they made their presence felt (Heb. 12:19-21).

At first, the shock would, understandably, have left John frozen into immobility, as his mind sought to come to terms with what was happening. Moses had at least some inkling of the trauma that was to follow (Exod.19:14-18), but the apostle was not given that opportunity. He just remained rooted to the spot, while the loud voice continued, heralding the fact that heaven had burst into time uninvited and unexpectedly.

It was unlikely that John recognized the voice immediately, despite its being one that once, long ago, had been very familiar to him; the suddenness with which it had penetrated his contemplation would have seen to that. If Cleopas and his friend had not recognized this voice shortly after the crucifixion (Luke 24:13-35), it was not surprising that decades later

John should not know it at first — that is, until revelation inspired reminiscence.

As if to remind the faithful old apostle, like the crash of thunder directly overhead and as fearful to hear, the 'great voice' began its message with the most significant of all expressions: 'I AM', the name of Almighty God himself, first revealed to Moses on the day of his call to be the leader of the Hebrews. He was commanded on that momentous occasion to tell them, 'I AM hath sent me unto you' (Exod. 3:14). Now, on the isle of Patmos, that name above every name was heard once more: 'I AM Alpha and Omega, the first and the last...' (Rev. 1:11).

For John, it clarified memories of much earlier times. The mighty city of Jerusalem in his younger days, his beloved Lord teaching captivated audiences in the temple precincts, the antagonistic priests, and that startling moment when Jesus astounded the assembly with words so 'blasphemous' the hearers were aghast, unable to believe their ears: 'Before Abraham was, I AM' (John 8:58). Stones had been thrown that day.

The sight of 'I AM'[1]

John would surely have been hesitant to turn around to confront the glory he knew lay behind him; in fact it was so glorious that he did not expect to see a face. Had not God said, 'There shall no man see me, and live'? (Exod. 33:20). He believed the voice was the nearest he could come to the being of the triune God (Rev. 1:12). Even to hear God's voice would in itself have been an honour above and beyond what most experience this side of eternity, for 'Who is there of all flesh, that hath heard the voice of the living God ... and lived?' (Deut. 5:26). John shared Moses' wonder.

If he looked behind him, what would he see? But his expectancy was limited, hoping only to 'see the voice', and nothing else (Rev. 1:12). All those years before, in Joseph of Arimathea's garden, Mary of Magdala had also heard a voice. She too had turned around and received the most wonderful of surprises (John 20:16). John was now about to experience something which far transcended a mere surprise.

Slowly, hesitantly, fearfully and scarcely daring to draw breath, he turned. He was on the point of seeing the one whose name is 'I AM'! But what would that mean? What would he see? How would he see? Was it possible to see, and would he live, having 'seen' even just the voice of the Almighty? (Deut. 5:26). John's mind must have been a kaleidoscope of unrelated thoughts, as it wrestled with the enormity of the experience. He was like one hurtling through space seeking solid ground upon which to rest his feet, yet spinning on a whirligig of seemingly endless queries. Had it been only seconds since the voice had first shaken his silent, prayerful contemplation? It surely must have seemed very much longer than that.

But, what a shock! Having turned, what greeted him was not the voice, but a vision of candlesticks! (Rev. 1:12). At first it must have appeared incongruous to him. Candlesticks? True, they were not ordinary candlesticks, but made of gold — the most precious of all materials — and there were seven of them — the most significant of all numbers, considered biblically as ideal (Gen. 2:2). However, any disappointment John may have felt initially was soon made up for as he came to understand the symbolic significance of his vision. As the golden seven-branched candlestick had stood in the holy place of the tabernacle (Exod. 25:31-37), and later in the temple in Jerusalem (1 Kings 7:49), signifying that Christ is the light of the world (John 12:46), what John now saw reflected that brilliance. The seven churches over which he had such an influence (Rev. 1:11), and which were so central to his heart and mind, were the beacons shining for the gospel throughout Asia Minor (Matt. 5:14-16). Furthermore, although John was absent from them by an enforced imprisonment, God had not forgotten them. On the contrary, collectively they bore his number (Rev. 4:5) and were to him as precious as 'gold'.

But where was the voice? It was the very least John had expected to communicate with, but it was silent. Instead, like Nebuchadnezzar five centuries earlier, who looked into a certain 'fiery furnace' and witnessed an astonishing miracle (Dan. 3:24-25), John also looked beyond the immediate and saw mystery. Within the fire had stood the Son of God, comforting and rescuing, and here at the centre of the Asian churches stood the Son of man, encouraging and rebuking (Rev. 1:13). Both were extraordinary moments to savour.

After a while old John was able to assess more objectively what he had seen, and whom. It was definitely Jesus, not as he had been whilst hanging on that cross almost seven decades before, bloodied and bruised, nor even as he had looked to John and his friends when mysteriously he 'appeared' after his resurrection (Luke 24:36), but now even more glorious, resplendent with the most exquisite beauty of all, the splendour of deity victoriously vindicated. Just think, John had looked for a voice, and instead met God himself!

It would have taken a little time for him to focus upon the radiance which met his gaze, but gradually his grasp of the situation clarified. There must surely have been a gasp, a sudden intake of breath, for he could scarcely believe what his eyes were telling him he was seeing. In fact, his mind took a little longer to register. Now here was a marvellous revelation, a breathtaking realization. The beginning ('Alpha') and the ending ('Omega') of all things (Rev. 1:11), the *raison d'être* for all existence within the cosmos (Col. 1:15-19), was standing in front of him and he found himself looking at a man! (Rev. 1:13). True, this was not just any man, but the Son of man (Dan. 7:9-14) whose Messianic appeal had spanned the centuries since the dawn of history (Gen. 3:15); nevertheless it was a man for all that: the Prophet (Deut. 18:15), the Priest (Zech. 6:12-13) and the King (Rev. 19:16).

The man

There was no doubting who it was. After all, they had been cousins, their mothers being sisters (John 19:25-26). John would have recognized his face, the voice and the build of the one he had known so well when a young man. Now here he was once more. Yet the obvious difference in his Lord's appearance, and the solemnity of the occasion, forbade an eager embrace. In the upper room that final evening together nearly seventy years earlier, John had leant his head affectionately against Jesus' chest (John 13:25), but now there was only one suitable reaction. The aged apostle fell to the ground, as Moses had done in the presence of Almighty God (Exod. 34:8), in the spirit of abject devotion. (Rev. 1:17). At that moment, John was given a glimpse of what humanity will experience when it rises to judgement (2 Cor. 5:10).

To begin with, the apostle found himself face to face with one with whom he could identify. He was not looking at a being outside of his realm, or completely devoid of his experience. The imperfect man was confronted with the perfect man, the God-man (Rev. 1:13). When sinners (of all religions or none at all) are called to the bar of judgement and face the God-man, they will be made aware of the stark reality of what it means to 'have sinned and come short of the glory of God' (Rom. 3:23). Man was originally a beautiful creature, made 'a little lower than the angels' and crowned with 'glory and honour' (Ps. 8:4-9), but tragically he fell and was driven from the presence of the Creator (Gen. 3:24).

Nothing short of perfection is what God has always demanded from his human creatures (Matt. 5:48), but failure is writ large across their lives, and the Ten Commandments underline that fact (Exod. 20:1-17). Those who die in their sins (John 8:24), unregenerate rebels, are cast unwillingly (Luke 12:20) into the immediate presence of the one described as 'the blessed and only Potentate, the King of kings, and Lord of lords', whose qualifications are immaculate, 'dwelling in the light which no man can approach unto; whom no man hath seen nor can see, to whom be honour and power everlasting' (1 Tim. 6:15-16; Exod. 33:20). The plight of those who fall unredeemed into the hands of the one who is in essence 'a consuming fire' is indeed fearful (Heb. 12:29).

The torment experienced in hell is the eternal awareness of the failure to meet the requirements (Matt. 5:29-30). God has rejected these people — unreservedly, finally, everlastingly. There is no possibility of mercy (Mark 9:43-50). In hell there is, as it were, the holding of heads and the gnashing of teeth, weeping and wailing (Matt. 25:29-31), hopeless despair. The bleakness is made more intense when the lost have eternally before them a view of what they could have been (Luke 16:23), and what those who are 'accepted in the beloved' (Eph. 1:6) will for ever enjoy. The former were often warned by the latter, but no notice was taken (Luke 16:27-31).

The condemnation is just. The God-man has entered the world. He was 'made flesh' (John 1:14) and identified himself with man. In order to illustrate this, Jesus employed an expression often mentioned in the New Testament, and did so most famously during his trial before the Sanhedrin — 'the Son of man' (Matt. 26:64). Ezekiel frequently heard God referring to him in this way (e.g. Ezek. 2:1; 3:1), in other words, as an 'ordinary man' (Ps. 8:4).

Who better to judge mankind than the ideal man (John 5:22), man as the Creator intended him to be? Daniel saw this same

Son of man being invested with absolute authority over 'all people, nations, and languages' (Dan. 7:13-14). He is the King of an unshakeable and glorious kingdom. All people live and die. All nations rise and fall. All languages flourish and wane, but this man, the appointed Judge of mankind (John 5:27), is King eternal.

The heart of the Priest

What attracted John's attention next was his Lord's clothing (Rev. 1:13). The rough outer garment, which had seen hard wear as Jesus strode the length and breadth of Israel, and beyond, during his three-year ministry, had faded away decades before in Roman hands. The robe, around which legends have grown, was carried from Calvary by a legionary who won it in a lottery (John 19:23-24). But now practicality had given way to spirituality, the bloodied 'coat' to shimmering splendour, the gruesome crucifixion to ascension majesty. Resplendent in the royal robe of heaven, the Prince of Peace (Isa. 9:6) had visited his imprisoned apostle (Rev. 1:9).

But the significance of what John had observed could not have escaped him; the golden breastplate would have seen to that. He would have cast his mind back to the days of Aaron, the first high priest, when the Hebrews wandered in the wilderness (Exod. 28). Having anointed, consecrated and sanctified his servant, God adorned him, and his priestly sons, with articles of clothing 'for glory and for beauty' befitting his remarkable role typifying the one before whom John now bowed.

Aaron had been dressed in symbolism, from the mitre bearing the noble inscription 'Holiness to the LORD', to the little golden bells hanging from the hem of his robe, which tinkled as he went about his duties, heralding each movement within the tabernacle's most holy place beyond the sight of man (Exod.

28:33-36). When that occurred, once annually on the Day of Atonement (Lev. 16), he too had worn a breastplate. Here mysteriously, through the 'Urim and Thummim', about which mystery remains, God revealed his commands (Exod. 28:30; Lev. 8:8).

But more importantly for the sinner, as Aaron carried six tribal names on each shoulder, engraved on two onyx stones, the breastplate was also representative of the Israelite tribes. Twelve precious, colourful jewels of differing kinds, neatly arranged in four rows of three apiece, encrusted this 'girdle' of gold. It must have caused sighs of relief to ascend sky-high. The people understood that Aaron was appearing before the God of Israel on their behalf, 'bearing their judgement' and their burdens (Exod. 28:30; Isa. 53:4), each individual carried, not in his head, but upon his heart 'continually'. It was a significant reminder that Jehovah was not just thinking about them, but loved them everlastingly (Deut. 7:7-8; Jer. 31:3).

As John gazed at his Lord, anointed in 'the glory and beauty' of all the perfections, Old Testament shadows faded into irrelevance in the 'marvellous light' of New Testament realities (1 Peter 2:9). They had played their part, but were no longer required. Priests, altars, and sacrifices of various kinds had all sunk for ever in the oceans of irrelevance, and from then on any of them still left bobbing about on the surface would merely be counterfeit (Heb. 9-10).

Over six decades earlier the apostle had witnessed a remarkable scene, his Lord's ascension to heaven. If there was 'great joy' and jubilation then (Luke 24:50-53), when his grasp of what God had accomplished was limited, in the period following Pentecost how overcome with awe he must have been! As he had once heard Peter declare, in circumstances which called for extreme courage, 'Neither is there salvation in any other: for there is none other name under heaven given among men, whereby we must be saved' (Acts 4:12). Highly exalted by God himself, Jesus is that name (Phil. 2:9), Christ (the Anointed One) his title.

As such he strode triumphantly to the throne of God (Heb. 4:14), with the expanse of heaven sharing in the apostles' worship, thanksgiving and praise (Rev. 5; 7), and took his seat at the right hand of the majesty on high, the great High Priest upon his throne (Heb. 12:2; Zech. 6:12-13). From that authoritative vantage-point he 'ever lives' (Heb. 7:25), the sole mediator between God and man (1 Tim. 2:5). His is the only redemptive act recognized in heaven: the fully sufficient atoning sacrifice (John 19:30); the blood of the everlasting covenant (Matt. 26:28); the gracious intercessor for his people (Heb. 4:14-16); the shoulders bearing their burdens (1 Peter 5:7); and the heart filled with their names (Rev. 20:15). He is 'I AM'.

The head and the hair

John would have been quick to observe something else about his Lord; the whiteness of his head and hair (Rev. 1:14), denoting eternal wisdom and perfect purity. These two virtues, wisdom and purity, have seldom been married to each other throughout the course of history, but in Christ they are, supremely so.

During his life in the flesh, profound suffering in his spirit had robbed him of physical attractions. The weight of responsibilities, the controversy, the hatred, the burden of soul — all guaranteed that there would be 'no beauty that we should desire him' (Isa. 53:2). In fact, his opponents considered him twenty years older than he actually was (John 8:57). Later, in the hands of the Romans notorious for their cruelty, Jesus' face had undergone vile treatment. Not only had it been hit and spat upon, but sharp thorns had slashed into the skin until it was blood-red. The prophecy is descriptive: 'I gave my back to the smiters, and my cheeks to them that plucked off the hair: I hid not my face from shame and spitting' (Isa. 50:6).

But all that was past. On Patmos, John realized he was looking at the personification of wisdom, the revelation of the mind and heart of God (John 1:18). Little wonder the apostle wept profusely (Rev. 5:1-4). Who is worthy even to cast a glance at Almighty God, to penetrate ultimate truth, to open 'the book' containing the secrets of heaven? Man certainly has no claim to do so. It cannot be wrenched with filthy hands from the divine grasp (Ps. 24:3-4), to be examined by intellects bathed in sin. Yet, had 'the book' not been opened, even if only partially (Deut. 29:29), only everlasting darkness would have remained. Salvation, even civilization, would have failed to exist. The sons of men owe everything to the Son of man (Dan. 7:9-14).

Does man desire to know God, to have some understanding of what he thinks or feels, if only a little of what it is permissible to know? (Deut. 29:29). Then it is to Christ alone he must go (John 1:14,18). His was the voice of Wisdom heard in eternity: 'I was set up from everlasting, from the beginning, or ever the earth was. When there were no depths, I was brought forth; when there were no fountains abounding with water. Before the mountains were settled, before the hills was I brought forth' (Prov. 8:23-25). He is the divine source in which are found 'all the treasures of wisdom and knowledge' (Col. 2:3), the mind behind the universe and the King of academia (1 Cor.1; 2).

Creation's colourful display, the vastness of seemingly limitless space, the sparkling galaxies, the petal on the smallest flower — they all testify to creative wisdom and divine energy (Col. 1:16). He it is who provides intellect and eyesight to the learned, who inhabits scientific laboratories and stands beside the astronomer's telescope, guiding them to 'their discoveries' within his creation. It matters not therefore what avenue of intellectual research is undertaken, or whether he is acknowledged or not; wisdom oversees it all.

How pitiful then that most of those who influence mankind today, being of nature rather than grace (1 Cor. 2:14), are unable to hear his poetic declaration: 'When he prepared the heavens, I was there; when he set a compass upon the face of the depth: when he established the clouds above: when he strengthened the foundations of the deep... Then I was by him, as one brought up with him: and I was daily his delight, rejoicing always before him' (Prov. 8:27-28,30). How foolish, therefore, is man when he thinks he can do without the wisdom of God, seeking even the erasure from his vocabulary of the name of Christ and lurching forward in the belief that this 'cosmic orphan' is wise enough to grope in the deepening darkness without a Father to guide him.

But the signs are not encouraging. Rejection of divine wisdom has produced appalling consequences to the world. Indifference to the Creator has produced a carelessness about his creation. The balance of nature has been irreparably damaged; the seas are dumping grounds for nuclear waste; poisoned fish float on many a river; wild animals are slaughtered for material gain, endangering entire species; rain forests are hacked down with little consideration for the future. The list is growing with the years. The wisdom of God has indeed 'made foolish the wisdom of this world' (1 Cor. 1:20).

The eyes

The Lord's eyes bored into John. Like sun shining on freshly fallen snow, the sight was dazzling. He could not look into the fiery eyes of 'I AM' (Rev. 1:14); nobody could have done so. The one for whom the hosts in heaven were created (Heb.

1:6), and to whom all praise and adoration is eternally directed, has no equal among men (Rev. 4:11; 5:12-14). They are defiled; he is pure. Their realm is 'beneath'; his is 'above' (John 8:23).

Those eyes are the mirrors reflecting the purity of his soul, and therefore a mere glance disturbs and embarrasses the sinner (Luke 22:61), and is enough to cause him to leave the room, or, as when the temple guards approached to arrest him, suddenly fall to the ground, as John did (John 18:6; Rev. 1:17).

Before his Lord spoke, the apostle experienced the searching and probing of every recess of his being. The one whose character fills heaven with holiness demands it also of each individual (Lev. 11:45; Matt. 5:48). Nothing could have been hidden from view, within the light emanating from eyes which scanned his mind and soul (Ps. 11:4). John's cherished privacy — the privacy behind which sinners hide their thoughts and secrete their sinful desires — was all laid bare; everything was open to the penetration of perfect righteousness (Ps. 90:6).

Of course, the eyes of Christ were not always aflame; they were capable of shedding tears too. The sensitivity of his spirit to the glory of his Father and the tenderness of his heart for lost sinners caused him to weep on more than one occasion (John 11:35; Luke 19:41). A profound love welled up inside him for the needy and distressed, and his eyes would have revealed the depth of his compassion. How gracious the gaze must have been, how comforting the glance, how warm the relationship! (Matt.15:30-32; 20:34).

For the 'few' (see Matt. 20:16), that same gracious affection will be evident, but magnified beyond their expectation and certainly beyond their deserving (Isa. 64:4; 1 Cor. 2:9) when, as Jesus promised at his 'trial' (Matt. 26:64), the Son of man makes his triumphant appearance at the consummation of all things (Matt. 24:30). Then, with his smile reflected in his eyes, they will hear assurances more wonderful than they could imagine: 'Come, ye blessed of my Father, inherit the kingdom prepared for you from the foundation of the world' (Matt. 25:34).

But what of the 'many' (Matt. 20:16), who heard the general call to repentance (Acts 17:30) but ignored it? Since God is a 'consuming fire' (Heb. 12:29), they will see eyes that blaze, pouring out flames (Rev. 19:12), and tremble upon hearing that they are 'cursed' in his sight for ever (Matt. 25:41). As fire creates terror in the hearts of those engulfed in it, so the sinner who appears at the bar of judgement knowing nothing of having Christ's righteousness imputed to him (see 2 Cor. 5:21) must face the full fury of holy wrath. It is indeed 'a fearful thing to fall' unsaved 'into the hands of the living God' (Heb. 10:31).

The feet

John lay upon the ground in complete submission to his Lord, and as he did so, could not help but notice the feet of 'I AM'. Although still nail-pierced (Luke 24:39), they possessed the radiance of molten bronze (Rev. 1:15). John did not require any instruction. It was plain what message needed to be learned. Ultimate authority belongs to the Son of man. His feet of bronze, which have left their footprints deep in the soil of humanity, are capable of trampling upon his enemies, whose feet are made of clay.

Many changes had taken place between the dark days of Calvary and the mysterious appearance on Patmos. Then, meek as a lamb, the Lamb of God had been taken to the slaughter without resisting (Isa. 53:4-11). But God had always promised his Son the 'heathen' for his inheritance, and 'the uttermost parts of the earth' for his possession (Ps. 2:8). Now the

Son has been invested with unique authority. He is the pivot around which all peoples and kingdoms revolve and before whom they must bow, whether they wish to or not. He is their only hope, as he is their only Judge (John 5:22).

Created to worship him but having failed to do so, the rebellious enter eternity to confront him, the King of all kings and Lord of all lords. All they have to offer is a life spent refusing to accept his claims, or in serving rivals to them (John 10:1). Those feet will crush every potential usurper to his throne (Rev. 19:11-16). As grapes within a winepress cannot hope to withstand the power, persistence and pressure of trampling feet (Rev. 14:18-20), neither can the eternally lost wriggle out from under those made of bronze.

The voice of the Prophet

There is that voice again! One cannot stand on earth without hearing it. Like the millions of gallons cascading down a giant waterfall, it is impossible to escape its thunderous presence (Rev. 1:15). No part of the globe has escaped. From birth (Luke 1:41) to death (John 8:24), and beyond the grave (John 5:28), the authoritative voice of the Son of man accompanies each citizen of planet Earth.

Not all will recognize the person of Christ behind it, never having heard his name or title, but the voice is 'heard' nevertheless. Have the 'sounds' and marvels of nature not reached them? Are they not familiar, even to the most primitive of peoples — the sky's dome of blue, the luxuriant foliage, the dense forests, the flight of the bird, the strength of the animal? Have not the mysteries of procreation, the cries of an infant and its development, been a source of wonder to even the most savage of tribes? It is a 'voice' from heaven which cannot, and dare not, be discounted (Rom. 1:19-20). Christ created it all, and by his eternal power it is held together (Col. 1:16-17; John 1:1-4).

Where the Christian faith is known, even if only partially, the attempt is made to avoid that voice — to feign indifference to its claims, to mock its warnings, to spurn its overtures of love — but as far as one might roam, that voice is heard (Jer. 23:24). Whether in Sunday school or classroom, college or place of employment, the 'sound of many waters' can be detected somewhere in the background, either fascinating the conscience or deeply disturbing it.

This is the Prophet who caused such turmoil when he strode the land of Israel proclaiming the truth which he had heard in eternity (Deut. 18:15; John 1:17; 8:26). The people were amazed, critical, hateful and divided (Matt. 7:28-29; Luke 7:39; Mark 3:6; John 7:43), but try as they might, they could not be indifferent. Now, standing before the apostle John was the voice of truth (John 14:6), absolute and divine, against which there can be no arguments and which brooks no rivals.

The hand

Until this point, John's spirit had been elevated to the highest pinnacle of all, viewing the exquisite grandeur of the divine — eternal Wisdom, burning holiness, ultimate authority and unrivalled revelation (Rev. 1:14-15). It was a fearful experience, yet a fascinating one, but the only comforting feature for a sinner to behold was the high-priestly garment and that precious and 'golden girdle' of a breastplate worn by this sole mediator between God and man (Rev. 1:13; 1 Tim. 2:5). There lay consolation — in fact the only one — the assurance of reconciliation between the two.

Now, though, something else attracted the elderly apostle's attention — the right hand of the Son of man, which denotes authority and divine power (Heb. 12:2; Exod. 15:6,12). Without doubt, John would have been comforted to see it, because it clasped 'seven stars' (Rev. 1:16), not in wrath's crushing embrace, but with love's assured protection (John 10:29). The apostle knew immediately, without need of words, the message he was receiving, one which must have given him great joy — that the 'angels' or pastors of his beloved seven churches in Asia Minor (the very precious 'golden candlesticks' of light in a dark world — Rev. 1:12,20) were safe and secure in the hand of the Church's Head (Col. 1:18).

But John's joy in his startling experience on the isle was not unique, because the message symbolically conveyed was not confined to that moment in time. Rather, it has been shared down the ages by successive generations of individual Christians, and by the church as a whole. The hand which irresistibly drew the soul to saving faith (John 6:44), 'wounding' in conviction and 'making whole' in Christ (Rom. 7:24; Job 5:18), now holds that soul eternally secure upon its palm (John 10:29).

That hand is often the instrument of correction, as every child of the Father knows (Prov. 3:11-12; Heb. 12:6-11), but within the covenant of grace the promise has been declared that it will never become a clenched fist (Rom. 8:1). The Son of man, seated in the heavens at the right hand of the most sublime majesty (Heb. 12:2), holds those whom he has redeemed through his blood firmly in his own hand, with him on that same eternal throne (1 John 1:7,9; Rev. 1:13,20; 3:21).

The mouth

Thus far, John had heard 'I AM' speak only once (Rev. 1:10-11), and then it had been by way of an introduction to their meeting. John's back had been turned when the voice had first spoken (Rev. 1:12), but since then the beauty of Christ had dazzled the elderly apostle into silence, one which the Son of man made no attempt to break into.

Instead, the mouth of 'I AM' remained open and from it protruded on this occasion, not a tongue (denoting verbal communication from the divine to the human — Deut. 8:3; Matt. 4:4), as John would have expected, but a double-edged sword! (Rev. 1:16). It was an apt reminder that truth revealed from heaven (John 1:14,17), the Word and the words of God, is lethal and capable of slicing through to the deepest recesses of man (Heb. 4:12). Equally, wielded by the Spirit, it is both the believer's greatest weapon and his most able defence (Eph. 6:17).

The two sides of this more than razor-sharp instrument cannot possibly be seen to starker effect than when the Son of man manifests himself at the end of the age. This will be in order to exercise his divine appointment as Ruler over all nations and individuals (Dan. 7:9-14). He will vindicate his glory, the truth he has revealed and his people who embrace it. No longer will he be rejected, neglected or cursed; no longer will his Word be trampled upon and his church persecuted. The insignia of his office as King of all kings and Lord of all lords is, significantly, a rod made of 'iron' (Rev. 19:15).

Every eye, both temporal and eternal, will see the heavens swept to one side by the giant hand of God, and witness the majesty of the Christ as King (Rev. 6:14-17; 1:7). The cries of angelic hosts are always like trumpet blasts to the ear (Exod. 19:16; Deut. 33:2), and the glorious appearing is not likely to be an exception (Titus 2:13; Jude 14). 'Holy, holy, holy, is the Lord of hosts, the whole earth is full of his glory' (Isa. 6:3). And the redeemed in glory reply, 'Great and marvellous are thy works, Lord God Almighty; just and true are thy ways, thou King of saints. Who shall not fear thee, O Lord, and glorify thy name? For thou only art holy: for all nations shall come and worship before thee; for thy judgements are made manifest' (Rev. 15:3-4).

Escape from 'this holy Lord God' is never possible (1 Sam. 6:20; Ps. 139:1-12); nor even standing upright before him. Many of those cringing in fear will have spent their lives committed to Marx, Mohammed, the Madonna, the Buddha, the Hindu gods, various eastern sages or exotic gurus — anybody, or anything, but the Christ of God. Their major contribution to religious activity will have been that they vainly attempted to redeem themselves, by rejecting the Word of Christ and the true way of salvation. Then that 'sword' in the mouth of the Son of man will slice through mankind, dividing wheat from tares and sheep from goats (Matt. 13:24-30; 25:32). But, as if to underline the horrendous nature of this ultimate divide, the agricultural metaphor is dropped in favour of a division with more chilling connotations, that between the 'blessed' and the 'cursed' (Matt. 25:34,41).

Like the valley between the mounts of blessing and cursing, Gerizim and Ebal (Deut. 11:29), the chasm is deep and wide. The 'sword' has two sharp cutting edges. On the one side, those without a saving relationship to Christ, adrift from truth (John 14:6;18:37) and the blood of the everlasting covenant (Heb. 13:20), will hear the most frightening words of all from Christ's mouth: 'Depart from me, ye cursed, into everlasting fire, prepared for the devil and his angels' (Matt. 25:41).

But on the other side of the divide, what bliss is to be expected! The 'precious', eternally separated from the 'vile' (see Jer.15:19), hear words of joyous welcome from their Lord's mouth which are sublime to their ears: 'Come, ye blessed of my Father, inherit the kingdom prepared for you from the foundation of the world' (Matt. 25:34). Each individual blood-bought saint has every reason to share humbly in the apostle Paul's 'blessed hope' as he awaited martyrdom: 'Henceforth, there is laid up for me a crown of righteousness, which the Lord, the righteous judge, shall give me at that day; and not to me only, but unto all them also that love his appearing' (2 Tim. 4:8; cf. Titus 2:13).

The face of the King

The rocky isle of Patmos, upon which on that remarkable Lord's day (Rev. 1:10) the Roman lash played host to a multitude of wretched guests, had melted away in John's mind during those sublime moments he spent with the Son of man (Dan. 7:13-14). How long they lasted is unknown; time was suspended, as it had been when he witnessed in his youth the majestic lustre of Christ 'transfigured' before him on a mountainside (2 Peter 1:16; Matt. 17:1-2).

One thing was certain, however: this experience was even more astonishing than the first, as the old apostle's spirit swept vertically upwards towards the most elevated plateau of all — the location where the face of God could be seen, in the person of 'I AM' (Rev. 1:16; Exod. 3:14). John had arrived at the final veil, through which he glimpsed the ultimate, 'Alpha and Omega' whose credentials are impeccable. He is the beginning and the end (Rev. 1:11); one cannot retreat or progress more penetratingly than that.

Perfection's glare was too much for John to withstand; the rays of infinite purity and power burned into his being, as if he sought to grapple with the sun (Rev. 1:16). To behold the face of God, the fount of truth (John 14:6), is to have reached the end of the line, from life's twisting pathways through many a maze of mysteries, where myriads of queries sleep peacefully and answers rest contentedly. Here everything is understood with crystal clarity — for most the understanding comes too late — in the presence of Spirit (John 4:24) whose sovereign energy lies behind the cosmos, beyond the furthest planet, or the loneliest galaxy at the very edge of the universe.

His exulting soul was unable to leap higher, his finite mind to absorb more profoundly, or his required obeisance to be more evident. John was overcome, as if he were dead (Rev. 1:17), overwhelmed by glory. He had 'died' to self (Gal. 2:20), and all else, and was wholly given over to his Lord. If they desired, those feet of burning bronze could trample him wrathfully into the dust, like grapes in a winepress (Isa. 63:3; Rev. 19:15). It was all he deserved (Job 25).

His imagination would have been justified in running amok. He would have remembered how his ancestors, having heard the voice of God, had rejoiced at being spared. Who indeed has heard it, and lived to relate the experience? (Deut. 5:24-26). But John had heard, and seen, much more than that. He had actually glanced at the face of the Son of man (Rev. 1:16), and yet God's warning to Moses was plain: 'There shall no man see me, and live' (Exod. 33:20). The apostle, therefore, shared Manoah's terror when he said, 'We shall surely die, because we have seen God' (Judg.13:22), and Jacob's awe when, believing he had arrived at heaven's gate, he exclaimed, 'How dreadful is this place!' (Gen. 28:17).

However, suddenly John's fears were assuaged, when he felt the gentle touch of a hand (Rev. 1:17), and heard again the reassuring voice which had at first disturbed his prayerful contemplation (Rev. 1:10-11). It was the tender compassion of heaven's High Priest, towards a child of the everlasting covenant whose sins he remembers no more (Heb. 4:15; 8:8-12; Jer. 31:34). John and Stephen would not be the only ones to receive such encouragement (Matt. 25:34; cf. Acts 7:56). An innumerable company would do so (Rev. 7:9). Just think — the one in whom heaven delighted prior to the advent of time (Prov. 8:23-31) and around whom the close of the age will pivot (Eph.1:10), the custodian of all matters concerning eternity — in fact, the risen and ascended Christ (Rev. 1:18) — was showing him kindness!

Long before, John had watched his Lord ascend to the skies in bright 'Shekinah' glory (Acts 1:9; cf. Exod. 40:34-35), heaven's High Priest entering eternity's most sacred spot on behalf of the redeemed (Heb. 1:3; cf. Lev. 16). His was the sacrifice acceptable to God, bound with the 'cords' of Calvary (2 Cor. 5:21; Ps. 118:27); his the blood presented to the Father to appease his wrath against sinners (Heb. 9:14), and his heart the golden 'breastplate' upon which in eternal aeons past the name of each blood-sprinkled child of his was written (Exod. 24:8; 28:29; 1 Peter 1:2; Rev. 20:14-15). John knew his name was there too, not by right of apostleship, but through electing mercy alone (Exod. 33:19).

There was much for him yet to hear (Rev. 1:19). But in the meantime Christ's testimony to each generation, a blessed comfort to the church and an alarm to the world, was heard loud and clear: 'I am he that liveth, and was dead; and, behold, I am alive for evermore...' (Rev. 1:18). It is the definitive reason why the garden tomb was empty, against which there can be no intelligent opposition. After all he, and he alone, possesses the keys of 'hell and of death'.

Notes

Chapter 2 — The third day

1. *The women at the tomb.* From John 20:2, it is evident Mary of Magdala's news to Peter and John was only about the fact of the empty tomb; that at that time she had not encountered angels. She must therefore have run from the tomb to tell her story immediately upon observing, with her friends, that the boulder had been removed.

Chapter 3 — The pace quickens

1. *Second-hand cloth.* Mary of Magdala's message having been given to Peter and John, they hurried to the tomb. There, the 'other disciple' (John, and Peter too, of course) 'saw, and believed'. As, at that time, 'They knew not the scripture, that he must rise again from the dead' (John 20:9), what did they see and believe? They saw that, indeed, the tomb was empty, and they believed Mary's story: 'They have taken away the Lord out of the sepulchre...' (John 20:2).

Apart from that basic knowledge, with the remainder of the apostles, Peter and John at that stage 'mourned' and 'wept' (Mark 16:10). It was later in the evening they understood, and truly believed (John 20:19-20).

Chapter 4 —News good, bad and indifferent

1. *A joyful reunion.* The four Gospels do not record any 'joyful reunion' among the women. However, Luke 24:10 informs us that all the women involved 'told these things unto the apostles'. We know, though, that Mary of Magdala's experience (John 20:1-12) differed from that of her friends (Mark 16:1-8). That being so, the women must have conferred together about what had happened before bursting in upon the apostles. Such a reunion could not have been other than extremely joyful!

2. *In search of Jesus.* Some commentators speculate that Luke 24:12 records the same experience as John 20:3 — Peter running to the tomb. However, this surely cannot be. The latter reference records Peter and John heading for the tomb after listening to Mary of Magdala; the former, in which John is not mentioned, relates the account of Peter hurrying to the tomb after hearing all the women tell their story (Luke 24:10-12). Therefore, we have good reason to believe Peter visited the empty tomb twice.

On the first occasion, he and John, having entered the tomb and examined the discarded clothing, 'went away again unto their own home' (John 20:10). The emphasis was upon Mary of Magdala's story — the empty tomb, and Jesus' missing body (John 20:2). It was important to tell his mother about the events of that remarkable day, and she lived in John's home (John 19:27).

But, on the second visit the emphasis differed. Then, Peter 'departed [from the empty tomb] wondering in himself' (Luke 24:12); the inference being, that after what all the women had excitedly told the apostles, not just about the empty tomb and Jesus' missing body, but of angelic visitations and of actually meeting the Lord, truth was slowly dawning.

Chapter 9 — One without equal

1. Some commentators suggest that two different events are recorded in Matthew 28:16-20 and 1 Corinthians 15:6: the Great Commission, and the occasion when 'above five hundred brethren at once' saw the risen Christ. Other commentators disagree. This book supports the latter view — that Matthew 28:16-20 and 1 Corinthians 15:6 refer to the one event.

The gathering of 'above five hundred brethren' could not have taken place in Judea, because shortly afterwards (at Pentecost) we are informed that there were only 120 disciples in the Jerusalem area (Acts 1:15). The hundreds of brethren must, therefore, have seen their risen Lord elsewhere. As Galilee was the area so closely associated with Jesus, where there would have been a large contingent of disciples, we can safely presume that was the area where 'above five hundred brethren' saw him.

Galilee was also the location of the Great Commission (Matt. 28:7,16); in which case, was there a need for the risen Christ to hold two such events in the same area?

Epilogue

1. The meeting on the isle of Patmos between the old apostle John and his risen and glorified Lord was one of the most remarkable of all moments. In this book, a sincere attempt has been made to try to understand how John must have felt upon receiving such an experience.